Public Administration

Public Administration

Dr. R.K. Duebey

Publishers
AMAN BOOK CENTER
Delhi–110053

ISBN	**:**	978-81-906593-6-9
Publisher	**:**	**Aman Book Center** L–20/13, Gali No. 5, Shivaji Marg Kartar Nagar, Delhi–110053 Delhi–110032
Frist Edition	**:**	**2012**
Price	**:**	**750.00**
Type Setting	**:**	**Editorial India, Delhi–92**
Printers	**:**	**Shiv Shakti Printers, Delhi–110032**

Public Administration (in English)

By Dr. R.K. Dubey

Contents

Preface

As economic and social intervention by governments has increased, the limitations of "incrementalism" as a public administration practice have become increasingly apparent. Incrementalism is the tendency of government to tinker with policies rather than to question the value of continuing them. A number of techniques have been introduced to make decisions more rational. One such technique, widely applied, is cost–benefit analysis.

Throughout the 20th century the study and practice of public administration has been essentially pragmatic and normative rather than theoretical and value free. This may explain why public administration, unlike some social sciences, developed without much concern about an encompassing theory. Not until the mid-20th century and the dissemination of the German sociologist Max Weber's theory of bureaucracy was there much interest in a theory of public administration.

Most recent bureaucratic theory, however, has been addressed to the private sector, and there has been little effort to relate organizational to political theory. A prominent principle of public administration has been economy and efficiency, that is, the provision of public services at the minimum cost. This has usually been the stated objective of administrative reform. Despite growing concern about other kinds of values, such as responsiveness to public needs, justice and equal treatment, and citizen involvement in government decisions, efficiency continues to be a major goal. In its concern with efficiency and improvement, public administration has focused frequently on questions of formal organization.

It is generally held that administrative ills can be at least partly corrected by reorganization. Many organizational principles originated with the military, a few from private business. They include, for example: (1) organizing departments, ministries, and agencies on the basis of common or closely related purposes, (2) grouping like activities in single units, (3) equating responsibility with authority, (4) ensuring unity of command (only one supervisor for each group of employees), (5) limiting the number of subordinates reporting to a single supervisor, (6) differentiating line (operating or end-purpose) activities from staff (advisory, consultative, or support) activities, (7) employing the principle of management by exception (only the unusual problem or case is brought to the top), and (8) having a clear-cut chain of command downward and of responsibility upward. Some critics have maintained that these and other principles of public administration are useful only as rough criteria for given organizational situations.

This book contains the fundamental and basic information of subject and the selection of contents makes it an appropriate book for the students.

—*Author*

1

Principles of Public Administration

Throughout the 20th century the study and practice of public administration has been essentially pragmatic and normative rather than theoretical and value free. This may explain why public administration, unlike some social sciences, developed without much concern about an encompassing theory. Not until the mid-20th century and the dissemination of the German sociologist Max Weber's theory of bureaucracy was there much interest in a theory of public administration.

Most recent bureaucratic theory, however, has been addressed to the private sector, and there has been little effort to relate organizational to political theory. A prominent principle of public administration has been economy and efficiency, that is, the provision of public services at the minimum cost. This has usually been the stated objective of administrative reform. Despite growing concern about other kinds of values, such as responsiveness to public needs, justice and equal treatment, and citizen involvement in government decisions, efficiency continues to be a major goal. In its concern with efficiency and improvement, public administration has focused frequently on questions of formal organization.

It is generally held that administrative ills can be at least partly corrected by reorganization. Many organizational principles originated with the military, a few from private business. They include, for example: (1) organizing departments, ministries, and agencies on the basis of common or closely related purposes, (2) grouping like activities in single units, (3) equating responsibility with authority, (4) ensuring unity of command (only one supervisor for each group of employees), (5) limiting the number of subordinates reporting to a single supervisor, (6) differentiating line (operating or end-purpose) activities from staff (advisory, consultative, or support) activities, (7) employing the principle of management by exception (only the unusual problem or case is brought to the top), and (8) having a clear-cut chain of command downward and of responsibility upward. Some critics have maintained that these and other principles of public administration are useful only as rough criteria for given organizational situations.

They believe that organizational problems differ and that the applicability of rules to various situations also differs. Nonetheless, and despite much more sophisticated analyses of organizational behaviour in recent decades, such principles as those enumerated above continue to carry force. Public administration has also laid stress upon personnel. In most countries administrative reform has involved civil service reform. Historically, the direction has been toward "meritocracy"—the best individual for each job, competitive examinations for entry, and selection and promotion on the basis of merit. Attention has increasingly been given to factors other than intellectual merit, including personal attitudes, incentives, personality, personal relationships, and collective bargaining. In addition, the budget has developed as a principal tool in planning future programs, deciding priorities, managing current programs, linking executive with legislature, and developing control and accountability.

The contest for control over budgets, particularly in the Western world, began centuries ago and at times was the main relationship between monarchs and their subjects. The modern executive budget system in which the executive recommends, the legislature appropriates, and the executive oversees expenditures originated in 19th-century Britain. In the United States during the 20th century, the budget became the principal vehicle for legislative surveillance of administration, executive control of departments, and departmental control of subordinate programs. It has been assuming a similar role in many of the developing countries of the world.

Recent Interpretations

The classical approach to public administration described above probably reached its fullest development in the United States during the 1930s, although since that time, through educational and training programs, technical assistance, and the work of international organizations, it has also become standard doctrine in many countries. However, some of its elements have been resisted by governments with British or continental-legal perspectives, and even during the 1930s it was being challenged from several quarters. Since that time study of the subject has greatly developed. It has also become somewhat confused as a result of certain inconsistencies in approach.

The orthodox doctrine rested on the premise that administration was simply the implementation of public policies determined by others. According to this view, administrators should seek maximum efficiency but should be otherwise neutral about values and goals. During the Great Depression of the 1930s, and even more so during World War II, however, it became increasingly evident that many new policies originated within the administration, that policy and value judgments were implicit in most significant administrative decisions, that many administrative officials worked on nothing except policy, and that, insofar as public policies were controversial, such work inevitably involved administrators in politics.

The supposed independence of administration from policy and politics was seen to be illusory. Since the 1930s there has thus been increasing concern with policy formation and the development of techniques to improve policy decisions. Although the concept of a value-free, neutral administration is regarded by many as no longer tenable, no fully satisfactory substitute has been offered. How to ensure that responsible and responsive policy decisions are made by career administrators, and how to coordinate their work with the policies of politically elected or appointive officials, remain key preoccupations, especially in democratic states. It was with governmental efforts to combat the Depression that new informational devices were introduced, including national income accounting and the scrutiny of gross national product as a major index of economic health.

The applied techniques of fiscal and monetary policy have become established specializations of public administration. Economists occupy key posts in the administrations of most nations, and many other administrators must have at least elementary knowledge of the economic implications of government operations. France, Sweden and other Scandinavian nations, Great Britain, and the United States were among the leaders in developing economic planning techniques. Such planning has become a dominating concern of public administration in many of the developing countries.

Responses to Incrementalism

As economic and social intervention by governments has increased, the limitations of "incrementalism" as a public administration practice have become increasingly apparent. Incrementalism is the tendency of government to tinker with policies rather than to question the value of continuing them. A number of techniques have been introduced to make decisions more rational. One such technique, widely applied, is cost–benefit analysis.

This involves identifying, quantifying, and comparing the costs and benefits of alternative proposals. Another, less successful, technique was the Planning, Programming, and Budgeting System (PPBS), introduced into the U.S. Department of Defence in 1961 and extended to the federal budget in 1965. According to PPBS, the objectives of government programs were to be identified, and then alternative means of achieving these objectives were to be compared according to their costs and benefits. In practice, PPBS made little difference in federal budgeting, partly because the objectives of governmental programs were difficult to specify and partly because comprehensive evaluation took too long. PPBS was abandoned in 1971, and similar attempts, such as Management by Objectives and Zero-Base Budgeting, both introduced in the

1970s, were equally short-lived and ineffective. Comparable schemes in western Europe, such as the method called "rationalization of budgetary choice" introduced into France in the late 1960s and the so-called Programme Analysis and Review in Great Britain in the 1970s, were likewise unsuccessful.

Quantitative economic measurement is useful up to a certain point, but the value of human life, of freedom from sickness and pain, of safety on the streets, of clean air, and of opportunity for achievement are hardly measurable in monetary terms. Public administration has thus increasingly concerned itself with developing better social indicators, quantitative and qualitative—that is, better indexes of the effects of public programs and new techniques of social analysis.

Another development has been an increasing emphasis on human relations. This originated in the 1930s when what became known as the Hawthorne research, involving the workers and management of an industrial plant near Chicago, brought out the importance to productivity of social or informal organization, good communications, individual and group behaviour, and attitudes (as distinct from aptitudes).

Awareness of the importance of human relations influenced the conduct of public administration. Many shibboleths of administration (hierarchy, directive leadership, set duties, treatment of employees as impersonal "units" of production, and monetary incentives) were challenged.

By the late 1930s the human relations approach had developed into a concept known as "organization development." Its primary goal was to change the attitudes, values, and structures of organizations so that they could meet new demands. Trained consultants, usually from outside the organization, undertook intensive interviewing of senior and junior staff, and sensitivity training and confrontation meetings were also held. Unlike the rationalistic PPBS approach, organization development stressed the identification of personal with organizational goals, the "self-actualization" of workers and managers, effective interpersonal communication, and broad participation in decision making. Its direct use within governmental agencies has been limited and has not always been successful, but it has had considerable indirect influence upon administrators.

Another modern movement in public administration has been the greater participation of citizens in government. It was stimulated during the 1950s and '60s by a growing feeling that governments were not responding to the needs of their citizens, particularly minority groups and the poor. A variety of experiments to involve citizens or their representatives in making governmental decisions were begun in the 1960s. These involved the delegation of decision making from central to local offices and, at the local level, the sharing of authority with citizen groups.

Public Policy Approach

From the early 1970s increasing analysis of the way government policies affected the public resulted in a concept called the "public policy approach" to administration. This examines to what extent each stage in devising and executing a policy affects the overall shape and impact of the policy. According to the concept, the way a problem is conceived in the first place influences the range of remedies considered. The nature of the decision-making process may determine whether a course of action is merely incremental or truly radical. Indeed, it has been argued that the nature of the decision-making process shapes the outcome of the decision itself, particularly when the process is dominated by a powerful interest group. Moreover, the willingness of the government to evaluate programs, and modify them if necessary, affects the outcome. Many supporters of the public policy approach regard the concept as an important tool for constructing a body of knowledge on which recommendations can be based.

Until World War II there was relatively little exchange among nations of ideas about public administration. As early as 1910, however, a professional organization, which eventually became the International Institute of Administrative Sciences (IIAS), had been established. At first its membership consisted principally of scholars and practitioners of administrative law in the countries of continental Europe. By the late 1980s the IIAS had a membership drawn from some 70 countries. Its triennial congresses have covered all aspects of the field.

Since World War II international interest in administrative systems has grown, precipitated by the necessity of cooperation during the war, by the formation of international organizations, by the occupation of conquered nations and the administration of economic recovery programs for Europe and the Far East, and by aid programs for developing countries. One by-product of aid programs was a renewed appreciation of how crucial effective administration is to national development. It has also become apparent how parochial and culture-bound styles of public administration have often remained within individual countries.

Another effect of this international communication and sharing of experiences has been the realization that development is not exclusive to the so-called underdeveloped countries. All countries have continued to develop, and public administration has increasingly been perceived as the administration of planned change in societies that themselves have undergone rapid change, not all of it planned. Government has no longer been merely the keeper of the peace and the provider of basic services: in the postindustrial era government has become a principal innovator, a determinant of social and economic priorities, and an entrepreneur on a major scale. On virtually every significant problem or challenge—from unemployment to clean air—people have looked to the government for solutions or assistance. The tasks of planning, organizing, coordinating, managing, and evaluating modern government have likewise become awesome in both dimension and importance

Comparative Administration

Public administration can be broadly described as the development, implementation and study of branches of government policy. The pursuit of the public good by enhancing civil society, ensuring a well-run, fair, and effective public service are some of the goals of the field. Though public administration has historically referred to as government management, since the 1990s the term is sometimes expanded to encompass non-governmental organizations (NGOs) that also operate with a similar, primary dedication to providing services to the public.

Public administration is carried out by public servants who work in public departments and agencies, at all levels of government, and perform a wide range of tasks. Public administrators collect and analyse data (statistics), monitor budgets,, draft legislation, develop policy, and execute legally mandated government activities.

Public administrators serve in many roles: ranging from "front-line" positions serving the public (e.g., parole officers and border guards); administrators (e.g., auditors); analysts (e.g., policy analysts); and managers and executives of government branches and agencies.

Public administration is also an academic field. In comparison with related fields such as political science, public administration is a relatively new, multidisciplinary field which only emerged in the 20th century. It draws on theories and concepts from economics, political science, sociology, administrative law, management, and a range of related fields. The goals of the field of public administration are related to the democratic values of improving equality, justice, security, efficiency, effectiveness of public services; business administration is primarily concerned with profit.

Types of Organization

An organization is a social arrangement which pursues collective goals, controls its own performance, and has a boundary separating it from its environment. The word itself is derived from the Greek word organon, itself derived from the better-known word ergon.

In the social sciences, organizations are studied by researchers from several disciplines, the most common of which are sociology, economics, political science, psychology, management, and organizational communication. The broad area is commonly referred to as organizational studies, organizational behaviour or organization analysis. Therefore, a number of different theories and perspectives exist, some of which are compatible,

- Organization – process-related: an entity is being (re-)organized (organization as task or action).
- Organization – functional: organization as a function of how entities like businesses or state authorities are used (organization as a permanent structure).
- Organization – institutional: an entity is an organization (organization as an actual purposeful structure within a social context).

Organization in Sociology

In sociology "organization" is understood as planned, coordinated and purposeful action of human beings to construct or compile a common tangible or intangible product. This action is usually framed by formal membership and form (institutional rules). Sociology distinguishes the term organization into planned formal and unplanned informal (i.e. spontaneously formed) organizations. Sociology analyses organizations in the first line from an institutional perspective. In this sense, organization is a permanent arrangement of elements. These elements and their actions are determined by rules so that a certain task can be fulfilled through a system of coordinated division of labour.

An organization is defined by the elements that are part of it (who belongs to the organization and who does not?), its communication (which elements communicate and how do they communicate?), its autonomy (Max Weber termed autonomy in this context: Autocephaly (which changes are executed autonomously by the organization or its elements?), and its rules of action compared to outside events (what causes an organization to act as a collective actor?).

By coordinated and planned cooperation of the elements, the organization is able to solve tasks that lie beyond the abilities of the single elements. The price paid by the elements is the limitation of the degrees of freedom of the elements.

Advantages of organizations are enhancement (more of the same), addition (combination of different features) and extension. Disadvantages can be inertness (through co-ordination) and loss of interaction.

Organization in Management and Organizational Studies

Management is interested in organization mainly from an instrumental point of view. For a company, organization is a means to an end to achieve its goals-which are to create value for its stakeholders (stockholders, employees, customers, suppliers, community).

Organization Theories

Among the theories that are or have been most influential are:

- Weberian organization theory (refer to Max Weber's chapter on Bureaucracy in his book 'Economy and Society')
- Marxist organization analysis
- Scientific management (mainly following Frederick W. Taylor)
- Human Relations Studies (going back to the Hawthorne studies, Maslow and Hertzberg)
- Administrative theories (with work by e.g. Henri Fayol and Chester Barnard)
- Contingency theory
- New institutionalise and new institutional economics
- Network analysis
- Economic sociology
- Organization ecology (or demography of organizations)
- Agency theory (sometimes called principal-agent theory)
- Studies of organization culture
- Labour Process Theory
- Critical Management Studies
- Complexity Theory and Organizations

- Transaction cost theory/Transaction cost Economics (TCE)
- Garbage can model
- Actor-Network Theory and the 'Montreal School'
- social entrepreneurship.

Organizational Chart

An organizational chart is a pictorial representation of a company's structure and reporting relationships. This chart can provide a great deal of information and may help organizational members understand the overall structure of the organization and its strategy. This entry describes how organizational charts are constructed, including the software that can be used to create them; what information the organizational chart provides; the benefits of making the chart available inside and outside of the organization; and the circumstances under which a chart is likely to change.

Constructing an Organizational Chart

All organizational charts have similar elements that allow them to be easily interpreted and understood by people inside and outside of the organization. Charts consist of shapes and lines that represent work units and their hierarchy. The basic building block of an organizational chart is the rectangle, which can represent a person or a work unit (e.g., a department). If the outline of the rectangle is dashed, this means that a position is open and must be filled, as with one of the manager positions. If a rectangle is divided, and two or more names are in it, this may indicate job sharing or that multiple people are responsible for the outcomes associated with this position. In the figure, W. Allen and P. Lloyd are comanagers in one area of the Production and Services Marketing Department, where they have a job sharing arrangement and each works part-time hours.

The boxes may contain as much or as little information as the organization prefers. They may include a job title, an employee's name, an employee's department, or even information such as job tenure, education, or salary.

Alternatively, a chart may be created without rectangles, with names or titles standing alone. The three employees in the Public and Community Relations Department are listed with their names not in rectangles. This often is done to save space on the chart. Rectangles on an organizational chart are linked with solid or dashed lines. A solid line indicates a formal, direct relationship and a dashed line indicates that one employee or department advises another or has some other sort of indirect relationship. When lines represent a tree structure—when two or more rectangles are linked to another with multiple lines—this indicates that several individuals or departments report to one supervisor. For instance, the tree structure represents the relationship between the CEO and the three top managers who report to the CEO. Finally, a rectangle that is attached horizontally outside of the vertical hierarchy typically indicates an assistant or staff person. In the example, this is represented by the executive secretary to the CEO.

While organizational charts can be created by hand, most are created using computer software. Although it may be labour intensive, organizational charts can be created using drawing tools in a word processing program. Microsoft's Power Point presentation software allows for the creation of organizational charts, although there is little space available to create large charts. Specific software exists for creating larger, more complex charts, and there are many different packages available for purchase. Some examples are Org Plus, Concept Draw V, Smart Draw, and Abra Org Chart. These software programs allow for quick and easy chart creation with point-and-click menus and automatic resizing and alignment. Many of these software programs also allow one to easily download charts into a word processing document, a presentation, or a Web site. Other features available in these programs include the ability to insert employee photographs, as well as information from other human resources computer programs, directly into charts.

Information in the Organizational Chart

The organizational chart provides a great deal of information about the organization as a whole and the interaction of its parts. From a chart, one can see the organization's structure, its hierarchy, the degree to which it is centralized or decentralized, and its chain of command. Each of these is summarized below.

Organizational Structure

First, organizational charts detail an organization's structure. It may be functional, in which work units are divided based on what they do and named after those functions (e.g., research and development, marketing, sales, etc.). The structure may be divisional, based on product, customers served, or geographic location. Finally, an organizational chart may represent a matrix structure, in which work units are organized by both function and division.

Organizational Hierarchy and Centralization

In addition to outlining the type of organizational structure, the organizational chart also indicates the number of management levels, whether the organizational structure is tall or flat, and the span of control at each level. Tall organizations have many levels of middle management and small spans of control. Each manager supervises and directs few employees, and the chain of command has many managers. Conversely, a flat organization has fewer management levels and larger spans of control. Because managers supervise more employees, employees tend to have more autonomy and discretion in their jobs. Organizational hierarchy and the number of management levels often indicates the degree of centralization within an organization. Centralized organizations are those in which most of the decision making occurs by a few people at the top of the hierarchy. This typically creates a top-down management structure, in which top-level managers strongly control the direction of the workplace through their decisions and supervision. Conversely, an organization with a decentralized structure allows greater decision-making and authority at lower organizational levels. Highly decentralized companies may have units that operate nearly independently of one another. The degree of hierarchy on an organization's chart normally will help one to determine the degree of centralization or decentralization within its structure. Typically, the taller the organization, the more centralized it is; flatter organizations generally require more decentralization, because managers each have broader spans of control and cannot direct and closely supervise so many people. Additionally, as previously described, the organization's structure may indicate the degree of centralization. Functional structures tend to be more centralized than do divisional structures.

Chain Of Command

The vertical and horizontal lines connecting the rectangles on an organizational chart indicate reporting relationships and chain of command. That is, they indicate which employees are directly responsible for the supervision of others and who has ultimate accountability for a group of employees.

Availability of the Organizational Chart

Many companies make their organizational chart available to their employees and to the public. The members of the public who may have an interest in a company's organizational chart include company shareholders, investors, distributors and suppliers, customers, potential job applicants, and even community members.

Employees typically have access to the organizational chart through materials provided by the organization (e.g., the employee handbook) or through a company Web site. Providing the organizational chart to employees allows them to see the structure of the organization and to better understand the entirety of the organization and how their position or work unit fits into it. Additionally, the observable chain of command can help an employee to understand to whom they are accountable. This may aid the company in diagnosing organizational problems by being able to pinpoint accountability.

Many organizations now make their organizational charts available for viewing by the general public, either online or in corporate literature for shareholders and prospective employees. By providing this information, these external stakeholders and other interested parties may gain a better understanding of the organization. The chart may give them a sense of the organization's operations, workforce, or even its strategy.

Changes to the Organizational Chart

There are a number of reasons that an organizational chart might change since the chart must reflect any alterations to the organizational structure. The structure may change due to a company's growth, decline, or restructuring.

Growth or Decline

All organizations progress through a life cycle of growth, maturity, and decline, and in each stage the organizational structure is likely to be different. In the growth stage, the company is expanding rapidly, gaining customers and market share. Growth will occur when a company is just beginning and products and services are gaining a foothold. It may also occur when an organization develops a new product or expands into new markets, perhaps in other countries. With growth, the organizational chart will change. Levels of management may be added, along with new departments.

In maturity, an organization is no longer growing at a rapid rate and is stable in its production and sales. The organization may introduce minor changes to a product or service, but there are unlikely to be major changes to its structure.

In the decline stage, the organization is losing ground in the marketplace. It may be that its products or services are becoming obsolete or that its competitors are taking over the market. In decline, the organization may shed levels of management or positions in all divisions. Additionally, it may outsource work in some areas and thus remove those departments from its structure. Or, as certain products or services are dropped from the organization, the work units needed for these products and services also may be eliminated. Thus, in the decline stage the organizational chart is likely to be streamlined or shrunken.

Restructuring

Restructuring occurs when an organization reduces its workforce by eliminating large numbers of management and line employees. Restructuring typically occurs when information technology can be used to achieve the same productivity outcomes with fewer people. With restructuring, management levels may be eliminated entirely, or entire departments may be removed. This particularly is true if outsourcing accompanies the restructuring.

Organizational Structure

Organizational structure refers to the way that an organization arranges people and jobs so that its work can be performed and its goals can be met. When a work group is very small and face-to-face communication is frequent, formal structure may be unnecessary, but in a larger organization decisions have to be made about the delegation of various tasks. Thus, procedures are established that assign responsibilities for various functions. It is these decisions that determine the organizational structure.

In an organization of any size or complexity, employees' responsibilities typically are defined by what they do, who they report to, and for managers, who reports to them. Over time these definitions are assigned to positions in the organization rather than to specific individuals. The relationships among these positions are illustrated graphically in an organizational chart. The best organizational structure for any organization depends on many factors including the work it does; its size in terms of employees, revenue, and the geographic dispersion of its facilities; and the range of its businesses (the degree to which it is diversified across markets).

There are multiple structural variations that organizations can take on, but there are a few basic principles that apply and a small number of common patterns. The following sections explain these patterns and provide the historical context from which some of them arose. The first section addresses organizational structure in the twentieth century. The second section provides additional details of traditional, vertically-arranged organizational structures. This is followed by descriptions of several alternate organizational structures including those arranged by product, function, and geographical or product markets. Next is a discussion of combination structures, or matrix organizations. The discussion concludes by addressing emerging and potential future organizational structures.

Organizational Structure During the Twentieth Century

Understanding the historical context from which some of today's organizational structures have developed helps to explain why some structures are the way they are. For instance, why are the old, but still operational steel mills such as U.S. Steel and Bethlehem Steel structured using vertical hierarchies? Why are newer steel mini-mills such as Chaparral Steel structured more horizontally, capitalizing on the innovativeness of their employees? Part of the reason, as this section discusses, is that organizational structure has a certain inertia—the idea borrowed from physics and chemistry that something in motion tends to continue on that same path. Changing an organization's structure is a daunting managerial task, and the immensity of such a project is at least partly responsible for why organizational structures change infrequently.

At the beginning of the twentieth century the United States business sector was thriving. Industry was shifting from job-shop manufacturing to mass production, and thinkers like Frederick Taylor in the United States and Henri Fayol in France studied the new systems and developed principles to determine how to structure organizations for the greatest efficiency and productivity, which in their view was very much like a machine. Even before this, German sociologist and engineer Max Weber had concluded that when societies embrace capitalism, bureaucracy is the inevitable result. Yet, because his writings were not translated into English until 1949, Weber's work had little influence on American management practice until the middle of the twentieth century.

Management thought during this period was influenced by Weber's ideas of bureaucracy, where power is ascribed to positions rather than to the individuals holding those positions. It also was influenced by Taylor's scientific management, or the "one best way" to accomplish a task using scientifically-determined studies of time and motion.

Also influential were Fayol's ideas of invoking unity within the chain-of-command, authority, discipline, task specialization, and other aspects of organizational power and job separation. This created the context for vertically-structured organizations characterized by distinct job classifications and top-down authority structures, or what became known as the traditional or classical organizational structure.

Job specialization, a hierarchical reporting structure through a tightly-knit chain-of-command, and the subordination of individual interests to the superordinate goals of the organization combined to result in organizations arranged by functional departments with order and discipline maintained by rules, regulations, and standard operating procedures.

This classical view, or bureaucratic structure, of organizations was the dominant pattern as small organizations grew increasingly larger during the economic boom that occurred from the 1900s until the Great Depression of the 1930s. Henry Ford's plants were typical of this growth, as the emerging Ford Motor Company grew into the largest U.S. automaker by the 1920s.

The Great Depression temporarily stifled U.S. economic growth, but organizations that survived emerged with their vertically-oriented, bureaucratic structures intact as public attention shifted to World War II. Postwar rebuilding reignited economic growth, powering organizations that survived the Great Depression toward increasing size in terms of sales revenue, employees, and geographic dispersion.

Along with increasing growth, however, came increasing complexity. Problems in U.S. business structures became apparent and new ideas began to appear. Studies of employee motivation raised questions about the traditional model. The "one best way" to do a job gradually disappeared as the dominant logic.

It was replaced by concerns that traditional organizational structures might prevent, rather than help, promote creativity and innovation—both of which were necessary as the century wore on and pressures to compete globally mounted.

Traditional Organizational Structure

While the previous section explained the emergence of the traditional organizational structure, this section provides additional detail regarding how this affected the practice of management. The structure of every organization is unique in some respects, but all organizational structures develop or are consciously designed to enable the organization to accomplish its work. Typically, the structure of an organization evolves as the organization grows and changes over time.

Researchers generally identify four basic decisions that managers have to make as they develop an organizational structure, although they may not be explicitly aware of these decisions. First, the organization's work must be divided into specific jobs. This is referred to as the division of labour. Second, unless the organization is very small, the jobs must be grouped in some way, which is called departmentalization. Third, the number of people and jobs that are to be grouped together must be decided. This is related to the number of people that are to be managed by one person, or the span of control—the number of employees reporting to a single manager. Fourth, the way decision-making authority is to be distributed must be determined.

In making each of these design decisions, a range of choices are possible. At one end of the spectrum, jobs are highly specialized with employees performing a narrow range of activities, while at the other end of the spectrum employees perform a variety of tasks. In traditional bureaucratic structures, there is a tendency to increase task specialization as the organization grows larger. In grouping jobs into departments, the manager must decide the basis on which to group them. The most common basis, at least until the last few decades, was by function. For example, all accounting jobs in the organization can be grouped into an accounting department, all engineers can be grouped into an engineering department, and so on. The size of the groupings also can range from small to large depending on the number of people the managers supervise. The degree to which authority is distributed throughout the organization can vary as well, but traditionally structured organizations typically vest final decision-making authority by those highest in the vertically structured hierarchy. Even as pressures to include employees in decision-making increased during the 1950s and 1960s, final decisions usually were made by top management. The traditional model of organizational structure is thus characterized by high job specialization, functional departments, narrow spans of control, and centralized authority. Such a structure has been referred to as traditional, classical, bureaucratic, formal, mechanistic, or command and control. A structure formed by choices at the opposite end of the spectrum for each design decision is called unstructured, informal, or organic.

The traditional model of organizational structure is easily represented in a graphical form by an organizational chart. It is a hierarchical or pyramidal structure with a president or other executive at the top, a small number of vice presidents or senior managers under the president, and several layers of management below this, with the majority of employees at the bottom of the pyramid. The number of management layers depends largely on the size of the organization. The jobs in the traditional organizational structure usually are grouped by function into departments such as accounting, sales, human resources, and so.

Basis for Departmentalization

As noted in the previous section, many organizations group jobs in various ways in different parts of the organization, but the basis that is used at the highest level plays a fundamental role in shaping the organization. There are four commonly used bases.

Functional Departmentalization

Every organization of a given type must perform certain jobs in order do its work. For example, key functions of a manufacturing company include production, purchasing, marketing, accounting, and personnel. The functions of a hospital include surgery, psychiatry, nursing, housekeeping, and billing. Using such functions as the basis for structuring the organization may, in some instances, have the advantage of efficiency. Grouping jobs that require the same knowledge, skills, and resources allows them to be done efficiently and promotes the development of greater expertise. A disadvantage of functional groupings is that people with the same skills and knowledge may develop a narrow departmental focus and have difficulty appreciating any other view of what is important to the organization; in this case, organizational goals may be sacrificed in favour of departmental goals. In addition, coordination of work across functional boundaries can become a difficult management challenge, especially as the organization grows in size and spreads to multiple geographical locations.

Geographic Departmentalization

Organizations that are spread over a wide area may find advantages in organizing along geographic lines so that all the activities performed in a region are managed together. In a large organization, simple physical separation makes centralized coordination more difficult. Also, important characteristics of a region may make it advantageous to promote a local focus. For example, marketing a product in Western Europe may have different requirements than marketing the same product in Southeast Asia. Companies that market products globally sometimes adopt a geographic structure. In addition, experience gained in a regional division is often excellent training for management at higher levels.

Product Departmentalization

Large, diversified companies are often organized according to product. All the activities necessary to produce and market a product or group of similar products are grouped together. In such an arrangement, the top manager of the product group typically has considerable autonomy over the operation. The advantage of this type of structure is that the personnel in the group can focus on the particular needs of their product line and become experts in its development, production, and distribution. A disadvantage, at least in terms of larger organizations, is the duplication of resources. Each product group requires most of the functional areas such as finance, marketing, production, and other functions. The top leadership of the organization must decide how much redundancy it can afford.

Customer/Market Departmentalization

An organization may find it advantageous to organize according to the types of customers it serves. For example, a distribution company that sells to consumers, government clients, large businesses, and small businesses may decide to base its primary divisions on these different markets. Its personnel can then become proficient in meeting the needs of these different customers. In the same way, an organization that provides services such as accounting or consulting may group its personnel according to these types of customers.

Matrix Organizational Structure

Some organizations find that none of the afore-mentioned structures meet their needs. One approach that attempts to overcome the inadequacies is the matrix structure, which is the combination of two or more different structures. Functional departmentalization commonly is combined with product groups on a project basis. For example, a product group wants to develop a new addition to its line; for this project, it obtains personnel from functional departments such as research, engineering, production, and marketing. These personnel then work under the manager of the product group for the duration of the project, which can vary greatly. These personnel are responsible to two managers.

One advantage of a matrix structure is that it facilitates the use of highly specialized staff and equipment. Rather than duplicating functions as would be done in a simple product department structure, resources are shared as needed. In some cases, highly specialized staff may divide their time among more than one project. In addition, maintaining functional departments promotes functional expertise, while at the same time working in project groups with experts from other functions fosters cross-fertilization of ideas.

The disadvantages of a matrix organization arise from the dual reporting structure. The organization's top management must take particular care to establish proper procedures for the development of projects and to keep communication channels clear so that potential conflicts do not arise and hinder organizational functioning.

In theory at least, top management is responsible for arbitrating such conflicts, but in practice power struggles between the functional and product manager can prevent successful implementation of matrix structural arrangements. Besides the product/function matrix, other bases can be related in a matrix. Large multinational corporations that use a matrix structure most commonly combine product groups with geographic units. Product managers have global responsibility for the development, manufacturing, and distribution of their own product or service line, while managers of geographic regions have responsibility for the success of the business in their regions.

Strategic Business Units

As corporations become very large they often restructure as a means of revitalizing the organization. Growth of a business often is accompanied by a growth in bureaucracy, as positions are created to facilitate developing needs or opportunities. Continued changes in the organization or in the external business environment may make this bureaucracy a hindrance rather than a help, not simply because of the size or complexity of the organization but also because of a sluggish bureaucratic way of thinking. One approach to encourage new ways of thinking and acting is to reorganize parts of the company into largely autonomous groups, called strategic business units (SBUs). Such units generally are set up like separate companies, with full profit and loss responsibility invested in the top management of the unit—often the president of the unit and/ or a senior vice president of the larger corporation.

This manager is responsible to the top management of the corporation. This arrangement can be seen as taking any of the aforementioned departmentalization schemes one step further. The SBUs might be based on product lines, geographic markets, or other differentiating factors.

Emerging Trends in Organizational Structure

Except for the matrix organization, all the structures described above focus on the vertical organization; that is, who reports to whom, who has responsibility and authority for what parts of the organization, and so on. Such vertical integration is sometimes necessary, but may be a hindrance in rapidly changing environments. A detailed organizational chart of a large corporation structured on the traditional model would show many layers of managers; decision making flows vertically up and down the layers, but mostly downward. In general terms, this is an issue of interdependence.

In any organization, the different people and functions do not operate completely independently. To a greater or lesser degree, all parts of the organization need each other. Important developments in organizational design in the last few decades of the twentieth century and the early part of the twenty-first century have been attempts to understand the nature of interdependence and improve the functioning of organizations in respect to this factor. One approach is to flatten the organization, to develop the horizontal connections and de-emphasize vertical reporting relationships. At times, this involves simply eliminating layers of middle management. For example, some Japanese companies—even very large manufacturing firms—have only four levels of management: top management, plant management, department management, and section management. Some U.S. companies also have drastically reduced the number of managers as part of a downsizing strategy; not just to reduce salary expense, but also to streamline the organization in order to improve communication and decision making.

In a virtual sense, technology is another means of flattening the organization. The use of computer networks and software designed to facilitate group work within an organization can speed communications and decision making. Even more effective is the use of intranets to make company information readily accessible throughout the organization. The rapid rise of such technology has made virtual organizations and boundarlyless organizations possible, where managers, technicians, suppliers, distributors, and customers connect digitally rather than physically.

A different perspective on the issue of interdependence can be seen by comparing the organic model of organization with the mechanistic model. The traditional, mechanistic structure is characterized as highly complex because of its emphasis on job specialization, highly formalized emphasis on definite procedures and protocols, and centralized authority and accountability. Yet, despite the advantages of coordination that these structures present, they may hinder tasks that are interdependent. In contrast, the organic model of organization is relatively simple because it de-emphasizes job specialization, is relatively informal, and decentralizes authority. Decision-making and goal-setting processes are shared at all levels, and communication ideally flows more freely throughout the organization.

A common way that modern business organizations move toward the organic model is by the implementation of various kinds of teams. Some organizations establish self-directed work teams as the basic production group. Examples include production cells in a manufacturing firm or customer service teams in an insurance company. At other organizational levels, cross-functional teams may be established, either on an ad hoc basis (e.g., for problem solving) or on a permanent basis as the regular means of conducting the organization's work. Aid Association for Lutherans is a large insurance organization that has adopted the self-directed work team approach. Part of the impetus toward the organic model is the belief that this kind of structure is more effective for employee motivation. Various studies have suggested that steps such as expanding the scope of jobs, involving workers in problem solving and planning, and fostering open communications bring greater job satisfaction and better performance.

Saturn Corporation, a subsidiary of General Motors (GM), emphasizes horizontal organization. It was started with a "clean sheet of paper," with the intention to learn and incorporate the best in business practices in order to be a successful U.S. auto manufacturer. The organizational structure that it adopted is described as a set of nested circles, rather than a pyramid. At the center is the self-directed production cell, called a Work Unit. These teams make most, if not all, decisions that affect only team members.

Several such teams make up a wider circle called a Work Unit Module. Representatives from each team form the decision circle of the module, which makes decisions affecting more than one team or other modules. A number of modules form a Business Team, of which there are three in manufacturing. Leaders from the modules form the decision circle of the Business Team. Representatives of each Business Team form the Manufacturing Action Council, which oversees manufacturing. At all levels, decision making is done on a consensus basis, at least in theory. The president of Saturn, finally, reports to GM headquarters.

The Future

Industry consolidation—creating huge global corporations through joint ventures, mergers, alliances, and other kinds of inter-organizational cooperative efforts—has become increasingly important in the twenty-first century. Among organizations of all sizes, concepts such as agile manufacturing, just-in-time inventory management, and ambidextrous organizations are impacting managers' thinking about their organizational structure.

Indeed, few leaders were likely to blindly implement the traditional hierarchical structure common in the first half of the century. The first half of the twentieth century was dominated by the one-size-fits-all traditional structure. The early twenty-first century has been dominated by the thinking that changing organizational structures, while still a monumental managerial challenge, can be a necessary condition for competitive success.

Organizational Structures

The study of organizations includes a focus on optimizing organizational structure. According to management science, most human organizations fall roughly into four types:

- Pyramids or hierarchies
- Committees or juries
- Matrix organizations
- Ecologies.

Pyramids or Hierarchies

A hierarchy exemplifies an arrangement with a leader who leads leaders. This arrangement is often associated with bureaucracy. Hierarchies were satirized in *The Peter Principle* (1969), a book that introduced *hierarchiology* and the saying that "in a hierarchy every employee tends to rise to his level of incompetence".

An extremely rigid, in terms of responsibilities, type of organization is exemplified by Führerprinzip.

Committees or Juries

These consist of a group of peers who decide as a group, perhaps by voting. The difference between a jury and a committee is that the members of the committee are usually assigned to perform or lead further actions after the group comes to a decision, whereas members of a jury come to a decision. In common law countries legal juries render decisions of guilt, liability and quantify damages; juries are also used in athletic contests, book awards and similar activities. Sometimes a selection committee functions like a jury. In the Middle Ages juries in continental Europe were used to determine the law according to consensus amongst local notables.

Committees are often the most reliable way to make decisions. Condorcet's jury theorem proved that if the average member votes better than a roll of dice, then adding more members increases the number of majorities that can come to a correct vote (however correctness is defined). The problem is that if the average member is *worse* than a roll of dice, the committee's decisions grow worse, not better: Staffing is crucial.

Parliamentary procedure, such as Robert's Rules of Order, helps prevent committees from engaging in lengthy discussions without reaching decisions.

Staff Organization or Cross-functional Team

A staff helps an expert get all his work done. To this end, a "chief of staff" decides whether an assignment is routine or not. If it's routine, he assigns it to a staff member, who is a sort of junior expert. The chief of staff schedules the routine problems, and checks that they are completed.

If a problem is not routine, the chief of staff notices. He passes it to the expert, who solves the problem, and educates the staff – converting the problem into a routine problem.

In a "cross functional team", like an executive committee, the boss *has* to be a non-expert, because so many kinds of expertise are required.

Organization: Cyclical Structure

A theory put forth by renowned scholar Stephen John has asserted that throughout the cyclical nature of one's life organizational patterns are key to success. Through various social and political constraints within society one must realize that organizational skills are paramount to success. Stephen John suggests that emphasis needs to be put on areas such as individual/group processes, functionality, and overall structures of institutions in order to maintain a proper organization. Furthermore, the individual's overall organizational skills are pre-determined by the processes undertaken.:

Matrix Organization

This organizational type assigns each worker two bosses in two different hierarchies. One hierarchy is "functional" and assures that each type of expert in the organization is well-trained, and measured by a boss who is super-expert in the same field. The other direction is "executive" and tries to get projects completed using the experts. Projects might be *organized by regions, customer types, or some other schema* matrix management

Ecologies

This organization has intense competition. Bad parts of the organization starve. Good ones get more work. Everybody is paid for what they actually do, and runs a tiny business that has to show a profit, or they are fired.

Companies who utilize this organization type reflect a rather one-sided view of what goes on in ecology. It is also the case that a natural ecosystem has a natural border-ecoregions do not in general compete with one another in any way, but are very autonomous.

The pharmaceutical company GlaxoSmithKline talks about functioning as this type of organization in this external article from The Guardian.

"Chaordic" Organizations

The chaordic model of organizing human endeavors emerged in the 1990s, based on a blending of chaos and order (hence "chaordic"), comes out of the work of Dee Hock and the creation of the VISA financial network. Blending democracy, complex system, consensus decision making, co-operation and competition, the chaordic approach attempts to encourage organizations to evolve from the increasingly nonviable hierarchical, command-and-control models.

Similarly, emergent organizations, and the principle of self-organization. See also group entity for an anarchist perspective on human organizations.

Organizations that are legal entities: government, international organization, non-governmental organization, armed forces, corporation, partnership, charity, not-for-profit corporation, cooperative, university.

The Organization of the Artist

The organization of the artist is a term first used by architect Frank Gehry to denote the organizational setup he enforces in order to ensure that the architect/artist is in control of design through construction. The organization of the artist deliberately eliminates the influence of politicians and business people on design. The purpose of the organization of the artist is to ensure that it is the design of the architect/artist that is actually implemented and not some compromise decided by political and business interests.

Gehry initially developed the concept of the organization of the artist as a reaction against what he calls the "marginalization of the architect/artist." Gehry explains:

"There's a tendency to marginalize and treat the creative people like women are treated, 'sweetie, us big business guys know how to do this, just give us the design and we'll take it from there.' That is the worst thing that can happen. It requires the organization of the artist to prevail so that the end product is as close as possible to the object of desire [the design] that both the client and architect have come to agree on."

Gehry argues that the organization of the artist, in addition to making possible artistic integrity, also helps keep his buildings on time and budget, which is rare for the type of innovative and complex designs that Gehry is known for. The organization of the artist thus serves the dual purpose of artistic freedom and economic prudence.

2

The Problems of Organization

Almost all of us belonged to some sick organization or another and at times all of us feel frustrated with them. Unfortunately, many of us are untrained in diagnosing what is going wrong in an organization. All we know is that it isn't working well. That sick feeling is from the Stewed Tomato Surprise you had last night, or that disastrous meeting this morning. To properly diagnose what is happening in an organization, we start like a doctor-with symptoms. Once we can describe what is going wrong, we look for causes, and recommend a prescription for what ails us.

Summary of Steps

The process has four steps as described below: 1) get started; 2) assess; 3) choose treatments and use them; and 4) periodically evaluate.

Get started: As in any situation, the first step is to recognize that a problem exists. Doctors call them symptoms; Organizations call them problems. These problems can range from declining productivity, quality or market share; dropped, disappearing projects that start marvelously well and end up in a black hole; increased absenteeism or turnover; group-related problems, such as frequent "Abilene paradoxes", group think, poorly run meetings, and frequent head-on collisions of style and priorities among management.

If (1) the symptoms outlined above strike home with you, and (2) your senior staff recognizes these are serious enough problems to invest time and resources, the next step is to decide what actions and resources are needed to diagnose and fix the problem(steps two through four).

At this point, people as patients and organizations as clients often diagnose themselves and take over-the-counter medications. Organizations take the equivalent: a few people go to a seminar and put on some training programs once they come back. *This works only if you want symptomatic relief!*

Organizations often go through the above process many times and for awhile they feel better. Unfortunately, the underlying causes haven't been assessed and changed, so the problem won't go away. People in organizations at this time get another disease: programmatic. Programmatic is the feeling of cynicism and indifference that happens when organizations plant different buzzword into the minds of employees without following through on implementation. After a few cycles, employees expect nothing from management, and the initial enthusiasm they have drains away.

Certainly the behavioural changes needed for teamwork must be done by employees and their management; In other words, the patient has to take his medicine. However, resources may be needed outside the organization to objectively assess the patient's health, provide guidance on treatment options and encourage the patient when he is feeling down. Outside resources are especially indicated when previous attempts by management to solve the problem either don't work or work only for a short time. These well-intentioned but short-lived solutions might include firing or transferring individual team members, training some of the team in meeting management skills, or browbeating/castigating the team.

Whoever this outside resource is, s/he should be politically neutral, knowledgeable in team assessment, and able to give guidance on the many treatment options. This person might be from another division, a sister company, or a professional consulting firm. This person should speak frankly and communicate the problems that your employees feel but are hesitant to say.

Assess breadth of the problem and identify causes: Via surveys, interviews and focus groups, determine the breadth and depth of your organizational symptoms. The breadth of organizational illness can be divided into three categories: Symptoms within just a few groups.

These causes generally focus around the goals, roles and relationships in the team. The team's charter or purpose may be vague, or in conflict with group members (or their department's) priorities. Who gets to do what, group membership, poor group skills and as well as personality conflicts are also potential causes. Symptoms between and within groups. Specific issues can arise between teams that create negative effects inside those teams. Such issues include disagreement over responsibilities, allocation of scarce resources, struggles for political power and the like. A typical triangle of conflict is between Marketing, Engineering and Manufacturing.

Symptoms across most of your organization. If illness is prevalent in your company, it implies that organizational systems are a primary cause of the symptoms. Organizational systems such as the organizational structure, compensation, management style, performance appraisal, employee selection process, authority/communication patterns, as well as organizational mission, vision and goals are the major (but often overlooked) causes of organizational ill health. A rule of thumb is that the more widespread the organizational sickness, the more likely that these systems are causing it.

Choose Treatments and Use Them

Treatments for Within-group Problems

Treatments for within-group issues include role clarification, goal setting and problem solving; individual coaching or removal of members; training in small group skills; and possibly disbanding the group.

Treatments for Inter-group Problems

Methods to treat inter-group issues include 1) inter-group teambuilding, where warring departments discuss their conflicts and agree upon solutions; 2) establishing cross-functional teams and matrix organizations to deal with "bridge" issues that cut across organizational lines; 3) and merging or dissolution of the groups.

Treatments for Changing Organization-wide, Systems Issues

Methods to treat organization-wide teamwork problems include changing organizational structure to a more product or customer-based focus, and away from the functional stovepipes; instituting gainsharing or profit sharing instead of individual merit reviews; changing market focus and the organization's strategic plan; and including line workers on the design and development of products.

Periodically Evaluate

Increasing organizational health is not a one-shot effort, but is continuous and on-going. Measures of success (such as re-assessing organizational health) should be established, and periodic checkups done at one, three, six and 12 months. If the organization progresses, these checkups can become less frequent; they may be more frequent if organizational health start to go downhill, or if the company faces new challenges.

Government Agency

A government agency is a permanent or semi-permanent organization in the machinery of government that is responsible for the oversight and administration of specific functions, such as an intelligence agency. There is a notable variety of types of agency. Although usage differs, a government agency is normally distinct both from a Department or Ministry, and other types of public body established by government. The functions of an agency are normally executive in character since different types of organisation (such as commissions) are normally used for advisory functions, but this distinction is often blurred in practice.

A government agency may be established by either a national government or a state government within a federal system. (The term is not normally used for an organization created by the powers of a local government body.) Agencies can be established by legislation or by executive powers. The autonomy, independence and accountability of government agencies also vary widely.

History

Early examples of organizations that would now be termed a government agency include the British Navy Board, responsible for ships and supplies, which was established 1546 by King Henry VIII and the British "Commissioners of Bankruptcy" established in 1570. The United States Library of Congress was founded in 1800 and is, unusually, an agency of the legislative branch of government.

From 1933, the New Deal saw rapid growth in US federal agencies, the "alphabet agencies" as they were used to deliver new programs mandated by legislation, such as federal emergency relief.

From the 1980s, as part of New Public Management, several countries including Australia and the United Kingdom developed the use of agencies to improve efficiency in public services.

India

The term *agency* in India has several meanings; For example, the Cabinet Secretariat describes itself as a "*nodal agency* for coordination amongst the ministries of the Govt.of India". Most notably as an international feature, what appear to be independent agencies (or *apex agencies*) include some that have active roles for Ministers: such as, the National Security Council, the Indian Council of Agricultural Research, and the Planning Commission, which is chaired ex-officio by the Prime Minister.

Sweden

The Government agencies in Sweden are state controlled organizations who act independently to carry out the policies of the Swedish Government. The Government Ministries are relatively small and merely policy-making organizations, allowed to control agencies by policy decisions but not by direct orders. A Minister is explicitly prohibited from interfering with the day-to-day operation in an agency or the outcome in individual cases. While no minister is allowed to give orders to agencies personally, they are subject to decisions made by the Government.

United Kingdom

Agencies in the United Kingdom are either executive agencies answerable to government ministers or non-departmental public bodies answerable directly to one of the parliaments or devolved assemblies of the United Kingdom.

Agencies can be created by enabling legislation by the Parliament of the United Kingdom, Scottish Parliament or the National Assembly for Wales.

Agencies in England usually answer to Westminster or the British Government. In Scotland they usually answer to the Scottish Executive or the Scottish Parliament and in Wales to the National Assembly for Wales. Some have remits that cover the entire UK and these organisations are funded by and answer to the British Government.

United States

The Congress and President of the United States delegate specific authority to government agencies to regulate the complex facets of the modern American federal state. Also, most of the 50 U.S. states have created similar government agencies.

The term "government agency" usually applies to one of the independent agencies of the United States government, which exercise some degree of independence from the President's control. Although the heads of independent agencies are often appointed by the President, they can usually can be removed only for cause. The heads of independent agencies work together in groups, such as a commission, board or council. Independent agencies often function as miniature versions of the tripartite federal government with the authority to legislate (through the issuing, or "promulgation" of regulations), to adjudicate disputes, and to enforce agency regulations (through enforcement personnel). Examples of independent agencies include the Federal Communication Commission (FCC), Federal Reserve Board, U.S. Securities and Exchange Commission (SEC), the National Labour Relations Board (NLRB) and the Federal Trade Commission (FTC).

A broader definition of the term "government agency" also means the United States federal executive departments that include the President's cabinet-level departments, and their sub-units. Examples of these agencies include the Department of Energy (DOE) and the Internal Revenue Service (IRS), which is a bureau of the Department of the Treasury.

Most federal agencies are created by Congress through statutes called "enabling acts" which define the scope of an agency's authority. Because the Constitution does not expressly mention federal agencies (as it does the three branches), some commentators have called agencies the "headless fourth branch" of the federal government. However, most independent agencies are technically part of the executive branch, with a few located in the legislative branch of government. By enacting the Administrative Procedure Act (APA) in 1946, Congress established some means to oversee government agency action. The APA established uniform administrative law procedures for a federal agency's promulgation of rules, and adjudication of claims. The APA also sets forth the process for judicial review of agency action.

The Organization in Practice

There is a left tradition of thinking about and taking action within two realms of activity: the mass level and the revolutionary political level. There are different ways to cash out these concepts, but they are distinguished basically by levels of unity and content. The mass level is where people come together based on common interests to take action in some form, with unions being the most obvious and traditional example. A higher level of unity is the revolutionary political level where people take action based on common ideas and practices. These concepts are tools or instruments that can help us make sense of the world, and better act to change it.

In so far as they do that, they work. If they don't, we get new ones. At the level of reality, this division is not so clear and in fact we see mixtures of unity and action everywhere. That being said, these concepts help us parse out how as revolutionaries we can relate to social groupings, and how we can intervene.

There is an additional level though that can help us in this manner, the intermediate level. As opposed to the political level, which is defined by attempted unity of ideas, and the mass level, which is defined by common practices with diversity of ideas, the intermediate level shares some features of both. The intermediate level is where people organize based on some basic level of unity of ideas to develop and coordinate their activity at the mass level.

Taking the example of the workers movement, we see unions at the mass level grouped together by common workplace issues, and a political level of revolutionary militants with unified ideology acting within the unions in some way or another. Within the unions there can be a plurality of political organizations, and even of individual militants who lack organizations. An intermediate level organization could come to unite class conscious workers around a strategy within their industry, workplace, etc. The intermediate level organization would not have the unity of a political organization, since its basis is bringing together militants for a common practice that doesn't require everyone having the same ideology and political program. Likewise, if we required every member in a mass organization to share a high level of class consciousness and militancy (independently of the ebb and flow of struggles), we would be doomed either to fractions or paper tigers.

There is also a distinction between levels and organizations. That is there's a mass level before the mass organization. The mass organization is made up of people who come together around common interests. That means there are people with common interests who exist before they come together in the mass organization. Often there is mass level activity and organizing (like spontaneous struggles, informal work groups, etc.), before there is mass organization. There's also a revolutionary (or at least leftist) level before the revolutionary organization-there are people with ideas and actions who exist before they come together into a conscious revolutionary body.

Likewise with the intermediate level, there are individuals and activities that precede organization. Presently there are organizations that sometimes play the role of intermediate organization (unconsciously), and there is prefigurative organizing and tendencies of potential future intermediate organizations. I want to hazard a thesis; in the United States today the intermediate level is the most important site for revolutionaries. In fact, I think this is true beyond the United States, but I lack the space here to prove it, and will leave it up to others in other places. The intermediate level is strategic at this time is due to the state of political and mass organizations. The revolutionary left has been isolated from the working class (as well as other oppressed classes) for at least decades.

The left is largely derived from the student and sub-cultural movements which serve as a training ground for the various institutional left bureaucracies (NGOs, unions, lobbying groups, political parties, sections of academia, etc.), or at the least these institutions remain dominant within the left. The left reflects a particular section of society, one that sets it apart from the working class in its activity, vision, and makeup. There's an inertia of dyspraxia; the ideas the left espouses do not reflect the activity of the left. Whether this is from the black block to the so-revolutionaries working to elect the left wing of capital, the left is characterized at this time by an alienation from the working class rather than an ability to "act in its interest".

On the other side the mass movements are dominated by those same forces that the left breeds in, the institutionalized bureaucracies which are integrated into capitalism. Few if any mass movements exist where the working class has collective engagement and leadership, and bring collective activity to bare down on capital. The mass movements alone don't have any guarantees. Workers have their own ideas and logic, some of which can be liberatory and others of which can be reactionary (and everything in between). Both spontaneity and vanguardism are fundamentally flawed ways of looking at the world. While the mass movements ultimately have the power to transform society, the opposite may be true as well (they can become reactionary defenders of capitalism, or worse put forward reactionary radical politics). Nor is the left is immune from all same forces that threaten the mass movements, in fact the official or institutional left's track record is worse. Generally the left has been behind the masses in times of upheaval, and often in the role of repressing these movements.

Nature, Transformation, and Struggle

Historically, there's a syllogism on the libertarian left about unions that reflects the division between the mass and political levels. The syllogism is some variant of this:

1. A union is organized by people to improve working conditions
2. In order for it to make good on their demands, the unions have to bring together large enough groups to be effective.
3. If workers must be anarchists/revolutionaries/communists before they join then either:
   a. It would be unnecessary since the workers are already revolutionary, and could just launch a revolution. The union would just be a duplicate of a political organization. (or)
   b. The members would merely be anarchists/revolutionaries/communists on paper.

Another variant:

1. Trade unions exist to win better working conditions
2. An organized working class creates antagonism with a better funded and organized capitalists class
3. Either trade unions:
   a. Retain their militancy, and are attacked without restraint
      i. Thereby rendering them less/ineffective at winning gains

b. Or they can attempt class collaboration, and (sometimes) wins ground
    i. This integrates unions into capitalism, and creates a union bureaucracy with interests separated from the workers
    ii. The union has an interest in maintaining capitalism, and therefore becomes reactionary.

The conclusions of these lines of thought vary, but they share some things in common. This orientation puts forward an ahistorical and overly schematic conception of the mass and political level. The implications of these theories are that either this is how things are or how they should be. The conclusion is that we should either try to convince mass movements to avoid politicization or that we should recognize their inability to do so and diverge from them. The upshot of this these lines of thought tend to orient us towards the mass and political level in ways that make us unprepared for the ways in which movements change across time and constitute themselves.

The history of the workers movement is quite different from the arguments above. Rather than seeing very clear cut divisions either between revolutionary political organizations and very general mass unions (or between collaborationist and militant unions), we see every possible permutation. That is to be expected, however the above arguments try to argue against mixing mass and political, saying it's a witches brew that will yield only failure. It's an argument about the nature or essence of mass and political, which then tries to change real mass organizations and political organizations in relation to their supposed nature.

The problem is that these organizations are not static, they change. They also do not change on a whim, but there are distinct ebbs and flows of struggle. When the struggle is pitched and society (or at least some section of it) erupts into resistance, we can see mass organizations become politicized, and workers can be radicalized (or become radicalized towards fascistic tendencies). Likewise political organization can take on mass characteristics. In low points of struggle however politicized workers organization have a difficult time acting as a mass organization (though they try!), and mass organizations can tend towards domination by class collaborationism and bureaucratic parasitism.

While too general to say anything systematic, this is a fundamental insight. The nature of struggle is not static, but changes with the rise and fall of resistance. Now, this doesn't negate that you can see militant radical mass movements in times when other struggles are absent (perhaps the MST in Brazil during some periods is a good example, or the underground CNT under Franco), but we should expect that the scope of these struggles will be limited, and that we need another orientation other than expecting them to grow step-by-step linearly. How people organize themselves changes alongside this. That being said, I will mention only in passing that I don't think either the mass organization alone or the political organization are sufficient to bring down capitalism and create a new society. Both the experiences of party dictatorship in the soviet states, and the failures of syndicalism in Spain and elsewhere provide some data about the limitations of rigidly adhering to organizational forms as vehicles of liberation.

Struggle itself can be transformative, both of people and of levels and organizations. People at the mass level come together in organization to fight, and can transform their consciousness through those struggles. The mass organization itself may change then, and intermediate and political organizations may evolve from those struggles. The political level may build mass organization, or intermediate organization consolidates into political organization. Ultimately the mass level is the lifeblood of all struggles. Without the mass level, the intermediate and political levels are merely chasing winds. If we recognize this dynamic, that people are transformed in struggle and organizations can be built through these transformations, it helps rupture these rigid conceptions of the separations of the political and mass organization, the dominance of the political organization, or fetishized forms of the mass revolutionary organization.

In our time, the alienation of the left from struggle has created a kind of abstract obsession with either structures or ideas. An intellectual and often political sect driven tendency focuses solely on political content, in terms of trying to convince, debate, win, or propagate revolutionary ideas irrespective of the form they take, their embodiment in struggle, etc. An activist tendency tends towards an obsession with form and structure (assemblies, councils, unions, etc.), and usually merely formal democracy, as being inherently revolutionary irrespective of the content and ideas of the people inside the structure, or even its direction.

The content of struggles is however crucial. Formal democracy with a racist working class could yield a radical democratic fascism for example. We want to see a lived democracy, which can't be guaranteed by structures alone, and ultimately we need a democracy with a certain content, anarchist communist content. This means we should seek out and strengthen struggles that develop that content in the struggle, which is different from getting people to verbalize radical ideas.

Synthesizing these two features of organization in society brings into focus the role of the intermediate level. At the present time, we live in a low point of struggle in the United States. Today mass organization is either spread out and localized, repressed, or co-opted. Political organization is generally isolated and deformed, while capital is unleashing massive restructuring, discipline, and rationalization. The two options usually presented have been to unreflectively build mass movements, or to build political organizations (sometimes to build them alongside or within the mass movements). At the level of mass struggle, it's worth saying that organizing is incredibly difficult, and the strength and repression of capital alone is the greatest threat.

However the potential of capital to incorporate and utilize repressive measures on struggle through the mass movements is poorly understood and unappreciated on the left (especially since the level of struggle is low anyhow). On the revolutionary political side we have isolation manifested in its spontaneist, insurrectionary, or intellectual forms. More secondarily there are attempts to build political organization out of the mass movements which generally don't exist or are organized against political organization. It becomes a chicken or the egg sort of game, we lack the struggle to rupture the stasis of the mass movements, but we lack the mass movements to generate the struggle. It is not possible to will into existence militant class conscious mass movements, nor is it responsible to sit on one's hands waiting for it to occur.

During low points of struggle then, the intermediate level presents an alternative. While we may not be able to sustain radical mass organization at all times, we can bring together the most conscious elements of the mass movements together with the most active and grounded elements of the revolutionary movements to provide continuity, organization, coordination, and education between struggles. The intermediate level organization then is the memory, training ground, and nursery of developing consciousness in struggle, which is not possible within the ebb and flows with the mass movements, and which has different activity and unity from the political level. Unlike the mass movements, the intermediate level does not seek to become the vehicle for mediation between capital and the working class, and because of this it has space for activity and development that the mass movement can not. That said, in practice the intermediate level should arise from and remain directly bound to the mass level. The intermediate level gets its vitality and strength from the lessons, challenges, and strength of the struggle, and maintains its unity through that fight. Abstract coalitions of self-identified leftists wanting to do things at the mass level is a recipe for dead end reading groups more than anything else.

The Intermediate Level Already Exists in Struggle

Concretely this alternative already presents itself in practice for those who are organizing. For example take struggles within the unions for greater militancy and democracy. Often these struggles take the form of union elections, coordinated activity in union meetings, and sometimes actions. For the workers organizing these actions (whatever their merits), there are a number of challenges to overcome. First there is the space to hold meetings where strategy and tactics can be discussed, assessments of the organizing, and also space to bring contacts for one-on-one discussions, or even larger mass meetings. While this is true of physical space, it is also true in terms of skills, abilities, and materials. Workers need some level of pooling of resources to train each other, maintain systematic organization, pass on lessons of struggle, and develop their vision of direction. This requires a level of organization that the boss will be hostile to, and the union being challenged is also likely to oppose. There are other points to consider. If the group wins the struggle, often the organization leading up to the fight is incorporated into the existing bureaucracy, dissolves itself, or is attacked. Yet all the same problems resurface down the line as the winds change, and the rank and file find themselves embattled again. The intermediate level organization is that space that allows militants the coordination, resources, education, and continuity to provide ongoing resistance and the development of new militants across these ups and downs.

Given the marginality of unions in the US at this point, a more general experience in the workplace is with a non-unionized environment, especially a precarious one. Three examples from the current IWW illuminate the potential of the intermediate level organization. While somewhat arbitrary I use these examples, because I was involved in all of them so am able to bring forward these reflections with more intimacy, and they provide symmetrical analogies and contradictions.

In the restaurant industry there is a high level of turnover, and generally speaking precarious work. Benefits are non-existent, loyalty to particular shops fairly low, and staff is dependent on tips for basic income while often divided amongst themselves. In a variety of contexts the IWW organized in the restaurant sector. Most shops are in units of less than 20 workers, which are not financially sustainable for any traditional union (run by paid staff) to organize contracts in. It is extremely unlikely that a union would be able to leverage enough power to win a contract, sustain membership and activity needed to maintain the contract, and keep a union in anything but name under these conditions. Consequently a strategy developed in some local branches of the IWW organizing in restaurants and food service. The organizing was oriented to fighting around particular grievances using direct action, and generally through clandestine organizing without the boss knowing a union is involved. A number of successes arose from this approach, in contrast to experiments with rank and file contract-based approaches in small shops.

The trajectory of this organizing however was limited. Hot shops produced one or two politicized leaders, but once the grievance passed the shop cooled, and business went back to normal. Often workers would quit anyway, and the leadership did too on a number of occasions. Where the union could recruit and develop the leadership, and convince them to carry the struggle to other shops, the beginning of an industrial network of militants developed. In one city this developed into a permanent organization outside the IWW, though organized with IWW militants, and won a number of successes, integrating more workers into their organization as militants. The IWW in this case began to shift from being a mass organization proper, to being an intermediate organization of class conscious revolutionary militants building a tendency within an industry, and eventually even a separate mass organization while retaining its autonomy. The intermediate organization grew out of mass level struggles and organization, and eventually reproduced mass level organization.

During the early 2000s the IWW in Portland had a series of victories in non-profit social service shops, ultimately winning contracts for a hand full of workers in small shops. While the shops remained organized in name, the social service industrial union branch that was built out of these shops swelled with unorganized social workers. Effectively the industrial union began to function as a network of social service worker militants rather than a representative body of employees (except for the handful of workers under contract). Membership peaked at around 200 for a period. With the strategy oriented primarily towards gaining contracts in small shops in an era of budget cuts, the project was to fail. However, during the peak one of the contract shops was threatened with a massive budget cut by the county, threatening the services provided and the workers deeply. Because this industrial network existed, the industrial union branch was able to organize a section of the social service industry to take action at county budget hearings. The hearing was picketed, and the county backed down. Social service workers from across the industry uniting for a public display of the contradictions of capital in it's mangled approach to trying to serve society. This was press that the county was not in the mood to deal with.

The county instantly restored full funding. While this was merely a transitory experience, it demonstrated an alternative to the contractual model of building unions. Ultimately the contract shop was not able to move beyond this activity as a defensive move, and expand their gains and reach, but it served as an example for organizers who participated and took the lessons of that struggle to a different approach. In this case the inability to see beyond the union building project was to be the death of the intermediate network, which otherwise may have been able to expand, clarify itself, and presented a rallying point and challenge to austerity and capitalism.

In the summer of 2004 wildcat strikes swept the ports of the US, bringing the transit of goods to a halt on a massive scale. The strikes were organized by a huge number of small groupings of truckers across the country, tenuously linked, and communicating via text, Nextel phones, community radio, and the internet. The workers were often hostile to the unions trying to organize them, due to bad blood over sweetheart deals for the employer and failed attempts decades earlier. The struggle was actually merely a particular intense flare up of similar fights happening over the 15+ years since the deunionization and deregulation of the ports, and the subsequent shifts in working conditions and class recomposition of the drivers. During that time, drivers had learned how to fight and win directly without intermediaries, and could for periods overcome interethnic competition to present a class-wide front for organization. The problem they faced was constantly that of coordination across the grouplets, sustaining the gains they made, and systematizing their often patched together organizing. The strike wave of 2004 was to fade away on account of these problems. At the time, a mass based militant organization was possible, though the foundation for that transition had not been laid. Both before and after the intermediate level organization could have served to build up to those fights, and sustain the victories through building the needed leadership, connections, and organization.

Exploring Alternatives

To conclude there are a few clear avenues I see open for the building of intermediate organization. I will borrow here from a recent Miami Autonomy and Solidarity organization strategy, and present that collective work as an addition to my individual arguments here. At its most general, our task is two-fold. Revolutionaries active in the mass level need to prioritize work that facilitates the radicalization of militants at the mass level. Miami Autonomy and Solidarity call this M-I (mass to intermediate). At the same time, though of lesser priority given the lower quality of the left, we need to work to engage revolutionaries at the mass level. Given the low level of activity at the mass level by revolutionaries this would be I-M. M-I and I-M gives us a broad perspective for our work with M-I as primary. These strategic priorities are those developed by MAS which I am drawing from and borrowing.

Within existing practice however the intermediate level shows promise with the potential for intermediate organization a close possibility. Within the workers movement, there's a libertarian tendency which could organize collectively to intervene as a force based on common practices irrespective of the site of struggle. This would require struggle, working out the strategy through practice, debate and even rupture with elements (especially those tied to the institutionalized workers movement) in the milieu, such an intermediate organization would be a potential force for presenting alternatives where the organization doesn't exist, and unions are unwilling. The massive budget cuts, layoffs, and austerity measures are glaring examples where the unions have so far generally chosen to lobby or collaborate, and new forms of struggles have not magically arisen.

The student movement has seen the rise of student-interests based organizing, which has the potential to become mass organization. At this point this work is largely driven by libertarian elements, and an intermediary classist organization could prepare the groundwork for these struggles. In the southern cone of South America similar libertarian or revolutionary student fronts exist presently. With huge cuts and people flooding into colleges to find respite from severe unemployment, a wide crisis is developing in education. There is potential likewise for this work to produce militants who can carry their lessons and organization onto their workplaces following graduation, assuming they don't integrate with capital.

Within housing and transit organizing likewise there is organizing (generally dominated by NGOs unfortunately) that has linked and developed militants with often libertarian methods. The fare strike movements and increasing militancy of transit workers, and the uncertain nature of transit costs, has created potentially explosive situations. The housing crisis and the relative success of direct action against capital has gained momentum and developed self-conscious militants. Intermediate organization could draw out and develop the anti-capitalist logic and tendencies within these struggles, and consolidate gains.

Staff and Line Organization

Organizational structure involves, in addition to task organizational boundary considerations, the designation of jobs within an organization and the relationships among those jobs. There are numerous ways to structure jobs within an organization, but two of the most basic forms include simple line structures and line-and-staff structures.

In a line organization, top management has complete control, and the chain of command is clear and simple. Examples of line organizations are small businesses in which the top manager, often the owner, is positioned at the top of the organizational structure and has clear "lines" of distinction between him and his subordinates. The line-and-staff organization combines the line organization with staff departments that support and advise line departments. Most medium and large-sized firms exhibit line-and-staff organizational structures. The distinguishing characteristic between simple line organizations and line-and-staff organizations is the multiple layers of management within line-and-staff organizations. The following sections refer primarily to line-and-staff structures, although the advantages and disadvantages discussed apply to both types of organizational structures.

Several advantages and disadvantages are present within a line-and-staff organization. An advantage of a line-and-staff organization is the availability of technical specialists. Staff experts in specific areas are incorporated into the formal chain of command. A disadvantage of a line-and-staff organization is conflict between line and staff personnel.

Line-and-staff Positions

A wide variety of positions exist within a line-and-staff organization. Some positions are primary to the company's mission, whereas others are secondary—in the form of support and indirect contribution. Although positions within a line-and-staff organization can be differentiated in several ways, the simplest approach classifies them as being either line or staff.

A line position is directly involved in the day-to-day operations of the organization, such as producing or selling a product or service. Line positions are occupied by line personnel and line managers. Line personnel carry out the primary activities of a business and are considered essential to the basic functioning of the organization.

Line managers make the majority of the decisions and direct line personnel to achieve company goals. An example of a line manager is a marketing executive. Although a marketing executive does not actually produce the product or service, he or she directly contributes to the firm's overall objectives through market forecasting and generating product or service demand. Therefore, line positions, whether they are personnel or managers, engage in activities that are functionally and directly related to the principal workflow of an organization.

Staff positions serve the organization by indirectly supporting line functions. Staff positions consist of staff personnel and staff managers. Staff personnel use their technical expertise to assist line personnel and aid top management in various business activities. Staff managers provide support, advice, and knowledge to other individuals in the chain of command.

Although staff managers are not part of the chain of command related to direct production of products or services, they do have authority over personnel. An example of a staff manager is a legal adviser. He or she does not actively engage in profit-making activities, but does provide legal support to those who do. Therefore, staff positions, whether personnel or managers, engage in activities that are supportive to line personnel.

Line-and-staff Authority

Authority within a line-and-staff organization can be differentiated. Three types of authority are present: line, staff, and functional. Line authority is the right to carry out assignments and exact performance from other individuals.

Line Authority

Line authority flows down the chain of command. For example, line authority gives a production supervisor the right to direct an employee to operate a particular machine, and it gives the vice president of finance the right to request a certain report from a department head.

Therefore, line authority gives an individual a certain degree of power relating to the performance of an organizational task.

Two important clarifications should be considered, however, when discussing line authority: (1) line authority does not ensure effective performance, and (2) line authority is not restricted to line personnel.

The head of a staff department has line authority over his or her employees by virtue of authority relationships between the department head and his or her directly-reporting employees.

Staff Authority

Staff authority is the right to advise or counsel those with line authority. For example, human resource department employees help other departments by selecting and developing a qualified workforce. A quality control manager aids a production manager by determining the acceptable quality level of products or services at a manufacturing company, initiating quality programs, and carrying out statistical analysis to ensure compliance with quality standards. Therefore, staff authority gives staff personnel the right to offer advice in an effort to improve line operations.

Functional Authority

Functional authority is referred to as limited line authority. It gives a staff person power over a particular function, such as safety or accounting. Usually, functional authority is given to specific staff personnel with expertise in a certain area. For example, members of an accounting department might have authority to request documents they need to prepare financial reports, or a human resource manager might have authority to ensure that all departments are complying with equal employment opportunity laws. Functional authority is a special type of authority for staff personnel, which must be designated by top management.

Line-and-staff Conflict

Due to different positions and types of authority within a line-and-staff organization, conflict between line and staff personnel is almost inevitable. Although minimal conflict due to differences in viewpoints is natural, conflict on the part of line and staff personnel can disrupt an entire organization. There are many reasons for conflict. Poor human relations, overlapping authority and responsibility, and misuse of staff personnel by top management are all primary reasons for feelings of resentment between line and staff personnel. This resentment can result in various departments viewing the organization from a narrow stance instead of looking at the organization as a whole. Fortunately, there are several ways to minimize conflict. One way is to integrate line and staff personnel into a work team. The success of the work team depends on how well each group can work together in efforts to increase productivity and performance. Another solution is to ensure that the areas of responsibility and authority of both line and staff personnel are clearly defined. With clearly defined lines of authority and responsibility, each group may better understand their role in the organization. A third way to minimize conflict is to hold both line and staff personnel accountable for the results of their own activities. In other words, line personnel should not be entirely responsible for poor performance resulting from staff personnel advice.

Line-and-staff organizations combine the direct flow of authority present within a line organization with staff departments that offer support and advice. A clear chain of command is a consistent characteristic among line-and-staff organizational structures. Problems of conflict may arise, but organizations that clearly delineate responsibility can help minimize such conflict.

The Principles of Administration

This chapter discusses how have principles of public administration been applied to positively advance each of the following fields: education, transportation, health care, community development, law enforcement, and environmental policy. Also, the chapter hypothesizes what would become of the aforementioned services in the absence of a public administration system.

The means by which public administration achieves its goals and the responsibilities vested on it are solely dependant on tactical principles and practices utilized to execute them. In order for the public administrators to achieve the set targets they must adhere to a set of orchestrated instruments or regulations by the government of the day so that they don't deviate from the initial intended objectives. The public sector plays crucial roles in ensuring that the general populace is well tended to and that their individual rights are respected. The administrators of public policies are governors who are as well governed through established government principles, to ensure that they don't compromise quality of vital aspects of public requirements. Policies implemented by the government to public administrators as devices though which the public sector is ale to reach out to the people. Principles codify value system that is intrinsically part of governments, social, political and legal arena. Through codified public policies governors adhere to the governing principles, upon which the responsibilities ascribed to the public governance are succinctly met.

Defining Public Administration

Public Administration is the development, implementation and study of branches of government policy linked to pursuing the public good by enhancing civil society and social justice. In the past public administration was synonymous to government management, however, with increased vigor in participation of private sector into public matters some NGO'S committed to serve the public have joined the public sector. Public administration has gained credibility over time owing to change in governance and management process.

Moreover, due to the sensitivity of the activities carried out by Public administrators and the participation of private sector change in quality of the services offered by the government became inevitable.

The public servants attain knowledge and skills of executing duties in a program through trained policy analysts v ho are thoroughly founded with the background information on how to manage the public resources. Through public servants, interests of the general public are served in a satisfactory cost-effective manner the public servants are mandated to oversee each implemented activity on daily.

Generally, public administration gears its efforts towards understanding public entities and how they interrelate with others and the immediate world. Organizations that work under public administration are organized and managed to realize deliberately structured goals in the near future. Through public policy programs the government responds to the needs and interests of the Nation through satisfying them with the available resources.

Principles of Public Administration

Public administration is a complex process, it involves social, economical, legal and political matters al interwoven together. Due to the complexity of its nature, management and regulation of the public sector becomes a hurdle. In order for the public administration to be well regulated and governed bracket laws had to be implemented to cover all spheres and aspects of the sector. A unifying common law to govern public sector has been a very controversial issue in the U.S, this could be accrued to the governors' reluctance to be restricted by statutes which could tether the added advantages associated with the public sector. With time however, due to emerge of democratic tendencies elements that initiate good management and governance have been embraced. Political evolution has led to accord on the key principles that can be implemented to ensure that the services delivered to the public by the government are excellent.

The key identified principles are:-

Reliability and predictability: This principle declares that in order for the government initiative in form of services or practice to be deemed as satisfactory it must be reliable by being consisted and accurate in meeting the potential needs for which it was intended for. The government programs should be predictable a factor that can only be attained through consisted effort whereby the government agencies in charge of the programs don't fluctuate in executing their duties in a systematic manner. On the same note the programs implemented by the government to serve the needs of public should have legal certainty or judicial security.

Openness and transparency: The government serves the society through tax levies and other customs exerted on them through added costs. In return, the government is supposed to govern the obtained resources, plan and allocate them to various public programs in order to satisfy the public needs better. The public is aware that the government derives its funds from their resources, so it becomes increasingly important for the public to know hoe the government tis using their resources to sponsor public programs. In order for the public to trust the government of the day, the government avails all the necessary details concerning the programs so that the government doesn't appear to have creepy motives

Accountability: The government sponsored programs are normally accountable for all activities and procedures carried out in their programs which are geared towards public satisfaction. Accountability, per se is whereby the government justifies the actions it pursues in its endeavor to serve the public and at the same time taking responsibility for the actions it pursues in achieving its objectives whether they have positive or negative implications.

Efficiency and effectiveness: Efficiency is a principle employed by the government sponsored programs to ensure that all the resources at the disposal of the government are utilized without wastage of time, increased expense or effort wastage. When the government embraces efficiency in its procedures it becomes effectual in meeting public needs without wasting time or effort or expense.

Public administration ideals and doctrine principles have enhanced better performance in public sector creating union amongst the many areas that need to be administered properly in order to serve the public better. In the U.S the government has been able to embrace the key principles vital for ensuing that all the programs that serve public interest run coherently and are able to meet the desired needs of the public. Each sector served by the government becomes effective in meeting the social needs by embracing the principles of public administration.

Positive Principles in Governance that Enhance Competence in Education Sector

The administration of primary and secondary public education in the United States is conducted primarily by state governments in conjunction with local school districts. All states with the exception of Hawaii employ the structure of local school districts as the direct administrators of public primary and secondary education. The significance of education to the

U.S populace was evidenced by inclusion in all 50 state constitutions of a clause.. This clause mandated the government of the day to pursue the responsibility of offering quality education by ensuring that the education programs are properly managed through school districts.

In the U.S State involvement in public education has grown significantly during the twentieth century for instance there has been additional programs implemented in the education sector such as. Computerized teaching programs, advanced vocational training, all inclusive education for the physically challenged and many more. Americans view education as a key element of civic engagement in a democratic society and as the basis for skill training necessary for gainful employment in a rapidly changing economy. Over time the government bodies in charge of education have become efficient through accountability for all the processes and procedures they carry out. Each department of the U.S education sector carries out research on how to improve public governance and gives the recommendations to the state in order for it to assimilate them in its operations. The general public has continuously made demands on improvement of educational sector a fact that has made the U.S government to step up its efficiency in delivering public education through integrations of, vocational education, improving curriculum and facilities, and increasing teacher preparedness through specialized training programs.

The principle of transparency has been embraced in the educational realm by allowing the public to have access to government reports concerning educational matters. The involvement of the general public in school governance through educational boards has helped a great deal in enhancing the educational program efficiency in meeting the needs of the citizens as well.

Positive Principles in Governance that Enhance Competence in Transport Sector

The government ensures that it's well aware of the current operations on the roads, railroads, at ports and airports at all the times through a systematic regulatory mechanism of the transport sector in order to boost efficiency through better management and operations. Some key sectors like the airport, water ways are prone to attack by the terrorists hence the government utilizes non-intrusive, automatic sensors, computers and communications in order to extract the necessary information and facts that could be used to deduce security threat.

On the road sector the government employs the principles of efficiency to enhance effectiveness through gathering and processing system use and condition information, forecasting conditions that will hamper travel, optimizing traffic signal and ramp meter timing based on actual conditions so that vehicle stops and delay are minimized, identifying and responding quickly to accidents and other incidents before queues can build, and coordinating traffic operations with other operators, including support to commercial and transit fleet managers for efficient routing around incidents/closures or for oversize trucks and hazardous cargoes. In addition to system management purposes, the data can also be used for performance measurement, planning, and traveller information.

The government has increased efficiency of the transport sector by enhancing better user services by providing vital information such as en-route information and route guidance, and travel services. The information availed to the travellers, shippers and fleet operators help them to obtain instant information for planning routes and selecting modes before and during trips. Through the traffic police, the government is able to make roads safe for commuters, with immediate notification of collisions, road and lane closures, and other conditions that might impact highway, transit or fleet operations. The over speeding road users, drunkards and the people violating traffic rules are taken under the custody of traffic police to ensure that they don't cause damage to other road users. Incase of a break down road users get informed on alternative routes and travel options. The government has also made the transport sector reliable for users and the travellers who seek fun by providing information on travel destinations and accommodations, such as gas stations, lodging, attractions, and restaurants. The general public is able to benefit massively by operational efficiency implemented by the public sector through road infrastructure development and enhanced transport facilities.

The transport sector is able to account for losses experienced through the transport sector; the government has implemented technologies real-time traffic, road, weather and other system conditions. The equipments used to enhance smooth flow of traffic and incident detection include detector loops, closed circuit TV, vehicle probes, and other sensors. The management of transport sector ensures that there are centers in place that are used to process incoming traffic information and helps the sector to respond promptly to any occurring incidences, by alerting the general public and also taking measures to ensure the occurring incidences don't stop the general flow of transport and communication. Computerized traffic signal systems, ramp meters, rail grade crossing and other traffic control systems have been implemented to help the transport sector manage the system of commuting.

Positive Principles in Governance that Enhance Competence in Community Development Sector

The government is actively involved in community based programmes through agencies that help the community by strengthening the health, safety, self-reliance and economic vitality of individuals and families. The public administrations reach out to the community through partnerships to provide service and material backing. From the level of federal to the state level there are programs implemented to reach out to low-income and vulnerable people who are integral to the development of thriving communities. A program to cater for crime victims called Crime Victims Advocacy is reaches out to the community to cater for the needs of crime victims the program serves the community through the following methodologies: by foremost providing advocacy services to the affected victims of crime, this they do by needed services and resources the program also administers funds for community programs working with crime victims; assists communities in planning and implementing services for crime victims.

Advising local and state government agencies of practices, policies, and priorities which impact crime victims. Victims of crime who feel that they have not been accorded justice or that their rights have been trodden on forward their grievances to the community advocacy to fight for them. Developmental Disabilities Council is a council which fights for the rights and well being of the disabled vulnerable community; it caters for their educational and physical needs and ensuring that they are well treated in their homes. This community based program is funded and managed by the federal state and trickles down to the other sectors of economy through community ramifications.

The principles of public administration employed to ensure that the community is well served by the federal state include efficiency through management agencies which scrutinize all the programs under community development to ensure that they execute the duties and tasks vested on them. This way the program becomes effective in meeting the needs of the community. Accountability is attained through auditing and generation of reports that are available for public and private viewing. Transparency in community development is attained through community members' involvement the agencies blend and integrate their views with the desires of the potential communities that await their support.

Programs like Work First's Community Jobs., and other work programs help the general populace to gain access to employment and get financially empowered to support the poor families. The young people who have vocational training are able to get jobs through such arrangements to minimize their reliance on welfare programs statistics indicate that more than a quarter of Americans are without assets living paycheck to paycheck without savings or investments in equity like a home or small business. The community development programs target this kind of populace so that they can train them and empower them through employments in order to break the vicious cycle of poverty and help them acquire financial stability.

Through community development initiative asset building is initiated and it provides ground-breaking ways to improve local economies and the lives of the vulnerable citizens who are not able to cater for their basic needs. Community development programs offers start-up support and free consultation for asset building activities in local communities. Through the principles of transparency, and accountability funds are disseminated to the needy populace and a follow up program to ensure tat the funds provided are put into proper use ensues. The Office of Community Planning and Development (CPD) seeks to develop viable communities by promoting integrated approaches that provide decent housing, a suitable living environment, and expand economic opportunities for low and moderate income persons. The community development programs initiated by the government are able to trickle down to the expected citizens through partnerships among all levels of government and the private sector, including for-profit and non-profit organizations

Community Mobilization program is effectively used to deter the young population from use or abuse of drug substances. The (CM). Community Mobilization provides visions to various community members participating in creating and sustaining healthy, safe, economically viable communities, free from alcohol, tobacco, and other drugs. Violence and involvement in illegal activities is combated through educative programs which give the youths an alternative to violent activities. CM achieves its mission through collaboration, cooperation, communication, commitment, and competency in dealing with diverse range of populace.

Positive Principles in Governance that Enhance Competence in Law Enforcement Sector

Innovative practices are employed by this sector to reach out to the public; strategies are employed by the federal government in respect to coordination and delivery of law enforcement and public safety. The government is able to ensure defence and security for the citizens at the same time ensuring that the citizens adhere to the rules and regulations of the state.

Through bodies like Department of Justice, Federal Bureau of Investigation, Drug Enforcement Administration, National

Institute of Justice, Secret Service, Immigrations Customs and Enforcement the government is able to administer to all legal needs of the U.S citizens. The public administration body endeavors to ensure that justice is accorded to all irrespective of their age and social standing. Moreover, the justice system is accountable for all the legal decisions made and tries to be efficient by ensuring that the rights of the citizens are followed whether they commit crime or not.

For accountability purposes the law enforcement body ensures that all reports are well kept and can be verifiable through established facts. Efficiency is created by use of qualified and dedicated personnel in the field of law enforcement. Through advanced technology the police are able to prevent crime, take law offenders under their custody and ensure that justice is accorded to the offended parties.

Transparency comes in when lawyers are involved in the cases of offenders and offended, the citizens get to hear and know facts before a verdict is passed on them. Crime prevention, policing and community safety.

Positive Principles in Governance that Enhance Competence in Health Care Sector

Through the United States Department of Health and Human Services (HHS), a U.S cabinet department the which pursues the government goal of protecting the American's health at the same time offering essential human services. The cabinet department was created by President Jimmy Cater in the year 1979. currently, the department is administered and regulated by the United States Secretary of Health and Human Services, is responsible for addressing matters concerning public health as authorized by the Secretary or by the Assistant Secretary of Health in addition to his primary mission of administering the Commissioned Corps.

Under HHS are so many branches which have specific tasks allocated to them to enhance specialization in offering good health care to the general public the human health service works through its main branches to meet the needs of the U.S citizens for instance Administration for Children and Families

(ACF) is a part of HHS which is mainly concerned with child welfare, through the families the office is able to reach out to the children and ensure that their health is well tended to and that issues like immunization are offered to children to reduce mortality rate. Agency for Healthcare Research and Quality (AHRQ) is an office in the health care fraternity which establishes facts through research and fact finding. The center enhance knowledge on particular disease and seeks to find out the best cure for diseases which are still puzzle to the medical fraternity. It works in conjunction with Centers for Disease Control and Prevention.

Integrity is employed when conducting research the office does not implement cruel methods in establishing effectiveness of s drug when they invent it, animal testing is thoroughly avoided and for ant respondents who are used to experiment on a new introduced drunk there is usually a written consent and they get compensation for it. HHS has spread its branches both in federal and state level in order to reach out to the masses in the U.S populace and provide efficient services. The principle of accountability which cuts across all the publicly administered departments is employed in public medical services, the services provided meet the required standards and the medical fraternity takes responsibility for any harm they may cause to public

The Substance Abuse and Mental Health Services Administration (SAMHSA) caters for the vulnerable population which offers from mental damage and are unable to do their duties normally, under public administration the needs of the mentally ill is catered for. Moreover, drug abusers who need to be rehabilitated back to normality, are also tended here the right professional are used to reach out to all the dire cases of mental illness and through them effective health service is offered.

Positive Principles in Governance that Enhance Competence in Environmental Policy

The federal government has set up environmental policies which basically deal with legislating the Clean Air Act, the

Clean Water Act, and the National Environmental Policy Act (NEPA). The stated acts enable the government to actively participate in environmental conservation to ensure that the environment doe not get deteriorated rather its conserved and well tended for the benefits of future generations. Currently the government works in consensus with the industrial sector to ensure that there is less emission into the air, this is an efficient way of ensuring that there is no more remission of green house gases into the atmosphere as it has dire repercussions on the environment.

Through the government budget funds have been allocated to help in the research effort carried out by the research institute on how to reduce emissions into the atmosphere, measures that would ensure that the environment does not get polluted. The government too has used the principle of accountability whereby it admits the errors of the past of not controlling the pollution rates and now it endeavors to offer excellent solutions to the escalating pollution of water air and the atmosphere through industrial activities.

Due to the increased public awareness of the ill impacts of air pollution the government works in consensus with the general public through enlightening projects which helps the public to realize the dangers of environmental pollution in order for them to take caution.

If the governance and control of the government was replaced by another body or was obliterated all together a lot of things would come to a sudden holt. To begin with the U.S citizens would be forced to pay extra money for all the services provided for free by the government, such services include, free medications and free access to education, consequently a lot of people who are classified as low and middle class will lack basic necessities like medicine and education which the state offers to them for free. On the other hand, the issue of insecurity will go way out of control because the private sector does not have enough machinery like the public administration, more over crime rates will go up since mechanisms to counter crimes will have been altered. There will be increased mortality rate since child health will not be well catered for, some of the people who cannot afford medications for themselves may die out of cronical diseases and this may lead to low life expectancy. A lot of young people will languish aimlessly with no jobs or means to support them and they may end up taking drugs because they will be idle and frustrated a fact that may force them to acquire bad habits. Unfortunately there will be no Medicare for free and such youths will be most likely unable to acquire medications for them and they will.

The transport sector will be all messed up, there will be no control mechanisms or means to nub the offenders, hence road accidents will increase and deaths attributed to accidents will increase. The mechanisms to check and report on incidences that may hamper road and other transport systems will not be in use therefore the transport sector will lack focus and eventually collapse and affect the U.S economy so badly.In nutshell, without the public administration every body would suffers one way or the other all the U.S citizens depend on the public administration, it will be impossible to lead a normal life without the public services well manned under public administration.

Public administration is the back bone of all the states provided services to the U.S citizens (Canadians, French, British-UK, Russia, any country in the world), the administration could never work well unless it was under regulations and it operated using policies which act as guidelines on how services are delivered.

If the aspect of principles and guidelines is overlooked in ensuring delivery of services, the public sector could never be able to meet the needs of the general citizens.

Through the established principles which act as blue print on the directions of the government goals, the government is not only able to manage the public services but it is also able to set goals and achieve them. This is the beauty, magic and efficiency of Public Administration.

The basic and important aspects of administration are called as the principles. These are the points that have to be remembered to make sure that the administration is able to work properly. These principles of administration are universal. They are all similar in all places and may change with time, but even the changes will be universal.

The principles of management are all very important to successfully manage an institution or an organization. They are also guidelines that help the administrators to follow and help in simplifying the process of administration.

The different principles of administration are:

1. Hierarchy: There is a hierarchy in every administration. This may change from place to place and organization to organization, but the basic principle of hierarchy remains the same. Usually the hierarchy is in the shape of a pyramid with the leader of the organization or the head is at the top and the support staff on the lower part of the pyramid.
2. Control: The decision making and various controls are made usually by the various heads of the departments in an organization that has many departments. The final decisions on matters that concern the organization are finally made by the board or the management led by the Chairman. In smaller organizations, the decisions are made by the head of the organization.
3. Unity of command: Each employee should be answerable to only one person. If there are two different people who a person needs to answer, then there will be confusion and the employee will not be able to work to the maximum of his ability.
4. Delegation of authority: Here the head of the organization divides the authority to various heads in the organization. This makes more people accountable and also helps the management of the organization easier.
5. Specialization: Each employee should be made to do a particular kind of work. If he is made to do many different kind of work, then the individual will not be able to concentrate on a particular kind of job leading to inefficiency.

6. Objectives: The organization should have objectives and the employees and the management should strive to achieve these objectives. This will help the organization to grow.
7. Centralization and decentralization: The authority if help by the people at the top of the organization, it is called centralization. Decentralization is when the authority is delegated at various levels. The organization should have a right balance of both of these to function in an optimal manner.

These are the important principles of administration that should be followed for the organization to function effectively.

e-Government

e-Government (short for electronic government, also known as e-gov, digital government, online government, connected government or transformational government) is creating a comfortable, transparent, and cheap interaction between government and citizens (G2C – government to citizens), government and business enterprises (G2B –government to business enterprises) and relationship between governments (G2G – inter-agency relationship).

Defining e-Government and e-Governance

Definitions of e-Government and e-Governance abound in literature. Definitions for e-Government and e-Governance range from the working definitions like "the ability for anyone visiting the city website to communicate and/or interact with the city via the Internet in any way more sophisticated than a simple email letter to the generic city (or webmaster) email address provided at the site" to "the use of technology to enhance the access to and delivery of government services to benefit citizens, business partners and employees". Focus of these definitions range from those focusing on ICTs to those focusing on ICT enabled government and governance transformation. Some examples of such definitions include:

- The use of ICTs, and particularly the Internet, as a tool to achieve better government.

- The use of information and communication technologies in all facets of the operations of a government organization.
- The continuous optimization of service delivery, constituency participation and governance by transforming internal and external relationships through technology, the Internet and new media.

Whilst e-Government has traditionally been understood as being centred around the operations of government, e-Governance is understood to extend the scope by including citizen engagement and participation in governance.

As such, following in line with the OECD definition of e-Government, e-Governance can be defined as the use of ICTs as a tool to achieve better governance.

Delivery Models and Activities of e-Government

The primary delivery models of e-Government can be divided into:

- Government-to-Citizen or Government-to-Consumer (G2C)
- Government-to-Business (G2B)
- Government-to-Government (G2G)
- Government-to-Employees (G2E)

Within each of these interaction domains, four kinds of activities take place:

- pushing information over the Internet, e.g: regulatory services, general holidays, public hearing schedules, issue briefs, notifications, etc.
- two-way communications between the agency and the citizen, a business, or another government agency. In this model, users can engage in dialogue with agencies and post problems, comments, or requests to the agency.
- conducting transactions, e.g: lodging tax returns, applying for services and grants.
- governance, e.g: online polling, voting, and campaigning.

Non-internet e-Government

While e-government is often thought of as "online government" or "Internet-based government," many non-Internet "electronic government" technologies can be used in this context. Some non-Internet forms include telephone, fax, PDA, SMS text messaging, MMS, wireless networks and services, Bluetooth, CCTV, tracking systems, RFID, biometric identification, road traffic management and regulatory enforcement, identity cards, smart cards and other Near Field Communication applications; polling station technology (where non-online e-voting is being considered), TV and radio-based delivery of government services, email, online community facilities, news groups and electronic mailing lists, online chat, and instant messaging technologies.

Potential Benefits and Risks of e-Government

Risks

There are many considerations and potential implications of implementing and designing e-government, including disintermediation of the government and its citizens, impacts on economic, social, and political factors, vulnerability to cyber attacks, and disturbances to the *status quo* in these areas.

Hyper-surveillance

Increased contact between government and its citizens goes both ways. Once e-government begins to develop and become more sophisticated, citizens will be forced to interact electronically with the government on a larger scale. This could potentially lead to a lack of privacy for civilians as their government obtains more and more information on them. In a worse case scenario, with so much information being passed electronically between government and civilians, a totalitarian-like system could develop. When the government has easy access to countless information on its citizens, personal privacy is lost.

Is Hyper-Surveillance Too Much?

Moore's law states, our rate of technological development

and advances in the semiconductor industry, the complexity of integrated circuits doubles every 24 months. Although in 1965 Moore's law was initially made in the form of an observation and prediction, the more widely it became accepted the more it served as a goal for an entire industry. This also rings true today; Moore's Law is a statement of how fast technology increases in complexity and efficiency each year.

With the speed that technology continues to increase, it has become economically feasible for government agencies (from the local level to the federal level), to implement all measures of surveillance. From simple video surveillance systems found in the red light traffic cameras that will automatically take a video of your vehicle running a red light, which then generates an automated ticket to be mailed to you home, to the complex internet surveillance systems used by homeland security and the FBI.

Hyper-Surveillance has become a part of our everyday lives. There isn't a day that goes by where we aren't monitored with some form of technology. Security cameras in our local supermarket are recording our presence; the firewall at our work is monitoring the web sites we visit, and in some cases, emails are monitored for key words that could be considered offensive.

Some may feel that certain aspects of E-Government's use of hyper-surveillance are encroaching on their civil liberties. While others feel that with the tragic events of 9/11, it's a necessary evil that we must all live with in order to keep our loved ones from harm. Whether the government has gone too far, or if enough safeguards are in place to protect citizens from abuse, is subjective and up to open for debate.

In Local government, Hyper-Surveillance is commonly found in the form of traffic or red light cameras in the more busy intersections. "According to the Insurance Institute for Highway Safety, annually nearly 2 million crashes occur in intersections. In 2005, red light running resulted in 800 fatalities and over 165,000 injuries nation-wide. Last year, [The City of] Lynnwood [in Washington state] experienced nearly 1,400 collisions, many of which occurred within or immediately around intersections. It is believed that an automated red light camera program will reduce the number of red light collisions and injuries associated with such crashes. "

"[In New York city,] on the heels of breaking up an alleged bomb terror plot, [the city] is planning to place high-tech security cameras, license plate readers, and "weapons sensors" in midtown Manhattan. Sensors will try to detect chemical, biological, and radiological threats."

There is some debate on whether the deployment of this hyper-surveillance equipment will deter terrorists. One of the places the federal government employs Hyper-Surveillance is most notably in the war on terror. One example of where hyper-surveillance has worked is in the foiled attempt of a terrorist plot to bomb the Holland tunnel. "[The] plot was discovered through the monitoring of Internet chat rooms."

Electronic ease dropping devices such as the Carnivore Surveillance tool are used to perform a digital wire tap of a user's internet activity and record information specific to that user. "Once installed it uses a packet-sniffing software program to trace emails sent and received by the targeted user. The program sifts through all the emails and conversations and records the data on a removable hard drive. In some cases the program can be setup to look for certain words or phrases."

Since 9/11 there have been 19 foiled terrorist attacks in part due to the use of hyper-surveillance technologies.

"If law enforcement agents use special software to sort though great numbers of emails essentially tolling the entire internet for the transmissions that they are authorized by the Title III [search] order to intercept. Does the search become even more intrusive, and should it be subject to even greater restrictions that a standard wiretap or reading of electronic mail? There appears to be no reason to do so, in fact, the actual sifting through email which is done by Carnivore does not, itself implicate the Fourth Amendment. It is equivalent to an FBI agent going to the post office and looking at the writing on the envelopes of the letters there is order to find the ones that are addressed to a specific individual". "On Jul 10, 2008, Congress passed the FISA Amendments Act of 2008, which provides blanket retroactive immunity to telecommunications companies that assisted the "terrorist surveillance program" (TSP). This provision allows the Attorney General to immunize these private parties from suit by certifying that President Bush requested their assistance and assured them that their actions were legal. "

With the passing of the FISA Amendments Act of 2008, it has been easier for the federal government to use hyper-surveillance to collect information, on suspected terrorists. Lawsuits have been filed stating the telecommunications companies have impeded civil rights in the use of this blanket immunity but to date most have been dismissed. Surveillance means continual observation of a person or group, especially one suspected of doing something illegal.

Cost

Although "a prodigious amount of money has been spent" on the development and implementation of e-government, some say it has yielded only a mediocre product. The outcomes and effects of trial Internet-based governments are often difficult to gauge or unsatisfactory.

Inaccessibility

An e-government site that provides web access and support often does not offer the "potential to reach many users including those who live in remote areas, are homebound, have low literacy levels, exist on poverty line incomes, suffer from chronic illness, are single parents or older adults."

False Sense of Transparency and Accountability

Opponents of e-government argue that online governmental transparency is dubious because it is maintained by the governments themselves. Information can be added or removed from the public eye (i.e. the Internet) with or without public notice. For example, after the World Trade Center in New York City was attacked on September 11, 2001, United States federal officials removed a large amount of government information from its websites in the name of national security. This act went relatively unnoticed by United States citizens. To this day, very few organizations monitor and provide accountability for these modifications. Those that do so, like the United States' OMBWatch and Government Accountability Project, are often nonprofit volunteers. Even the governments themselves do not always keep track of the information they insert and delete.

Benefits

It is convenient and cost-effective for businesses, and the public benefits by getting easy access to the most current information available without having to spend time, energy and money to get it.

E-government helps simplify processes and makes access to government information more easily accessible for public sector agencies and citizens. For example, the Indiana Bureau of Motor Vehicles simplified the process of certifying driver records to be admitted in county court proceedings. Indiana became the first state to allow government records to be digitally signed, legally certified and delivered electronically by using Electronic Postmark technology. In addition to its simplicity, e-democracy services can reduce costs. Alabama Department of Conservation & Natural Resources, Wal-Mart and NIC developed an online hunting and fishing license service utilizing an existing computer to automate the licensing process. More than 140,000 licenses were purchased at Wal-Mart stores during the first hunting season and the agency estimates it will save $200,000 annually from service.

The anticipated benefits of e-government include efficiency, improved services, better accessibility of public services, and more transparency and accountability.

Democratization

One goal of e-government will be greater citizen participation. Through the internet, people from all over the country can interact with politicians or public servants and make their voices heard. Blogging and interactive surveys will allow politicians or public servants to see the views of the people they represent on any given issue. Chat rooms can place citizens in real-time contact with elected officials, their offices or provide them with the means to replace them by interacting directly with public servants, allowing voters to have a direct impact and influence in their government. These technologies can create a more transparent government, allowing voters to immediately see how and why their representation in the capital is voting the way they are. This helps voters better decide who to vote for in the future or how to help the public servants become more productive.

A government could theoretically move more towards a true democracy with the proper application of e-government. Government transparency will give insight to the public on how decisions are made and hold elected officials or public servants accountable for their actions. The public could become a direct and prominent influence in government legislature to some degree.

Environmental Bonuses

Proponents of e-government argue that online government services would lessen the need for hard copy forms. Due to recent pressures from environmentalist groups, the media, and the public, some governments and organizations have turned to the Internet to reduce this paper use.

Speed, Efficiency, and Convenience

E-government allows citizens to interact with computers to achieve objectives at any time and any location, and eliminates the necessity for physical travel to government agents sitting behind desks and windows.

Improved accounting and record keeping can be noted through computerization, and information and forms can be easily accessed, equaling quicker processing time. On the administrative side, access to help find or retrieve files and linked information can now be stored in databases versus hardcopies stored in various locations. Individuals with disabilities or conditions no longer have to be mobile to be active in government and can be in the comfort of their own homes.

Public Approval

Recent trials of e-government have been met with acceptance and eagerness from the public. Citizens participate in online discussions of political issues with increasing frequency, and young people, who traditionally display minimal interest in government affairs, are drawn to e-voting procedures. Although internet-based governmental programs have been criticized for lack of reliable privacy policies, studies have shown that people value prosecution of offenders over personal confidentiality. Ninety percent of United States adults approve of Internet tracking systems of criminals, and fifty-seven percent are willing to forgo some of their personal internet privacy if it leads to the prosecution of criminals or terrorists.

Technology-specific e-Government

There are also some technology-specific sub-categories of e-government, such as m-government (mobile government), u-government (ubiquitous government), and g-government (GIS/GPS applications for e-government.

E-government portals and platforms The primary delivery models of e-Government are classified depending on who benefits. In the development of public sector or private sector portals and platforms, a system is created that benefits all constituents. Citizens needing to renew their vehicle registration have a convenient way to accomplish it while already engaged in meeting the regulatory inspection requirement. On behalf of a government partner, business provides what has traditionally, and solely, managed by government and can use this service to generate profit or attract new customers. Government agencies are relieved of the cost and complexity of having to process the transactions.

To develop these public sector portals or platforms, governments have the choice to internally develop and manage, outsource, or sign a self-funding contract. The self-funding model creates portals that pay for themselves through convenience fees for certain e-government transactions, known as self-funding portals. Early players in this space include given Solutions, First Data Government Solutions and NIC, a company built on the self-funded model. Social networking is an emerging area for e-democracy. The social networking entry point is within the citizens' environment and the engagement is on the citizens' terms. Proponents of e-government perceive government use of social networks as a medium to help government act more like the public it serves. Examples of state usage can be found at The Official Commonwealth of Virginia Homepage, where citizens can find Google tools and open social forums. Government and its agents also have the opportunity to follow citizens to monitor satisfaction with services they receive. Through List Servs, RSS feeds, mobile messaging, micro-blogging services and blogs, government and its agencies can share information to citizens who share common interests and concerns. Government is also beginning to Twitter. In the state of Rhode Island, Treasurer Frank T. Caprio is offering daily tweets of the state's cash flow. Interested people can sign up at here. For a full list of state agencies with Twitter feeds, visit Real Life. Live document. For more information, visit transparent-gov.

UN e-Government Readiness Index

There are several international rankings of e-government maturity. The Eurostat rankings, Economist, Brown University, and the UN e-Government Readiness Index are among the most frequently cited. The United Nations conduct an annual e-Government survey which includes a section titled *e-Government Readiness*. It is a comparative ranking of the countries of the world according to two primary indicators: i) the state of e-government readiness; and ii) the extent of e-participation. Constructing a model for the measurement of digitized services, the Survey assesses the 191 member states of the UN according to a quantitative composite index of e-government readiness based on website assessment; telecommunication infrastructure and human resource endowment.

Ethics, Transparency and Accountability

The end of the cold war; spreading democratization; a shift in balance among the state, the market and civil society;

globalization; and changing social mores — among other factors — are altering the environment in which governments are operating. The explosion of new information and communication technologies is also allowing for a rapid, global diffusion of ideas and practices, enabling the public to demand higher standards of ethics, transparency and accountability in the public sector. These prerequisite values of good governance and sustainable development not only buttress responsive public policy and high levels of public sector performance but also play a crucial role in preventing the onset of systemic corruption. There is now international recognition that corruption impedes economic development, undermines stability and erodes trust in public institutions. The pernicious effects of corruption — the lack or poor quality of essential public infrastructure and services — are borne by those the least able to do so: the poor.

Given its mandate of fostering good governance and sound public administration in development, the Division for Public Administration and Development Management (DPADM) supports setting international standards, carries out comparative policy research and analysis, and assists in building capacity in institutions safeguarding public sector ethics, transparency and accountability. The Division's activities are predicated on the analysis that corruption is one symptom of poor administration and mismanagement.

These situations allow unscrupulous public officials to exploit opportunities for putting self above public interest, contrary to the spirit of public service. Moreover, the Division's activities also seek to preserve the integrity of other "honest" public officials by putting into place an "ethics infrastructure" that not only provides guidance for good conduct but also administratively and legally punishes misconduct. The "ethics infrastructure" includes measures to enhance and preserve organizational integrity, access to information that promotes transparency and accountability, and oversight by independent institutions and the public at large. In conducting its activities in this area, the Division has tried to best leverage the United Nations' uniquely global membership, through fostering international dialogue and the exchange of experiences.

3

Leadership in Organizations

Leadership in Formal Organizations

An organization that is established as an instrument or means for achieving defined objectives has been referred to as a formal organization. Its design specifies how goals are subdivided and reflected in subdivisions of the organization. Divisions, departments, sections, positions, jobs, and tasks make up this work structure.

Thus, the formal organization is expected to behave impersonally in regard to relationships with clients or with its members. According to Weber's definition, entry and subsequent advancement is by merit or seniority. Each employee receives a salary and enjoys a degree of tenure that safeguards him from the arbitrary influence of superiors or of powerful clients. The higher his position in the hierarchy, the greater his presumed expertise in adjudicating problems that may arise in the course of the work carried out at lower levels of the organization. It is this bureaucratic structure that forms the basis for the appointment of heads or chiefs of administrative subdivisions in the organization and endows them with the authority attached to their position.

Leadership in Informal Organizations

In contrast to the appointed head or chief of an administrative unit, a leader emerges within the context of the informal organization that underlies the formal structure. The informal organization expresses the personal objectives and goals of the individual membership. Their objectives and goals may or may not coincide with those of the formal organization. The informal organization represents an extension of the social structures that generally characterize human life — the spontaneous emergence of groups and organizations as ends in themselves. In prehistoric times, man was preoccupied with his personal security, maintenance, protection, and survival. Now man spends a major portion of his waking hours working for organizations.

His need to identify with a community that provides security, protection, maintenance, and a feeling of belonging continues unchanged from prehistoric times. This need is met by the informal organization and its emergent, or unofficial, leaders. Leaders emerge from within the structure of the informal organization. Their personal qualities, the demands of the situation, or a combination of these and other factors attract followers who accept their leadership within one or several overlay structures. Instead of the authority of position held by an appointed head or chief, the emergent leader wields influence or power. Influence is the ability of a person to gain cooperation from others by means of persuasion or control over rewards. Power is a stronger form of influence because it reflects a person's ability to enforce action through the control of a means of punishment.

Leader in Organizations

An individual who is appointed to a managerial position has the right to command and enforce obedience by virtue of the authority of his position. However, he must possess adequate personal attributes to match his authority, because authority is only potentially available to him.

In the absence of sufficient personal competence, a manager may be confronted by an emergent leader who can challenge his role in the organization and reduce it to that of a figurehead. However, only authority of position has the backing of formal sanctions. It follows that whoever wields personal influence and power can legitimize this only by gaining a formal position in the hierarchy, with commensurate authority.

Hybrid Organizations

A hybrid organization is a body that operates in both the public sector and the private sector, simultaneously fulfilling public duties and developing commercial market activities. As a result the hybrid organization becomes a mixture of both a part of government and a private corporation.

Management Levels

Managers are organizational members who are responsible for the work performance of other organizational members. Managers have formal authority to use organizational resources and to make decisions. In organizations, there are typically three levels of management: top-level, middle-level, and first-level. These three main levels of managers form a hierarchy, in which they are ranked in order of importance. In most organizations, the number of managers at each level is such that the hierarchy resembles a pyramid, with many more first-level managers, fewer middle managers, and the fewest managers at the top level. Each of these management levels is described below in terms of their possible job titles and their primary responsibilities and the paths taken to hold these positions. Additionally, there are differences across the management levels as to what types of management tasks each does and the roles that they take in their jobs. Finally, there are a number of changes that are occurring in many organizations that are changing the management hierarchies in them, such as the increasing use of teams, the prevalence of outsourcing, and the flattening of organizational structures.

Top-level Managers

Top-level managers, or top managers, are also called senior management or executives. These individuals are at the top one or two levels in an organization, and hold titles such as: Chief Executive Officer (CEO), Chief Financial Officer (CFO), Chief Operational Officer (COO), Chief Information Officer (CIO), Chairperson of the Board, President, Vice president, Corporate head. Often, a set of these managers will constitute the top management team, which is composed of the CEO, the

COO, and other department heads. Top-level managers make decisions affecting the entirety of the firm. Top managers do not direct the day-to-day activities of the firm; rather, they set goals for the organization and direct the company to achieve them. Top managers are ultimately responsible for the performance of the organization, and often, these managers have very visible jobs.

Top managers in most organizations have a great deal of managerial experience and have moved up through the ranks of management within the company or in another firm. An exception to this is a top manager who is also an entrepreneur; such an individual may start a small company and manage it until it grows enough to support several levels of management. Many top managers possess an advanced degree, such as a Masters in Business Administration, but such a degree is not required.

Some CEOs are hired in from other top management positions in other companies. Conversely, they may be promoted from within and groomed for top management with management development activities, coaching, and mentoring. They may be tagged for promotion through succession planning, which identifies high potential managers.

Middle-level Managers

Middle-level managers, or middle managers, are those in the levels below top managers. Middle managers' job titles include: General manager, Plant manager, Regional manager, and Divisional manager.

Middle-level managers are responsible for carrying out the goals set by top management. They do so by setting goals for their departments and other business units. Middle managers can motivate and assist first-line managers to achieve business objectives. Middle managers may also communicate upward, by offering suggestions and feedback to top managers. Because middle managers are more involved in the day-to-day workings of a company, they may provide valuable information to top managers to help improve the organization's bottom line. Jobs in middle management vary widely in terms of responsibility and salary. Depending on the size of the company and the number of middle-level managers in the firm, middle managers may supervise only a small group of employees, or they may manage very large groups, such as an entire business location. Middle managers may be employees who were promoted from first-level manager positions within the organization, or they may have been hired from outside the firm. Some middle managers may have aspirations to hold positions in top management in the future.

First-level Managers

First-level managers are also called first-line managers or supervisors. These managers have job titles such as: Office manager, Shift supervisor, Department manager, Foreperson, Crew leader, Store manager. First-line managers are responsible for the daily management of line workers—the employees who actually produce the product or offer the service. There are first-line managers in every work unit in the organization. Although first-level managers typically do not set goals for the organization, they have a very strong influence on the company. These are the managers that most employees interact with on a daily basis, and if the managers perform poorly, employees may also perform poorly, may lack motivation, or may leave the company.

Management Levels and the Four Managerial Functions

Managers at different levels of the organization engage in different amounts of time on the four managerial functions of planning, organizing, leading, and controlling. Planning is choosing appropriate organizational goals and the correct directions to achieve those goals. Organizing involves determining the tasks and the relationships that allow employees to work together to achieve the planned goals. With leading, managers motivate and coordinate employees to work together to achieve organizational goals. When controlling, managers monitor and measure the degree to which the organization has reached its goals. The degree to which top, middle, and supervisory managers perform each of these functions is presented in Exhibit 1. Note that top managers do considerably more planning, organizing, and controlling than do managers at any other level. However, they do much less leading. Most of the leading is done by first-line managers. The amount of planning, organizing, and controlling decreases down the hierarchy of management; leading increases as you move down the hierarchy of management.

Management Roles

In addition to the broad categories of management functions, managers in different levels of the hierarchy fill different managerial roles. These roles were categorized by researcher Henry Mintzberg, and they can be grouped into three major types: decisional, interpersonal, and informational.

Decisional Roles

Decisional roles require managers to plan strategy and utilize resources. There are four specific roles that are decisional. The *entrepreneur* role requires the manager to assign resources to develop innovative goods and services, or to expand a business. Most of these roles will be held by top-level managers, although middle managers may be given some ability to make such decisions. The *disturbance handler* corrects unanticipated problems facing the organization from the internal or external environment. Managers at all levels may take this role. For example, first-line managers may correct a problem halting the assembly line or a middle level manager may attempt to address the aftermath of a store robbery. Top managers are more likely to deal with major crises, such as requiring a recall of defective products. The third decisional role, that of *resource allocator,* involves determining which work units will get which resources. Top managers are likely to make large, overall budget decisions, while middle mangers may make more specific allocations. In some organizations, supervisory managers are responsible for determine allocation of salary raises to employees. Finally, the *negotiator* works with others, such as suppliers, distributors, or labour unions, to reach agreements regarding products and services. First-level managers may negotiate with employees on issues of salary increases or overtime hours, or they may work with other supervisory managers when needed resources must be shared. Middle managers also negotiate with other managers and are likely to work to secure preferred prices from suppliers and distributors. Top managers negotiate on larger issues, such as labour contracts, or even on mergers and acquisitions of other companies.

Interpersonal Roles

Interpersonal roles require managers to direct and supervise employees and the organization. The *figurehead* is typically a top of middle manager. This manager may communicate future organizational goals or ethical guidelines to employees at company meetings. A *leader* acts as an example for other employees to follow, gives commands and directions to subordinates, makes decisions, and mobilizes employee support. Managers must be leaders at all levels of the organization; often lower-level managers look to top management for this leadership example. In the role of *liaison,* a manger must coordinate the work of others in different work units, establish alliances between others, and work to share resources. This role is particularly critical for middle managers, who must often compete with other managers for important resources, yet must maintain successful working relationships with them for long time periods.

Informational Roles

Informational roles are those in which managers obtain and transmit information. These roles have changed dramatically as technology has improved. The *monitor* evaluates the performance of others and takes corrective action to improve that performance. Monitors also watch for changes in the environment and within the company that may affect individual and organizational performance. Monitoring occurs at all levels of management, although managers at higher levels of the organization are more likely to monitor external threats to the environment than are middle or first-line managers. The role of *disseminator* requires that managers inform employees of changes that affect them and the organization. They also communicate the company's vision and purpose.

Managers at each level disseminate information to those below them, and much information of this nature trickles from the top down. Finally, a *spokesperson* communicates with the external environment, from advertising the company's goods and services, to informing the community about the direction of the organization. The spokesperson for major announcements, such as a change in strategic direction, is likely to be a top manager. But, other, more routine information may be provided by a manager at any level of a company. For example, a middle manager may give a press release to a local newspaper, or a supervisor manager may give a presentation at a community meeting.

Management Skills

Regardless of organizational level, all managers must have five critical skills: technical skill, interpersonal skill, conceptual skill, diagnostic skill, and political skill.

Technical Skill

Technical skill involves understanding and demonstrating proficiency in a particular workplace activity. Technical skills are things such as using a computer word processing program, creating a budget, operating a piece of machinery, or preparing a presentation.

The technical skills used will differ in each level of management. First-level managers may engage in the actual operations of the organization; they need to have an understanding of how production and service occur in the organization in order to direct and evaluate line employees. Additionally, first-line managers need skill in scheduling workers and preparing budgets. Middle managers use more technical skills related to planning and organizing, and top managers need to have skill to understand the complex financial workings of the organization.

Interpersonal Skill

Interpersonal skill involves human relations, or the manager's ability to interact effectively with organizational members. Communication is a critical part of interpersonal skill, and an inability to communicate effectively can prevent career progression for managers. Managers who have excellent technical skill, but poor interpersonal skill are unlikely to succeed in their jobs. This skill is critical at all levels of management.

Conceptual Skill

Conceptual skill is a manager's ability to see the organization as a whole, as a complete entity. It involves understanding how organizational units work together and how the organization fits into its competitive environment.

Conceptual skill is crucial for top managers, whose ability to see "the big picture" can have major repercussions on the success of the business. However, conceptual skill is still necessary for middle and supervisory managers, who must use this skill to envision, for example, how work units and teams are best organized.

Diagnostic Skill

Diagnostic skill is used to investigate problems, decide on a remedy, and implement a solution. Diagnostic skill involves other skills—technical, interpersonal, conceptual, and politic. For instance, to determine the root of a problem, a manager may need to speak with many organizational members or understand a variety of informational documents. The difference in the use of diagnostic skill across the three levels of management is primarily due to the types of problems that must be addressed at each level.

For example, first-level managers may deal primarily with issues of motivation and discipline, such as determining why a particular employee's performance is flagging and how to improve it. Middle managers are likely to deal with issues related to larger work units, such as a plant or sales office. For instance, a middle-level manager may have to diagnose why sales in a retail location have dipped. Top managers diagnose organization-wide problems, and may address issues such as strategic position, the possibility of outsourcing tasks, or opportunities for overseas expansion of a business.

Political Skill

Political skill involves obtaining power and preventing other employees from taking away one's power. Managers use power to achieve organizational objectives, and this skill can often reach goals with less effort than others who lack political skill. Much like the other skills described, political skill cannot stand alone as a manager's skill; in particular, though, using political skill without appropriate levels of other skills can lead to promoting a manager's own career rather than reaching organizational goals. Managers at all levels require political skill; managers must avoid others taking control that they should have in their work positions. Top managers may find that they need higher levels of political skill in order to successfully operate in their environments. Interacting with competitors, suppliers, customers, shareholders, government, and the public may require political skill.

Changes in Management Hierarchies

There are a number of changes to organizational structures that influence how many managers are at each level of the organizational hierarchy, and what tasks they perform each day.

Flatter Organizational Structures

Organizational structures can be described by the number of levels of hierarchy; those with many levels are called "tall" organizations. They have numerous levels of middle management, and each manager supervises a small number of employees or other managers. That is, they have a small span of control. Conversely, "flat" organizations have fewer levels of middle management, and each manager has a much wider span of control. Examples of organization charts that show tall and flat organizational structures are presented in Exhibit 2.

Many organizational structures are now more flat than they were in previous decades. This is due to a number of factors. Many organizations want to be more flexible and increasingly responsive to complex environments. By becoming flatter, many organizations also become less centralized. Centralized organizational structures have most of the decisions and responsibility at the top of the organization, while decentralized organizations allow decision-making and authority at lower levels of the organization. Flat organizations that make use of decentralization are often more able to efficiently respond to customer needs and the changing competitive environment. As organizations move to flatter structures, the ranks of middle-level managers are diminishing. This means that there a fewer opportunities for promotion for first-level managers, but this also means that employees at all levels are likely to have more autonomy in their jobs, as flatter organizations promote decentralization. When organizations move from taller to flatter hierarchies, this may mean that middle managers lose their jobs, and are either laid off from the organization, or are demoted to lower-level management positions. This creates a surplus of labour of middle level managers, who may find themselves with fewer job opportunities at the same level.

Increased Use of Teams

A team is a group of individuals with complementary skills who work together to achieve a common goal. That is, each team member has different capabilities, yet they collaborate to perform tasks. Many organizations are now using teams more frequently to accomplish work because they may be capable of performing at a level higher than that of individual employees. Additionally, teams tend to be more successful when tasks require speed, innovation, integration of functions, and a complex and rapidly changing environment.

Another type of managerial position in an organization that uses teams is the team leader, who is sometimes called a project manager, a program manager, or task force leader. This person manages the team by acting as a facilitator and catalyst. He or she may also engage in work to help accomplish the team's goals. Some teams do not have leaders, but instead are self-managed. Members of self-managed teams hold each other accountable for the team's goals and manage one another without the presence of a specific leader.

Outsourcing

Outsourcing occurs when an organization contracts with another company to perform work that it previously performed itself. Outsourcing is intended to reduce costs and promote efficiency. Costs can be reduced through outsourcing, often because the work can be done in other countries, where labour and resources are less expensive than in the United States. Additionally, by having an out-sourcing company aid in production or service, the contracting company can devote more attention and resources to the company's core competencies. Through outsourcing, many jobs that were previously performed by American workers are now performed overseas. Thus, this has reduced the need for many first-level and middle-level managers, who may not be able to find other similar jobs in another company.

There are three major levels of management: top-level, middle-level, and first-level. Managers at each of these levels have different responsibilities and different functions. Additionally, managers perform different roles within those managerial functions. Finally, many organizational hierarchies are changing, due to changes to organizational structures due to the increasing use of teams, the flattening of organizations, and outsourcing.

Management and Executive Development

Manager effectiveness has an enormous impact on a firm's success. Therefore, companies must provide instruction for managers and high-potential management candidates in order to help them perform current and future jobs with the utmost proficiency. Management development has long been an important component of corporate strategic planning. In fact, many companies consider the identification and development of next-generation managers to be their top human resource challenge.

Management development is important for new managers because these individuals really need instruction on how to perform their new supervisory jobs. Even so, companies often allow employees to make the transition to management with little or no training, leaving them with feelings of frustration, inadequacy, and dismay.

More experienced managers also benefit from management development. A majority of first-line managers have their sights set on higher-level management jobs. Given these ambitions, companies need to provide lower-level and mid-level managers with formal development programs in order to help them climb the corporate ladder.

Management instruction programs should bridge gaps between what individuals already know and what they need to know for their new positions. Managers need different skills at each managerial level.

First-line managers need training in;

- basic supervision
- motivation
- career planning
- performance feedback.

Middle managers need training in;

- designing and implementing effective group and intergroup work and information systems
- defining and monitoring group-level performance indicators
- diagnosing and resolving problems within and among work groups
- designing and implementing reward systems that support cooperative behaviour.

Executives need training in;

- broadening their understanding of how factors such as competition, world economies, politics, and social trends influence the effectiveness of the organization.

A variety of approaches are used to teach these subjects. Some are in traditional classroom-type settings, while others are taught outside of the classroom via career resource centers, job rotation, mentoring, and special projects.

Classroom Instruction

Classroom training takes place within the organization or outside at seminars and universities.

Lecture

Most training experts criticize lectures because they are passive learning devices, focusing on one-way communication to learners who do not have the opportunity to clarify material. Lectures generally fail to gain and maintain learner attention unless they are given by someone who is able to make the material meaningful and promote questions and discussions. Lectures are most appropriate for situations where simple knowledge acquisition is the goal (e.g., describing company history during a new employee orientation session). However, lectures are not well suited to serve as the sole training method for teaching management skills, because the format does not provide trainees with feedback or the opportunity for practice.

Job Duties and Responsibilities: Trainees learn what they must do to fulfill the company's expectations of them.

Policies and Procedures: Trainees learn company police and procedures.

Employee Familiarization: Trainees become familiar with the job functions of their employees. The training provides specific instructions on how to review job descriptions, performance standards, personnel files, and so forth.

Attitudes and Confidence: The training attempts to establish new attitudes toward the job employees, and the manager, and to build the confidence necessary for managers to be effective on the job.

Handling Employee Interactions: Trainees are taught how to handle interpersonal problems effectively through such techniques as behaviour modelling.

Career Development: Trainees learn about career opportunities in higher levels of management and how they may advance in the future.

General Management Training: These courses typically

cover labour relations, management theory and practice, labour economics, and general management functions.

Human Relations/Leadership Programs: These topics are narrower than general management programs. They focus on the human relations problems of leadership, supervision, attitude toward employees, and communication.

Self-Awareness Program: The content of these programs is understanding one's own behaviour and how that behaviour is viewed by others, identifying the so-called games people play, and learning about one's strengths and weaknesses.

Problem-Solving/Decision-Making Programs: The emphasis is on teaching generalized problem-solving and decision-making skills that would be applicable to the wide range of work problems that managers encounter.

Case Method

As the name suggests, the case method requires management trainees to analyse cases or scenarios depicting realistic job situations. Cases often are structured like a play that opens in the middle of a story and uses flashbacks to describe the action that led up to the opening scene, where an employee has just made a key decision. The rest of the case lays out the documentation and data available to the decision maker at the time of the decision. Questions are posed at the end of the case that ask the trainees to analyse the situation and recommend a solution. For instance, they may be asked to state the nature of the problem, identify the events that led to the problem, and indicate what the individual should do to resolve the problem.

The case method rests on the assumption that people are most likely to retain and use what they learn if they reach an understanding through "guided discovery." Trainers act as guides or facilitators. Cases typically do not have right or wrong answers. Therefore, the aim of the method is not to teach trainees the "right" answer, but rather to teach them how to identify potential problems and recommend realistic actions. Critics of this method balk at the lack of direction trainees receive when analysing a case. What if they arrive at a poor decision? Moreover, trainees do not get the opportunity to practice their skills. For instance, after analysing a case involving a subordinate who has repeatedly arrived at work late, the trainees may conclude that the manager should have said something sooner and must now provide counsel. However, the case method does not afford trainees the opportunity to practice their counseling skills.

Role-playing

As an instructional technique, role-playing presents a hypothetical problem involving human interaction. Trainees spontaneously act out that interaction face-to-face. Participants are then given feedback by the trainer and the rest of the group on their performance so they may gain insight regarding the impact of their behaviour on others. The issues addressed during feedback typically revolve around these types of questions:

- What was correct about the participant's behaviour?.
- What was incorrect about the participant's behaviour?
- How did the participant's behaviour make the other participants feel?
- How could the trainee have handled the situation more effectively?

Role-playing may be used to develop skill in any area that involves human interaction. The method is most often used for teaching human relations skills and sales techniques. Role-playing provides management trainees with an opportunity to practice the skill being taught. It thus goes beyond the case method, which merely requires the trainee to make a decision regarding how to handle a situation. These two methods are often used in conjunction with one another. That is, after analysing a case and recommending a solution, trainees are asked to act out the solution in the form of a role-play.

Critics of the role-playing method point out that role-players are often given little guidance beforehand on how to handle transactions. This may cause them to make mistakes, resulting in embarrassment and a loss of self-confidence. When their mistake-ridden role-play is finished, they sit, never getting the opportunity to do it correctly.

Behaviour Modelling

Behaviour modelling is based on the idea that workers learn best when they see how a task should be performed and then practice the task with feedback until they are competent. This method is similar to role-playing in that the trainees act out situations playing certain roles. However, the methods differ in two important ways. First, behaviour modelling teaches trainees a preferred way to perform a task. Second, the interactions occurring during behaviour modelling are practice sessions, not role plays. The trainees practice only the right way. If they make a mistake, the trainer immediately corrects them and asks them to repeat the step correctly.

A behaviour modelling program typically consists of the following steps:

Present an overview of the material. This usually consists of a brief lecture that describes training objectives and the importance of the skill to be learned.

Describe the procedural steps. The trainee learns the one best way (or at least an effective way) to handle a situation. Case and role-playing methods, on the other hand, stress the variety of effective ways to handle a situation and do not emphasize any one particular approach.

Model or demonstrate the procedural steps. The trainee is shown a "model" of how the task is to be performed correctly. The model usually is presented in the form of a videotape or live demonstration.

Allow guided practice. Trainees then practice the modeled behaviours. As previously stated, these sessions are similar to role-plays, except that trainees are given feedback by the instructor (or classmates) during the skill practice session, rather than after. This procedure forces trainees to correct mistakes as soon as they are made, assuring them an opportunity to practice the correct way of performing the task.

Practice sessions start with simple problems, similar to those depicted in the model. Later practice sessions are made more realistic by adding complexity to the situation.

Provide on-the-job reinforcement. Participants' managers often go through identical training programs to ensure that they will understand what their employees are learning and, hence, support these new behaviours back on the job.

Behaviour modelling has become very popular. Research examining its effectiveness has been quite favourable. Behaviour modelling works because it successfully incorporates each of the aforementioned learning principles: it captures and maintains trainees' attention and provides ample opportunity for practice and feedback.

Nonclassroom Methods

Nonclassroom methods include career resource centers, job rotation, coaching and mentoring, and special assignments.

Career Resource Centers

Some organizations make learning opportunities available to interested candidates by establishing career resource centers, which usually include an in-house library with relevant reading material. In some companies, candidates simply are given recommended readings lists. Other companies provide management candidates with comprehensive career-planning guides that contain company-related information about available resources, career options, and counselling contacts. These individuals also may be given workbooks that provide written assignments.

Job Rotation

Job rotation exposes management trainees to various organizational settings by rotating them through a number of departments. Thus, trainees have an opportunity to gain an overall perspective of the organization and learn how various parts interrelate. Additionally, they face new challenges during these assignments that may foster new skill development. Trainees usually have full management responsibility during these assignments. For example, in one hospital new department supervisors rotate through all major departments on a monthly basis, serving in a managerial capacity during their "tours." Although they often learn a lot from such training, they also may make harmful mistakes during their learning period because they lack knowledge of the functional area that they are supervising.

Coaching And Mentoring

Coaching is a method of management development that is conducted on the job, in which experienced managers or peers advise and guide trainees in solving managerial problems. Typically, less experienced managers are coached by their direct supervisor or a coworker on their specific performance of managerial tasks. An upper-level manager is likely to coach several lower-level managers at once, offering feedback, helping them to find expert advice, and providing resources.

Mentoring is different from coaching in several ways. Mentors are experienced supervisors who establish close, one-on-one relationships with new managers, called proteges. A mentor usually is someone two or three levels higher in the organization than the protege who teaches, guides, advises, counsels, and serves as a role model; the mentor is not necessarily the protege's direct supervisor.

Mentoring can help the protege to form common values with the organization's senior leadership and better understand his or her role in the company. Additionally, proteges are often advocated for and protected by a mentor. A mentor may ensure that the protege is assigned high-visibility projects, or even change negative opinions about the protege that may be held by others in the company. While a coach focuses on job-specific advice, a mentor is likely to give advice on a broader range of topics related to the protege's career success.

Special Assignment

Companies sometimes assign special, nonroutine job duties to trainees in order to prepare them for future assignments. One such special project is called action learning, which derives its name from the fact that the trainees can learn by doing.

Candidates are given real problems generated by management. Trainees might be given a written assignment that specifies objectives, action plans, target dates, and the name of the person responsible for monitoring the completion of the assignment. For instance, trainees might be asked to study the company's budgeting procedures and submit a written critique.

Another type of special project is the task force, where trainees are grouped together and asked to tackle an actual organizational problem. For example, the task force may be asked to develop a new performance appraisal form, solve a quality problem, or design a program to train new employees. Trainees not only gain valuable experience by serving on a task force, they also have the opportunity to "show their stuff" to others within the organization.

Management Succession Planning

Most organizations base their management development and training efforts on succession planning, a systematic process of defining future management requirements and identifying the candidates who best meet them. Unfortunately, many companies take a very informal approach to succession planning. Identification of high-potential candidates is largely subjective, based on the opinions of the nominating managers, who choose "fast-track" or "superstar" employees with little consideration of the actual requirements of future positions. Research has found that promotions within the management ranks are often based on employee behaviours that have no bearing on managerial effectiveness; specifically, networking had the greatest influence on managerial promotions, even though networking made no contribution to actual performance. Additionally, ill-conceived succession planning activities can have disastrous consequences; as many as 30 percent of all newly placed executives are unprepared for their jobs and ultimately fail to meet company expectations.

Elements of an effective succession planning program involve human resource planning, defining qualifications for positions, identifying career paths, and developing replacement charts. The first step in succession planning is human resource planning, in which forecasting is used to determine projected staffing needs for the next several years. Based on these needs, management succession plans should specify key management positions for which staffing should be targeted. Succession plans should next define pertinent individual qualifications needed for each targeted position, which are based on information derived from a job analysis. A firm then identifies individuals with high potential for promotion into or through the management ranks. This is accomplished by assessing employee abilities and career interests through records of career progress, experience, past performance, and self-reported interests regarding future career steps.

Following the above steps, an organization identifies a career path for each high-potential candidate (i.e., those who have the interest and ability to move upward in the organization).

A career path typically appears as a flow chart, indicating the sequencing of specific jobs that may lead one up the organizational ladder to a targeted job. The final step is to develop replacement charts that indicate the availability of candidates and their readiness to step into the various management positions. Such charts usually are depicted as diagrams superimposed onto the organizational chart. These show possible replacement candidates, in rank order, for each management position. Rank orders are often based on the candidates' "overall potential scores," derived on the basis of their past performance, experience, test scores, and so on.

Organizational Culture

Organizational culture is an idea in the field of Organizational studies and management which describes the psychology, attitudes, experiences, beliefs and values (personal and cultural values) of an organization. It has been defined as "the specific collection of values and norms that are shared by people and groups in an organization and that control the way they interact with each other and with stakeholders outside the organization."

This definition continues to explain organizational values also known as "beliefs and ideas about what kinds of goals members of an organization should pursue and ideas about the appropriate kinds or standards of behaviour organizational members should use to achieve these goals. From organizational values develop organizational norms, guidelines or expectations that prescribe appropriate kinds of behaviour by employees in particular situations and control the behaviour of organizational members towards one another."

Organizational culture is not the same as corporate culture. It is wider and deeper concepts, something that an organization 'is' rather than what it 'has'.

Corporate culture is the total sum of the values, customs, traditions and meanings that make a company unique. Corporate culture is often called "the character of an organization" since it embodies the vision of the company's founders. The values of a corporate culture influence the ethical standards within a corporation, as well as managerial behaviour.

Senior management may try to determine a *corporate culture*. They may wish to impose corporate values and standards of behaviour that specifically reflect the objectives of the organization. In addition, there will also be an extant internal culture within the workforce. Work-groups within the organization have their own behavioural quirks and interactions which, to an extent, affect the whole system. Roger Harrison's four-culture typology, and adapted by Charles Handy, suggests that unlike organizational culture, corporate culture can be 'imported'. For example, computer technicians will have expertise, language and behaviours gained independently of the organization, but their presence can influence the culture of the organization as a whole.

Strong/Weak Cultures

Strong culture is said to exist where staff respond to stimulus because of their alignment to organizational values. In such environments, strong cultures help firms operate like well-oiled machines, cruising along with outstanding execution and perhaps minor tweaking of existing procedures here and there.

Conversely, there is weak culture where there is little alignment with organizational values and control must be exercised through extensive procedures and bureaucracy.

Where culture is strong—people do things because they believe it is the right thing to do—there is a risk of another phenomenon, Group think. "Group think" was described by Irving L. Janis. He defined it as "...a quick and easy way to refer to a mode of thinking that people engage when they are deeply involved in a cohesive ingroup, when members' strivings for unanimity override their motivation to realistically appraise alternatives of action." This is a state where people, even if they have different ideas, do not challenge organizational thinking, and therefore there is a reduced capacity for innovative thoughts. This could occur, for example, where there is heavy reliance on a central charismatic figure in the organization, or where there is an evangelical belief in the organization's values, or also in groups where a friendly climate is at the base of their identity (avoidance of conflict). In fact group think is very common, it happens all the time, in almost every group. Members that are defiant are often turned down or seen as a negative influence by the rest of the group, because they bring conflict.

Innovative organizations need individuals who are prepared to challenge the status quo—be it group think or bureaucracy, and also need procedures to implement new ideas effectively.

Typologies of Organizational Cultures

Several methods have been used to classify organizational culture. Some are described below: Demonstrated that there are national and regional cultural groupings that affect the behaviour of organizations. Hofstede looked for national differences between over 100,000 of IBM's employees in different parts of the world, in an attempt to find aspects of culture that might influence business behaviour.

Hofstede identified five dimensions of culture in his study of national influences:

- *Power distance*-The degree to which a society expects there to be differences in the levels of power. A high score suggests that there is an expectation that some individuals wield larger amounts of power than others. A low score reflects the view that all people should have equal rights.

- *Uncertainty avoidance* reflects the extent to which a society accepts uncertainty and risk.
- *Individualism vs. collectivism*-individualism is contrasted with collectivism, and refers to the extent to which people are expected to stand up for themselves, or alternatively act predominantly as a member of the group or organization. However, recent researches have shown that high individualism may not necessarily mean low collectivism, and vice versa. Research indicates that the two concepts are actually unrelated. Some people and cultures might have both high individualism and high collectivism, for example. Someone who highly values duty to his or her group does not necessarily give a low priority to personal freedom and self-sufficiency
- *Masculinity vs. femininity*-refers to the value placed on traditionally male or female values. Male values for example include competitiveness, assertiveness, ambition, and the accumulation of wealth and material possessions.
- *Long vs. short term orientation*-describes a society's "time horizon," or the importance attached to the future versus the past and present. In long term oriented societies, thrift and perseverance are valued more; in short term oriented societies, respect for tradition and reciprocation of gifts and favors are valued more. Eastern nations tend to score especially high here, with Western nations scoring low and the less developed nations very low; China scored highest and Pakistan lowest.

Deal and Kennedy

Deal and Kennedy defined organizational culture as *the way things get done around here*. They measured organizations in respect of:

- Feedback-quick feedback means an instant response. This could be in monetary terms, but could also be seen in other ways, such as the impact of a great save in a soccer match.
- Risk-represents the degree of uncertainty in the organization's activities.

Using these parameters, they were able to suggest four classifications of organizational culture:

- The Tough-Guy Macho Culture. Feedback is quick and the rewards are high. This often applies to fast moving financial activities such as brokerage, but could also apply to a police force, or athletes competing in team sports. This can be a very stressful culture in which to operate.
- The Work Hard/Play Hard Culture is characterized by few risks being taken, all with rapid feedback. This is typical in large organizations, which strive for high quality customer service. It is often characterized by team meetings, jargon and buzzwords.
- The Bet your Company Culture, where big stakes decisions are taken, but it may be years before the results are known. Typically, these might involve development or exploration projects, which take years to come to fruition, such as oil prospecting or military aviation.
- The Process Culture occurs in organizations where there is little or no feedback. People become bogged down with how things are done not with what is to be achieved. This is often associated with bureaucracies. While it is easy to criticize these cultures for being overly cautious or bogged down in red tape, they do produce consistent results, which is ideal in, for example, public services.

Charles Handy

Charles Handy (1985) popularized the 1972 work of Roger Harrison of looking at culture which some scholars have used to link organizational structure to organizational culture. He describes Harrison's four types thus:

- a Power Culture which concentrates power among a few. Control radiates from the center like a web. Power Cultures have few rules and little bureaucracy; swift decisions can ensue.
- In a Role Culture, people have clearly delegated authorities within a highly defined structure. Typically, these organizations form hierarchical bureaucracies. Power derives from a person's position and little scope exists for expert power.
- By contrast, in a Task Culture, teams are formed to solve particular problems. Power derives from expertise as long as a team requires expertise. These cultures often feature the multiple reporting lines of a matrix structure.
- A Person Culture exists where all individuals believe themselves superior to the organization. Survival can become difficult for such organizations, since the concept of an organization suggests that a group of like-minded individuals pursue the organizational goals. Some professional partnerships can operate as person cultures, because each partner brings a particular expertise and clientele to the firm.

Edgar Schein

Edgar Schein, an MIT Sloan School of Management professor, defines organizational culture as:

"A pattern of shared basic assumptions that the group learned as it solved its problems of external adaptation and internal integration, that has worked well enough to be considered valid and, therefore, to be taught to new members as the correct way you perceive, think, and feel in relation to those problems".

According to Schein, culture is the most difficult organizational attribute to change, outlasting organizational products, services, founders and leadership and all other physical attributes of the organization. His organizational model illuminates culture from the standpoint of the observer, described by three cognitive levels of organizational culture.

At the first and most cursory level of Schein's model is organizational attributes that can be seen, felt and heard by the uninitiated observer-collectively known as *artifacts*. Included are the facilities, offices, furnishings, visible awards and recognition, the way that its members dress, how each person visibly interacts with each other and with organizational outsiders, and even company slogans, mission statements and other operational creeds. The next level deals with the professed culture of an organization's members-the *values*. At this level, local and personal values are widely expressed within the organization. Organizational behaviour at this level usually can be studied by interviewing the organization's membership and using questionnaires to gather attitudes about organizational membership.

At the third and deepest level, the organization's tacit assumptions are found. These are the elements of culture that are unseen and not cognitively identified in everyday interactions between organizational members. Additionally, these are the elements of culture which are often taboo to discuss inside the organization.

Many of these 'unspoken rules' exist without the conscious knowledge of the membership. Those with sufficient experience to understand this deepest level of organizational culture usually become acclimatized to its attributes over time, thus reinforcing the invisibility of their existence. Surveys and casual interviews with organizational members cannot draw out these attributes—rather much more in-depth means is required to first identify then understand organizational culture at this level. Notably, culture at this level is the underlying and driving element often missed by organizational behaviourists.

Using Schein's model, understanding paradoxical organizational behaviours becomes more apparent. For instance, an organization can profess highly aesthetic and moral standards at the second level of Schein's model while simultaneously displaying curiously opposing behaviour at the third and deepest level of culture.

Superficially, organizational rewards can imply one organizational norm but at the deepest level imply something completely different. This insight offers an understanding of the difficulty that organizational newcomers have in assimilating organizational culture and why it takes time to become acclimatized. It also explains why organizational change agents usually fail to achieve their goals: underlying tacit cultural norms are generally not understood before would-be change agents begin their actions. Merely understanding culture at the deepest level may be insufficient to institute cultural change because the dynamics of interpersonal relationships (often under threatening conditions) are added to the dynamics of organizational culture while attempts are made to institute desired change.

Arthur F Carmazzi

The Blame culture This culture cultivates distrust and fear, people blame each other to avoid being reprimanded or put down, this results in no new ideas or personal initiative because people don't want to risk being wrong.

Multi-directional culture This culture cultivates minimized cross-department communication and cooperation. Loyalty is only to specific groups (departments). Each department becomes a clique and is often critical of other departments which in turn creates lots of gossip. The lack of cooperation and Multi-Direction is manifested in the organization's inefficiency.

Live and let live culture This culture is Complacency, it manifests Mental Stagnation and Low Creativity. People here have little future vision and have given up their passion. There is average cooperation and communication, and things do work, but they do not grow. People have developed their personal relationships and decided who to stay away from, there is not much left to learn.

Brand congruent culture People in this culture believe in the product or service of the organization, they feel good about what their company is trying to achieve and cooperate to achieve it. People here are passionate and seem to have similar goals in the organisation. They use personal resources to actively solve problems and while they don't always accept the actions of management or others around them, they see their job as important. Most everyone in this culture is operating at the level of Group.

Leadership enriched culture People view the organization as an extension of themselves, they feel good about what they personally achieve through the organization and have exceptional Cooperation. Individual goals are aligned with the goals of the organization and people will do what it takes to make things happen. As a group, the organization is more like family providing personal fulfillment which often transcends ego so people are consistently bringing out the best in each other. In this culture, Leaders do not develop followers, but develop other leaders. Most everyone in this culture is operating at the level of Organization.

Carmazzi's model requires application of his Directive Communication psychology to evolve the culture. While the idea of having a Leadership Enriched organization is inspirational, it would require substantial Leadership resources to develop. The concept of Evolving the culture assumes that "Every Individual in the organization wants to do a good job", and the behaviours that result in poor performance are manifestations of psychology the group or organization has created through policies, leadership and poor communication.

Robert A. Cooke

The Organizational Culture Inventory: Culture Clusters.

Robert A. Cooke, PhD, defines culture as the behaviours that members believe are required to fit in and meet expectations within their organization. The Organizational Culture Inventory? measures twelve behavioural of norms that are grouped into three general types of cultures:

- Constructive Cultures, in which members are encouraged to interact with people and approach tasks in ways that help them meet their higher-order satisfaction needs.
- Passive/Defensive Cultures, in which members believe they must interact with people in ways that will not threaten their own security.

- Aggressive/Defensive Cultures, in which members are expected to approach tasks in forceful ways to protect their status and security.

The Constructive Cluster

The Constructive Cluster includes cultural norms that reflect expectations for members to interact with others and approach tasks in ways that will help them meet their higher order satisfaction needs for affiliation, esteem, and self-actualization. The four cultural norms in this cluster are:

- Achievement
- Self-Actualizing
- Humanistic-Encouraging
- Affiliative.

Organizations with Constructive cultures encourage members to work to their full potential, resulting in high levels of motivation, satisfaction, teamwork, service quality, and sales growth. Constructive norms are evident in environments where quality is valued over quantity, creativity is valued over conformity, cooperation is believed to lead to better results than competition, and effectiveness is judged at the system level rather than the component level. These types of cultural norms are consistent with (and supportive of) the objectives behind empowerment, total quality management, transformational leadership, continuous improvement, reengineering, and learning organizations.

The Passive/Defensive Cluster

Norms that reflect expectations for members to interact with people in ways that will not threaten their own security are in the Passive/Defensive Cluster.

The four Passive/Defensive cultural norms are:

- Approval
- Conventional
- Dependent
- Avoidance.

In organizations with Passive/Defensive cultures, members feel pressured to think and behave in ways that are inconsistent with the way they believe they should in order to be effective. People are expected to please others (particularly superiors) and avoid interpersonal conflict. Rules, procedures, and orders are more important than personal beliefs, ideas, and judgment. Passive/Defensive cultures experience a lot of unresolved conflict and turnover, and organizational members report lower levels of motivation and satisfaction.

The Aggressive/Defensive Cluster

The Aggressive/Defensive Cluster includes cultural norms that reflect expectations for members to approach tasks in ways that protect their status and security.

The Aggressive/Defensive cultural norms are:

- Oppositional
- Power
- Competitive
- Perfectionistic.

Organizations with Aggressive/Defensive cultures encourage or require members to appear competent, controlled, and superior. Members who seek assistance, admit shortcomings, or concede their position are viewed as incompetent or weak. These organizations emphasize finding errors, weeding out "mistakes," and encouraging members to compete against each other rather than competitors. The short-term gains associated with these strategies are often at the expense of long-term growth.

Elements

G. Johnson described a cultural web, identifying a number of elements that can be used to describe or influence Organizational Culture:

- The Paradigm: What the organization is about; what it does; its mission; its values.
- Control Systems: The processes in place to monitor what is going on. Role cultures would have vast

rulebooks. There would be more reliance on individualism in a power culture.

- Organizational Structures: Reporting lines, hierarchies, and the way that work flows through the business.
- Power Structures: Who makes the decisions, how widely spread is power, and on what is power based?
- Symbols: These include organizational logos and designs, but also extend to symbols of power such as parking spaces and executive washrooms.
- Rituals and Routines: Management meetings, board reports and so on may become more habitual than necessary.
- Stories and Myths: build up about people and events, and convey a message about what is valued within the organization.

These elements may overlap. Power structures may depend on control systems, which may exploit the very rituals that generate stories which may not be true.

Organizational Culture and Change

There are a number of methodologies specifically dedicated to organizational culture change such as Peter Senge's *Fifth Discipline* and Arthur F Carmazzi's *Directive Communication.* These are also a variety of psychological approaches that have been developed into a system for specific outcomes such as the *Fifth Discipline's* "learning organization" or *Directive Communication's* "corporate culture evolution." Ideas and strategies, on the other hand, seem to vary according to particular influences that affect culture.

Burman and Evans (2008) argue that it is 'leadership' that affects culture rather than 'management', and describe the difference. When one wants to change an aspect of the culture of an organization one has to keep in consideration that this is a long term project. Corporate culture is something that is very hard to change and employees need time to get used to the new way of organizing. For companies with a very strong and specific culture it will be even harder to change.

Cummings & Worley give the following six guidelines for cultural change, these changes are in line with the eight distinct stages mentioned by Kotter (1995):

Formulate a clear strategic vision: In order to make a cultural change effective a clear vision of the firm's new strategy, shared values and behaviours is needed. This vision provides the intention and direction for the culture change (Cummings & Worley, 2005).

Display Top-management commitment: It is very important to keep in mind that culture change must be managed from the top of the organization, as willingness to change of the senior management is an important indicator. The top of the organization should be very much in favour of the change in order to actually implement the change in the rest of the organization. De Caluwe & Vermaak provide a framework with five different ways of thinking about change.

Model culture change at the highest level: In order to show that the management team is in favour of the change, the change has to be notable at first at this level. The behaviour of the management needs to symbolize the kinds of values and behaviours that should be realized in the rest of the company. It is important that the management shows the strengths of the current culture as well, it must be made clear that the current organizational does not need radical changes, but just a few adjustments.

Modify the organization to support organizational change

The fourth step is to modify the organization to support organizational change.

Select and socialize newcomers and terminate deviants: A way to implement a culture is to connect it to organizational membership, people can be selected and terminate in terms of their fit with the new culture.

Changes in culture can lead to tensions between organizational and individual interests, which can result in ethical and legal problems for practitioners. This is particularly relevant for changes in employee integrity, control, equitable treatment and job security.

Change of culture in the organizations is very important and inevitable. Culture innovations is bound to be because it entails introducing something new and substantially different from what prevails in existing cultures.

Cultural innovation is bound to be more difficult than cultural maintenance. People often resist changes hence it is the duty of the management to convince people that likely gain will outweigh the losses. Besides institutionalization, deification is another process that tends to occur in strongly developed organizational cultures. The organization itself may come to be regarded as precious in itself, as a source of pride, and in some sense unique. Organizational members begin to feel a strong bond with it that transcends material returns given by the organization, and they begin to identify with in. The organization turns into a sort of clan.

Entrepreneurial Culture

Stephen McGuire defined and validated a model of organizational culture that predicts revenue from new sources. An Entrepreneurial Organizational Culture (EOC) is a system of shared values, beliefs and norms of members of an organization, including valuing creativity and tolerance of creative people, believing that innovating and seizing market opportunities are appropriate behaviours to deal with problems of survival and prosperity, environmental uncertainty, and competitors' threats, and expecting organizational members to behave accordingly.

Elements of Entrepreneurial Culture

- People and enpowerment focused
- Value creation through innovation and change
- Attention to the basics
- Hands-on management
- Doing the right thing
- Freedom to grow and to fail
- Commitment and personal responsibility
- Emphasis on the future.

Critical Views

Writers from Critical management studies have tended to express skepticism about the functionalist and unitarist views of culture put forward by mainstream management thinkers. Whilst not necessarily denying that organizations are cultural phenomena, they would stress the ways in which cultural assumptions can stifle dissent and reproduce management propaganda and ideology.

After all, it would be naive to believe that a single culture exists in all organizations, or that cultural engineering will reflect the interests of all stakeholders within an organization. In any case, Parker has suggested that many of the assumptions of those putting forward theories of organizational culture are not new.

They reflect a long-standing tension between cultural and structural (or informal and formal) versions of what organizations are. Further, it is perfectly reasonable to suggest that complex organizations might have many cultures, and that such sub-cultures might overlap and contradict each other. The neat typologies of cultural forms found in textbooks rarely acknowledge such complexities, or the various economic contradictions that exist in capitalist organizations.

One of the strongest and widely recognised criticisms of theories that attempt to categorize or 'pigeonhole' organizational culture is that put forward by Linda Smircich. She uses the metaphor of a plant root to represent culture, describing that it drives organizations rather than vice versa.

Organizations are the product of organizational culture, we are unaware of how it shapes behaviour and interaction (also recognised through Scheins (2002) underlying assumptions) and so how can we categorize it and define what it is?

Organizational Communication Perspective on Culture

The organizational communication perspective on culture is divided into three areas:

- Traditionalism: Views culture through objective things such as stories, rituals, and symbols
- Interpretivism: Views culture through a network of shared meanings (organization members sharing subjective meanings)
- Critical-Interpretivism: Views culture through a network of shared meanings as well as the power struggles created by a similar network of competing meanings

There are many different types of communication that contribute in creating an organizational culture:

- Metaphors such as comparing an organization to a machine or a family reveal employees' shared meanings of experiences at the organization.
- Stories can provide examples for employees of how to or not to act in certain situations.
- Rites and ceremonies combine stories, metaphors, and symbols into one. Several different kinds of rites that affect organizational culture:
  - Rites of passage: employees move into new roles
  - Rites of degradation: employees have power taken away from them
  - Rites of enhancement: public recognition for an employee's accomplishments
  - Rites of renewal: improve existing social structures
  - Rites of conflict reduction: resolve arguments between certain members or groups
  - Rites of integration: reawaken feelings of membership in the organization
- Reflexive comments are explanations, justifications, and criticisms of our own actions. This includes:
  - Plans: comments about anticipated actions
  - Commentaries: comments about action in the present
  - Accounts: comments about an action or event that has already occurred

Such comments reveal interpretive meanings held by the speaker as well as the social rules they follow.

- Fantasy Themes are common creative interpretations of events that reflect beliefs, values, and goals of the organization. They lead to rhetorical visions, or views of the organization and its environment held by organization members.

Schema

Schemata (plural of schema) are knowledge structures a person forms from past experiences allowing them to respond to similar events more efficiently in the future by guiding the processing of information. Schemata are created through interaction with others and thus inherently involve communication.

Stanley G. Harris argues that five categories of in-organization schemata are necessary for organizational culture:

- Self-in-organization schemata: a person's concept of themselves within the context of the organization, including their personality, roles, and behaviour
- Person-in-organization schemata: a person's memories, impressions and expectations of other individuals within the organization
- Organization schemata: subset of person schemata, a person's generalized perspective on others as a whole in the organization
- Object/concept-in-organization schemata: knowledge an individual has of organization aspects other than other people
- Event-in-organization schemata: a person's knowledge of social events within an organization

All of these categories together represent a person's knowledge of an organization. Organizational culture is created when the schemata's of individuals within an organization come to resemble each other. This is primarily done through organizational communication as individuals directly or indirectly share knowledge and meanings.

Mergers, Organizational Culture, and Cultural Leadership

One of the biggest obstacles in the way of the merging of two organizations is organizational culture. Each organization has its own unique culture and most often, when brought together, these cultures clash. When mergers fail employees point to issues such as identity, communication problems, human resources problems, ego clashes, and inter-group conflicts, which all fall under the category of "cultural differences". One way to combat such difficulties is through cultural leadership. Organizational leaders must also be cultural leaders and help facilitate the change from the two old cultures into the one new culture. This is done through cultural innovation followed by cultural maintenance.

- Cultural innovation includes:
  - o Creating a new culture: recognizing past cultural differences and setting realistic expectations for change
  - o Changing the culture: weakening and replacing the old cultures
- Cultural maintenance includes:
  - o Integrating the new culture: reconciling the differences between the old cultures and the new one
  - o Embodying the new culture: Establishing, affirming, and keeping the new culture.

4

Dynamic Leadership, Discipline and Policy-formation

Leadership is stated as the "process of social influence in which one person can enlist the aid and support of others in the accomplishment of a common task." Definitions more inclusive of followers have also emerged. Alan Keith of Genentech states that, "Leadership is ultimately about creating a way for people to contribute to making something extraordinary happen." Tom DeMarco says that leadership needs to be distinguished from posturing. Leadership remains one of the most relevant aspects of the organizational context. However, defining leadership has been challenging and definitions can vary depending on the situation.

According to Ann Marie E. McSwain, Assistant Professor at Lincoln University, "leadership is about capacity: the capacity of leaders to listen and observe, to use their expertise as a starting point to encourage dialogue between all levels of decision-making, to establish processes and transparency in decision-making, to articulate their own values and visions clearly but not impose them. Leadership is about setting and not just reacting to agendas, identifying problems, and initiating change that makes for substantial improvement rather than managing change." The following sections discuss several important aspects of leadership including a description of what leadership is and a description of several popular theories and styles of leadership. This article also discusses topics such as the role of emotions and vision, as well as leadership effectiveness and performance, leadership in different contexts, how it may differ from related concepts (i.e., management), and some critiques of leadership as generally conceived.

Theories of Leadership

Students of leadership have produced theories involving traits, situational interaction, function, behaviour, power, vision and values, charisma, and intelligence among others.

Trait Theory

Trait theory tries to describe the characteristics associated with effective leadership.

Early History

The search for the characteristics or traits of leaders has been ongoing for centuries. History's greatest philosophical writings from Plato's *Republic* to Plutarch's *Lives* have explored the question of "What qualities distinguish an individual as a leader?" Underlying this search was the early recognition of the importance of leadership and the assumption that leadership is rooted in the characteristics that certain individuals possess. This idea that leadership is based on individual attributes is known as the "trait theory of leadership."

This view of leadership, the trait theory, was explored at length in a number of works in the previous century. Most notable are the writings of Thomas Carlyle and Francis Galton, whose works have prompted decades of research. In *Heroes and Hero Worship* (1841), Carlyle identified the talents, skills, and physical characteristics of men who rose to power.

In Galton's (1869) *Hereditary Genius*, he examined leadership qualities in the families of powerful men. After showing that the numbers of eminent relatives dropped off when moving from first degree to second degree relatives, Galton concluded that leadership was inherited. In other words, leaders were born, not developed. Both of these notable works lent great initial support for the notion that leadership is rooted in characteristics of the leader. For decades, this trait-based perspective dominated empirical and theoretical work in leadership. Using early research techniques, researchers conducted over a hundred studies proposing a number of characteristics that distinguished leaders from nonleaders: intelligence, dominance, adaptability, persistence, integrity, socioeconomic status, and self-confidence just to name a few.

The Rise of Alternative Leadership Theories

In the late 1940s and early 1950s, however, a series of qualitative reviews of these studies (e.g., Bird, 1940; Stogdill, 1948; Mann, 1959) prompted researchers to take a drastically different view of the driving forces behind leadership.

In reviewing the extant literature, Stogdill and Mann found that while some traits were common across a number of studies, the overall evidence suggested that persons who are leaders in one situation may not necessarily be leaders in other situations. Subsequently, leadership was no longer characterized as an enduring individual trait, as situational approaches posited that individuals can be effective in certain situations, but not others. This approach dominated much of the leadership theory and research for the next few decades.

The Re-emergence of the Trait Theory

New methods and measurements were developed after these influential reviews that would ultimately reestablish the trait theory as a viable approach to the study of leadership. For example, improvements in researchers' use of the round robin research design methodology allowed researchers to see that individuals can and do emerge as leaders across a variety of situations and tasks. Additionally, during the 1980s statistical advances allowed researchers to conduct meta-analyses, in which they could quantitatively analyse and summarize the findings from a wide array of studies. This advent allowed trait theorists to create a comprehensive and parsimonious picture of previous leadership research rather than rely on the qualitative reviews of the past. Equipped with new methods, leadership researchers revealed the following:

- Individuals can and do emerge as leaders across a variety of situations and tasks

- Significant relationships exist between leadership and such individual traits as:
- intelligence
- adjustment
- extraversion
- conscientiousness
- openness to experience
- general self-efficacy

Current Criticisms of the Trait Theory

While the trait theory of leadership has certainly regained popularity, its re-emergence has not been accompanied by a corresponding increase in sophisticated conceptual frameworks.

Specifically, Zaccaro (2007) noted that trait theories still:

1. Focus on a small set of individual attributes such as Big Five personality traits, to the neglect of cognitive abilities, motives, values, social skills, expertise, and problem-solving skills
2. Fail to consider patterns or integrations of multiple attributes
3. Do not distinguish between those leader attributes that are generally not malleable over time and those that are shaped by, and bound to, situational influences
4. Do not consider how stable leader attributes account for the behavioural diversity necessary for effective leadership.

Leader Attribute Pattern Approach

Considering the criticisms of the trait theory outlined above, several researchers have begun to adopt a different perspective of leader individual differences-the leader attribute pattern approach.

In contrast to the traditional approach, the leader attribute pattern approach is based on theorists' arguments that the influence of individual characteristics on outcomes is best understood by considering the person as an integrated totality rather than a summation of individual variables. In other words, the leader attribute pattern approach argues that integrated constellations or combinations of individual differences may explain substantial variance in both leader emergence and leader effectiveness beyond that explained by single attributes, or by additive combinations of multiple attributes.

Behavioural and Style Theories

In response to the early criticisms of the trait approach, theorists began to research leadership as a set of behaviours, evaluating the behaviour of 'successful' leaders, determining a behaviour taxonomy and identifying broad leadership styles. David McClelland, for example, Leadership takes a strong personality with a well developed positive ego. Not so much as a pattern of motives, but a set of traits is crucial. To lead; self-confidence and a high self-esteem is useful, perhaps even essential. [Kevin Mick]

Kurt Lewin, Ronald Lipitt, and Ralph White developed in 1939 the seminal work on the influence of leadership styles and performance. The researchers evaluated the performance of groups of eleven-year-old boys under different types of work climate. In each, the leader exercised his influence regarding the type of group decision making, praise and criticism (feedback), and the management of the group tasks (project management) according to three styles: (1) authoritarian, (2) democratic and (3) laissez-faire.

Authoritarian climates were characterized by leaders who make decisions alone, demand strict compliance to his orders, and dictate each step taken; future steps were uncertain to a large degree. The leader is not necessarily hostile but is aloof from participation in work and commonly offers personal praise and criticism for the work done. *Democratic climates* were characterized by collective decision processes, assisted by the leader. Before accomplishing tasks, perspectives are gained from group discussion and technical advice from a leader. Members are given choices and collectively decide the division of labour. Praise and criticism in such an environment are objective, fact minded and given by a group member without necessarily having participated extensively in the actual work. *Laissez faire climates* gave freedom to the group for policy determination without any participation from the leader. The leader remains uninvolved in work decisions unless asked, does not participate in the division of labour, and very infrequently gives praise. The results seemed to confirm that the democratic climate was preferred. The managerial grid model is also based on a behavioural theory. The model was developed by Robert Blake and Jane Mouton in 1964 and suggests five different leadership styles, based on the leaders' concern for people and their concern for goal achievement.

B.F. Skinner is the father of Behaviour Modification and developed the concept of positive reinforcement. Positive reinforcement occurs when a stimulus is presented contingent upon a behaviour which results in a higher probability of that behaviour increasing in the future. The following is an example of how positive reinforcement can be used in a business setting. Assume praise is a positive reinforcer for a particular employee. This employee does not show up to work on time every day. The manager of this employee decides to praise the employee for showing up on time every day the employee actually shows up to work on time. As a result, the employee comes to work on time more often because the employee likes to be praised. In this example, praise (i.e. stimulus) is a positive reinforcer for this employee because the employee arrives (i.e. behaviour) to work on time more frequently after being praised for showing up to work on time.

The use of positive reinforcement is a successful and growing technique used by leaders to motivate and attain desired behaviours from subordinates. Organizations such as Frito-Lay, 3M, B.F. Goodrich, Michigan Bell, and Emery Air Freight have all used reinforcement to increase productivity. Empirical research covering the last 20 years suggests that reinforcement theory has a 17 percent increase in performance. Additionally, many reinforcement techniques such as the use of praise are inexpensive which can result in higher performances for low monetary costs.

Situational and Contingency Theories

Situational theory also appeared as a reaction to the trait theory of leadership. Social scientists argued that history was more than the result of intervention of great men as Carlyle suggested. Herbert Spencer (1884) said that the times produce the person and not the other way around. This theory assumes that different situations call for different characteristics; according to this group of theories, no single optimal psychographic profile of a leader exists. According to the theory, "what an individual actually does when acting as a leader is in large part dependent upon characteristics of the situation in which he functions."

Some theorists started to synthesize the trait and situational approaches. Building upon the research of Lewin et al., academics began to normatize the descriptive models of leadership climates, defining three leadership styles and identifying in which situations each style works better. The *authoritarian leadership style*, for example, is approved in periods of crisis but fails to win the "hearts and minds" of their followers in the day-to-day management; the *democratic leadership style* is more adequate in situations that require consensus building; finally, the *laissez faire leadership style* is appreciated by the degree of freedom it provides, but as the leader does not "take charge", he can be perceived as a failure in protracted or thorny organizational problems. Thus, theorists defined the style of leadership as contingent to the situation, which is sometimes classified as contingency theory. Four contingency leadership theories appear more prominently in the recent years: Fiedler contingency model, Vroom-Yetton decision model, the path-goal theory, and the Hersey-Blanchard situational theory.

The Fiedler contingency model bases the leader's effectiveness on what Fred Fiedler called *situational contingency*. This results from the interaction of leadership style and situational favorableness (later called "situational control"). The theory defined two types of leader: those who tend to accomplish the task by developing good-relationships with the group (*relationship-oriented*), and those who have as their prime concern carrying out the task itself (*task-oriented*). According to Fiedler, there is no ideal leader. Both task-oriented and relationship-oriented leaders can be effective if their leadership orientation fits the situation. When there is a good leader-member relation, a highly structured task, and high leader position power, the situation is considered a "favourable situation". Fiedler found that task-oriented leaders are more effective in extremely favourable or unfavourable situations, whereas relationship-oriented leaders perform best in situations with intermediate favourability.

Victor Vroom, in collaboration with Phillip Yetton (1973) and later with Arthur Jago (1988), developed a taxonomy for describing leadership situations, taxonomy that was used in a normative decision model where leadership styles where connected to situational variables, defining which approach was more suitable to which situation. This approach was novel because it supported the idea that the same manager could rely on different group decision making approaches depending on the attributes of each situation. This model was later referred as situational contingency theory.

The path-goal theory of leadership was developed by Robert House (1971) and was based on the expectancy theory of Victor Vroom. According to House, the essence of the theory is "the meta proposition that leaders, to be effective, engage in behaviours that complement subordinates' environments and abilities in a manner that compensates for deficiencies and is instrumental to subordinate satisfaction and individual and work unit performance. The theory identifies four leader behaviours, *achievement-oriented*, *directive*, *participative*, and *supportive*, that are contingent to the environment factors and follower characteristics. In contrast to the Fiedler contingency model, the path-goal model states that the four leadership behaviours are fluid, and that leaders can adopt any of the four depending on what the situation demands. The path-goal model can be classified both as a contingency theory, as it depends on the circumstances, but also as a transactional leadership theory, as the theory emphasizes the reciprocity behaviour between the leader and the followers.

The situational leadership model proposed by Hersey and Blanchard suggests four leadership-styles and four levels of follower-development. For effectiveness, the model posits that the leadership-style must match the appropriate level of followership-development. In this model, leadership behaviour becomes a function not only of the characteristics of the leader, but of the characteristics of followers as well.

Functional Theory

Functional leadership theory is a particularly useful theory for addressing specific leader behaviours expected to contribute to organizational or unit effectiveness. This theory argues that the leader's main job is to see that whatever is necessary to group needs is taken care of; thus, a leader can be said to have done their job well when they have contributed to group effectiveness and cohesion. While functional leadership theory has most often been applied to team leadership, it has also been effectively applied to broader organizational leadership as well (Zaccaro, 2001).

A variety of leadership behaviours are expected to facilitate these functions. In initial work identifying leader behaviour, Fleishman (1953) observed that subordinates perceived their supervisors' behaviour in terms of two broad categories referred to as consideration and initiating structure. Consideration includes behaviour involved in fostering effective relationships. Examples of such behaviour would include showing concern for a subordinate or acting in a supportive manner towards others. Initiating structure involves the actions of the leader focused specifically on task accomplishment. This could include role clarification, setting performance standards, and holding subordinates accountable to those standards.

Transactional and Transformational Theories

The transactional leader (Burns, 1978) is given power to perform certain tasks and reward or punish for the team's performance. It gives the opportunity to the manager to lead the group and the group agrees to follow his lead to accomplish a predetermined goal in exchange for something else. Power is given to the leader to evaluate, correct and train subordinates when productivity is not up to the desired level and reward effectiveness when expected outcome is reached.

The transformational leader (Burns, 1978) motivates its team to be effective and efficient. Communication is the base for goal achievement focusing the group on the final desired outcome or goal attainment. This leader is highly visible and uses chain of command to get the job done. Transformational leaders focus on the big picture, needing to be surrounded by people who take care of the details. The leader is always looking for ideas that move the organization to reach the company's vision.

Leadership and Emotions

Leadership can be perceived as a particularly emotion-laden process, with emotions entwined with the social influence process. In an organization, the leaders' mood has some effects on his/her group. These effects can be described in 3 levels:

1. The mood of individual group members. Group members with leaders in a positive mood experience more positive mood than do group members with leaders in a negative mood. The leaders transmit their moods to other group members through the mechanism of emotional contagion. Mood contagion may be one of the psychological mechanisms by which charismatic leaders influence followers.
2. The affective tone of the group. Group affective tone represents the consistent or homogeneous affective reactions within a group. Group affective tone is an aggregate of the moods of the individual members of the group and refers to mood at the group level of analysis. Groups with leaders in a positive mood have a more positive affective tone than do groups with leaders in a negative mood.
3. Group processes like coordination, effort expenditure, and task strategy. Public expressions of mood impact how group members think and act. When people experience and express mood, they send signals to

> others. Leaders signal their goals, intentions, and attitudes through their expressions of moods. For example, expressions of positive moods by leaders signal that leaders deem progress toward goals to be good. The group members respond to those signals cognitively and behaviourally in ways that are reflected in the group processes.

In research about client service, it was found that expressions of positive mood by the leader improve the performance of the group, although in other sectors there were other findings.

Beyond the leader's mood, her/his behaviour is a source for employee positive and negative emotions at work. The leader creates situations and events that lead to emotional response. Certain leader behaviours displayed during interactions with their employees are the sources of these affective events. Leaders shape workplace affective events. Examples – feedback giving, allocating tasks, resource distribution. Since employee behaviour and productivity are directly affected by their emotional states, it is imperative to consider employee emotional responses to organizational leaders. Emotional intelligence, the ability to understand and manage moods and emotions in the self and others, contributes to effective leadership in organizations. Leadership is about being responsible.

Neo-emergent Theory

The Neo-emergent leadership theory (from the Oxford school of leadership) espouses that leadership is created through the emergence of information by the leader or other stakeholders, not through the true actions of the leader himself. In other words, the reproduction of information or stories form the basis of the perception of leadership by the majority. It is well known that the great naval hero Lord Nelson often wrote his own versions of battles he was involved in, so that when he arrived home in England he would receive a true hero's welcome. In modern society, the press, blogs and other sources report their own views of a leader which may be based on reality, but may also be based on a political command, a payment or an inherent interest of the author, media or leader. Therefore, it can be contended that the perception of all leaders is created and in fact does not reflect their true leadership qualities at all.

Environmental Leadership Theory

The Environmental leadership model (Carmazzi) describes leadership from a Group dynamics perspective incorporating group psychology and self awareness to nurture "Environments" that promote self sustaining group leadership based on personal emotional gratification from the activities of the group. The Environmental Leader creates the psychological structure by which employees can find and attain this gratification through work or activity.

It stems from the idea that each individual has various environments that bring out different facets from their own Identity, and each facet is driven by emotionally charged perceptions within each environment... The Environmental Leader creates a platform through education and awareness where individuals fill each others emotional needs and become more conscious of when, and how they affect personal and team emotional gratifications. This is accomplished by knowing why people "react" to their environment instead of act intelligently.

"Environmental Leadership is not about changing the mindset of the group or individual, but in the cultivation of an environment that brings out the best and inspires the individuals in that group.

It is not the ability to influence others to do something they are not committed to, but rather to nurture a culture that motivates and even excites individuals to do what is required for the benefit of all. It is not carrying others to the end result, but setting the surrounding for developing qualities in them to so they may carry each other." Carmazzi

The role of an Environmental Leader is to instill passion and direction to a group and the dynamics of that group. This leader implements a psychological support system within a group that fills the emotional and developmental needs of the group.

Leadership Styles

Leadership style refers to a leader's behaviour. It is the result of the philosophy, personality and experience of the leader.

Kurt Lewin's Leadership Styles

Kurt Lewin and colleagues identified different styles of leadership:

- Dictator
- Autocratic
- Participative
- Laissez-Faire.

Autocratic or Authoritarian Leaders

Under the autocratic leadership style, all decision-making powers are centralized in the leader, as with dictator leaders.

They do not entertain any suggestions or initiatives from subordinates. The autocratic management has been successful as it provides strong motivation to the manager. It permits quick decision-making, as only one person decides for the whole group and keeps each decision to themself until they feel it is needed by the rest of the group.

Participative or Democratic Leaders

The democratic leadership style favors decision-making by the group as shown, such as leader gives instruction after consulting the group.

They can win the cooperation of their group and can motivate them effectively and positively. The decisions of the democratic leader are not unilateral as with the autocrat because they arise from consultation with the group members and participation by them.

Laissez-Faire or Free Rein Leaders

The phrase is French and literally means "let do", but, in a leadership context, can be roughly translated as "free rein". A free rein leader does not lead, but leaves the group entirely to itself as shown; such a leader allows maximum freedom to subordinates, i.e., they are given a free hand in deciding their own policies and methods.

Different situations call for different leadership styles. In an emergency when there is little time to converge on an agreement and where a designated authority has significantly more experience or expertise than the rest of the team, an autocratic leadership style may be most effective; however, in a highly motivated and aligned team with a homogeneous level of expertise, a more democratic or laissez-faire style may be more effective. The style adopted should be that which most effectively achieves the objectives of the group while balancing the interests of its individual members.

Leadership Performance

In the past, some researchers have argued that the actual influence of leaders on organizational outcomes is overrated and romanticized as a result of biased attributions about leaders. Despite these assertions however, it is largely recognized and accepted by practitioners and researchers that leadership is important, and research supports the notion that leaders do contribute to key organizational outcomes. To facilitate successful performance it is important to understand and accurately measure leadership performance.

Job performance generally refers to behaviour that is expected to contribute to organizational success (Campbell, 1990). Campbell identified a number of specific types of performance dimensions; leadership was one of the dimensions that he identified. There is no consistent, overall definition of leadership performance (Yukl, 2006). Many distinct conceptualizations are often lumped together under the umbrella of leadership performance, including outcomes such as leader effectiveness, leader advancement, and leader emergence (Kaiser et al., 2008). For instance, leadership performance may be used to refer to the career success of the individual leader, performance of the group or organization, or even leader emergence. Each of these measures can be considered conceptually distinct. While these aspects may be related, they are different outcomes and their inclusion should depend on the applied/research focus.

Contexts of Leadership

Leadership in Organizations

An organization that is established as an instrument or means for achieving defined objectives has been referred to as a formal organization. Its design specifies how goals are subdivided and reflected in subdivisions of the organization. Divisions, departments, sections, positions, jobs, and tasks make up this work structure. Thus, the formal organization is expected to behave impersonally in regard to relationships with clients or with its members. According to Weber's definition, entry and subsequent advancement is by merit or seniority. Each employee receives a salary and enjoys a degree of tenure that safeguards her/him from the arbitrary influence of superiors or of powerful clients. The higher his position in the hierarchy, the greater his presumed expertise in adjudicating problems that may arise in the course of the work carried out at lower levels of the organization. It is this bureaucratic structure that forms the basis for the appointment of heads or chiefs of administrative subdivisions in the organization and endows them with the authority attached to their position.

In contrast to the appointed head or chief of an administrative unit, a leader emerges within the context of the informal organization that underlies the formal structure. The informal organization expresses the personal objectives and goals of the individual membership. Their objectives and goals may or may not coincide with those of the formal organization. The informal organization represents an extension of the social structures that generally characterize human life — the spontaneous emergence of groups and organizations as ends in themselves.

In prehistoric times, humanity was preoccupied with personal security, maintenance, protection, and survival. Now humanity spends a major portion of waking hours working for organizations. Her/His need to identify with a community that provides security, protection, maintenance, and a feeling of belonging continues unchanged from prehistoric times. This need is met by the informal organization and its emergent, or unofficial, leaders.

Leaders emerge from within the structure of the informal organization. Their personal qualities, the demands of the situation, or a combination of these and other factors attract followers who accept their leadership within one or several overlay structures. Instead of the authority of position held by an appointed head or chief, the emergent leader wields influence or power. Influence is the ability of a person to gain co-operation from others by means of persuasion or control over rewards. Power is a stronger form of influence because it reflects a person's ability to enforce action through the control of a means of punishment.

A leader is a person who influences a group of people towards a specific result. It is not dependent on title or formal authority. (elevos, paraphrased from Leaders, Bennis, and Leadership Presence, Halpern & Lubar). Leaders are recognized by their capacity for caring for others, clear communication, and a commitment to persist. An individual who is appointed to a managerial position has the right to command and enforce obedience by virtue of the authority of his position. However, she or he must possess adequate personal attributes to match his authority, because authority is only potentially available to him. In the absence of sufficient personal competence, a manager may be confronted by an emergent leader who can challenge her/his role in the organization and reduce it to that of a figurehead. However, only authority of position has the backing of formal sanctions. It follows that whoever wields personal influence and power can legitimize this only by gaining a formal position in the hierarchy, with commensurate authority. Leadership can be defined as one's ability to get others to willingly follow. Every organization needs leaders at every level.

Leadership Versus Management

Over the years the philosophical terminology of "management" and "leadership" have, in the organisational context, been used both as synonyms and with clearly differentiated meanings. Debate is fairly common about whether the use of these terms should be restricted, and generally reflects an awareness of the distinction made by Burns (1978) between "transactional" leadership (characterised by e.g. emphasis on procedures, contingent reward, management by exception) and "transformational" leadership (characterised by e.g. charisma, personal relationships, creativity).

Leadership by a Group

In contrast to individual leadership, some organizations have adopted group leadership. In this situation, more than one person provides direction to the group as a whole. Some organizations have taken this approach in hopes of increasing creativity, reducing costs, or downsizing. Others may see the traditional leadership of a boss as costing too much in team performance. In some situations, the maintenance of the boss becomes too expensive-either by draining the resources of the group as a whole, or by impeding the creativity within the team, even unintentionally.

A common example of group leadership involves cross-functional teams. A team of people with diverse skills and from all parts of an organization assembles to lead a project. A team structure can involve sharing power equally on all issues, but more commonly uses *rotating leadership*. The team member(s) best able to handle any given phase of the project become(s) the temporary leader(s). Additionally, as each team member has the opportunity to experience the elevated level of empowerment, it energizes staff and feeds the cycle of success. Leaders who demonstrate persistence, tenacity, determination and synergistic communication skills will bring out the same qualities in their groups. Good leaders use their own inner mentors to energize their team and organizations and lead a team to achieve success.

According to the National School Boards Association (USA)

These Group Leadership or Leadership Teams have specific characteristics:

Characteristics of a Team

- There must be an awareness of unity on the part of all its members.
- There must be interpersonal relationship. Members must have a chance to contribute, learn from and work with others.
- The member must have the ability to act together toward a common goal.

Ten characteristics of well-functioning teams:

- Purpose: Members proudly share a sense of why the team exists and are invested in accomplishing its mission and goals.
- Priorities: Members know what needs to be done next, by whom, and by when to achieve team goals.
- Roles: Members know their roles in getting tasks done and when to allow a more skillful member to do a certain task.
- Decisions: Authority and decision-making lines are clearly understood.
- Conflict: Conflict is dealt with openly and is considered important to decision-making and personal growth.
- Personal traits: members feel their unique personalities are appreciated and well utilized.
- Norms: Group norms for working together are set and seen as standards for every one in the groups.
- Effectiveness: Members find team meetings efficient and productive and look forward to this time together.
- Success: Members know clearly when the team has met with success and share in this equally and proudly.
- Training: Opportunities for feedback and updating skills are provided and taken advantage of by team members.

Leadership Among Primates

Richard Wrangham and Dale Peterson, in *Demonic Males: Apes and the Origins of Human Violence* present evidence that only humans and chimpanzees, among all the animals living on earth, share a similar tendency for a cluster of behaviours: violence, territoriality, and competition for uniting behind the one chief male of thc land. This position is contentious. Many animals beyond apes are territorial, compete, exhibit violence, and have a social structure controlled by a dominant male (lions, wolves, etc.), suggesting Wrangham and Peterson's evidence is not empirical. However, we must examine other species as well, including elephants (which are matriarchal and follow an alpha female), meerkats (who are likewise matriarchal), and many others.

It would be beneficial, to examine that most accounts of leadership over the past few millennia (since the creation of Christian religions) are through the perspective of a patriarchal society, founded on Christian literature. If one looks before these times, it is noticed that Pagan and Earth-based tribes in fact had female leaders. It is important also to note that the peculiarities of one tribe cannot necessarily be ascribed to another, as even our modern-day customs differ. The current day patrilineal custom is only a recent invention in human history and our original method of familial practices were matrilineal (Dr. Christopher Shelley and Bianca Rus, UBC). The fundamental assumption that has been built into 90% of the world's countries is that patriarchy is the 'natural' biological predisposition of homo sapiens. Unfortunately, this belief has led to the widespread oppression of women in all of those countries, but in varying degrees. (Whole Earth Review, Winter, 1995 by Thomas Laird, Michael Victor). The Iroquoian First Nations tribes are an example of a matrilineal tribe, along with Mayan tribes, and also the society of Meghalaya, India. (Laird and Victor,).

By comparison, bonobos, the second-closest species-relatives of man, do *not* unite behind the chief male of the land. The bonobos show deference to an alpha or top-ranking female that, with the support of her coalition of other females, can prove as strong as the strongest male in the land. Thus, if leadership amounts to getting the greatest number of followers, then among the bonobos, a female almost always exerts the strongest and most effective leadership. However, not all scientists agree on the allegedly "peaceful" nature of the bonobo or its reputation as a "hippie chimp".

Historical Views on Leadership

Sanskrit literature identifies ten types of leaders. Defining characteristics of the ten types of leaders are explained with examples from history and mythology.

Aristocratic thinkers have postulated that leadership depends on one's blue blood or genes: monarchy takes an extreme view of the same idea, and may prop up its assertions against the claims of mere aristocrats by invoking divine sanction: see the divine right of kings. Contrariwise, more democratically-inclined theorists have pointed to examples of meritocratic leaders, such as the Napoleonic marshals profiting from careers open to talent.

In the autocratic/paternalistic strain of thought, traditionalists recall the role of leadership of the Roman *pater familias*. Feminist thinking, on the other hand, may object to such models as patriarchal and posit against them emotionally-attuned, responsive, and consensual empathetic guidance, which is sometimes associated with matriarchies.

Comparable to the Roman tradition, the views of Confucianism on "right living" relate very much to the ideal of the (male) scholar-leader and his benevolent rule, buttressed by a tradition of filial piety.

Leadership is a matter of intelligence, trustworthiness, humaneness, courage, and discipline... Reliance on intelligence alone results in rebelliousness. Exercise of humaneness alone results in weakness. Fixation on trust results in folly. Dependence on the strength of courage results in violence. Excessive discipline and sternness in command result in cruelty. When one has all five virtues together, each appropriate to its function, then one can be a leader. — Sun Tzu

In the 19th century, the elaboration of anarchist thought called the whole concept of leadership into question. (Note that the *Oxford English Dictionary* traces the word "leadership" in English only as far back as the 19th century.) One response to this denial of elitism came with Leninism, which demanded an elite group of disciplined cadres to act as the vanguard of a socialist revolution, bringing into existence the dictatorship of the proletariat.

Other historical views of leadership have addressed the seeming contrasts between secular and religious leadership. The doctrines of Caesaro-papism have recurred and had their detractors over several centuries. Christian thinking on leadership has often emphasized stewardship of divinely-provided resources-human and material-and their deployment in accordance with a Divine plan. Compare servant leadership.

Action Oriented Team Leadership Skills

This is a unique approach to team leadership that is aimed at action oriented environments where effective functional leadership is required to achieve critical or reactive tasks by small teams deployed into the field. In other words leadership of small groups often created to respond to a situation or critical incident.

In most cases these teams are tasked to operate in remote and changeable environments with limited support or backup (action environments). Leadership of people in these environments requires a different set of skills to that of front line management. These leaders must effectively operate remotely and negotiate both the needs of the individual, team and task within a changeable environment. This has been termed Action Oriented Leadership. Some example action oriented leadership is demonstrated in the following ways: extinguishing a rural fire, locating a missing person, leading a team on an outdoor expedition or rescuing a person from a potentially hazardous environment.

Titles Emphasizing Authority

At certain stages in their development, the hierarchies of social ranks implied different degrees or ranks of leadership in society. Thus a knight led fewer men in general than did a duke; a baronet might in theory control less land than an earl. In the course of the 18th and 20th centuries, several political operators took non-traditional paths to become dominant in their societies. They or their systems often expressed a belief in strong individual leadership, but existing titles and labels ("King", "Emperor", "President" and so on) often seemed inappropriate, insufficient or downright inaccurate in some circumstances. The formal or informal titles or descriptions they or their flunkies employ express and foster a general veneration for leadership of the inspired and autocratic variety. The definite article when used as part of the title (in languages that use definite articles) emphasizes the existence of a sole "true" leader.

Critical Thought on the Concept of Leadership

Noam Chomsky and others have brought critical thinking to the very concept of leadership and have provided an analysis which asserts that people abrogate their responsibility to think and will actions for themselves. While the conventional view of leadership is rather satisfying to people who "want to be told what to do", these critics say that one should question why they are being subjected to a will or intellect other than their own if the leader is not a Subject Matter Expert

The fundamentally anti-democratic nature of the leadership principle is challenged by the introduction of concepts such as autogestion, employeeship, common civic virtue, etc., which stress individual responsibility and/or group authority in the work place and elsewhere by focusing on the skills and attitudes that a person needs in general rather than separating out leadership as the basis of a special class of individuals.

Similarly various historical calamities are attributed to a misplaced reliance on the principle of leadership.

Personnel Policy

Administration is the means of translating the state policies into programmatic action.

An administration can discharge its role only through the media of required resources, the most important of which is the human resource or human capital. Public Administration must, therefore, so fashion its policies and programmes that the resources upon which it depends are not only adequately mobilised but also effectively utilised. The same is true of the human resource also. Management of human resources, therefore, is an important ingredient in the management system of the government. For managing the human resource of the system, what is inescapably necessary is a well co-ordinated policy framework which integrates different aspects of personnel as an input.

The human input in management as a basic resource and not just a material commodity, has been a rather late realisation with the top management. For a long time, personnel in the administration has been taken for granted, they had not been taken as something which required to be treated with special consideration and distinctive differentiation. Personnel were considered to be nothing but mere cog in the organisational mechanism-which had it (counter-Productive toll on the system-efficiency. All this was due to wrong and misplaced policy-perception about the important contribution made by the personnel. This unit will try to highlight the meaning of personnel policy and constitutional policy especially in Indian context.

The unit will deal with modem personnel functions and reports of the Estimates Committee and Administrative Reforms Commission on Personnel Organisation. A brief discussion on Department of Personnel and new policy perspective will also be made.

Policy Making: Meaning

'Policy making' is one of the common terminologies used in the discipline of Public Administration and management, though more popular one is the 'decision-making', the differences between the two being those of depth and sweep, and not of quality of process. Decisions are taken by everybody, every moment, on every thing-whether they are of great significance or on comparatively inconsequential matters. Though, from a normative angle, decisions ought to refer to planned and calculated exercise in rationality in actual practice they are often subjective, probabilistic and arbitrary, as more often they are arrived at individually and not collectively. Policy making is also a variety of decision-making, differentiated by the fact that policies are "generally taken to belong to the jurisdiction of more substantive or heavier significance, valid for a longer time-range and operative as a guiding framework for more sweeping action".

Thus, policy making has been defined as "that dynamic process for a normative event, arrived at through assessment of relevant facts and evaluation of judgement, providing major guidelines for further action directed at the future with the object of achieving a given objective by the best possible means." The stages that are resorted to in this procedural exercise are- (i) isolation of issues, (ii) identification of problems, (iii) analysing the problems and looking for ideas, (iv) incubation (re-analysis of problems and development of ideas), (v) synthesisation, (vi) evaluation, (vii) adoption of programme, (viii) implementation and (ix) follow-up.

However, though every decision and every policy are expected to be made on any subject after taking into account all available, relevant facts and evaluating requisite dimensions and alternatives involved, all the stages mentioned above are generally not relied upon in the actual practice. Under imperfect conditions of Public Administration, often the required data are not either available or made available to the policy-makers who, consequently, depend on their own particularistic experience, individualistic knowledge and professionalised expertise, combined with intuition, to come to what could be described as 'optimal' decision-cum-policy-making.

It is not as if such decisions are necessarily 'bad decisions or policies' arrived at on such considerations are 'irrational policies'. The real issue in decision/policy-making in Public Administration is not that it is not formulated in accordance with a proper procedure but it is often formulated in an ad hoc manner, as a reactive response to certain emerging situations rather than in a pro-active manner based on futuristic planning, fore-thought or far-sight. This is also true of Indian Public Administration and policy-making in the country.

Indian Public/Personnel Scenario

Public Administration in India inevitably suffers from the same vices or inadequacies in forms of well-integrated, well co-ordinated and comprehensive policy framework. The public personnel administration is also characterised by similar ad hocism, confusion, chaos and haphazardness.

It is a common knowledge that Public Administration in this country has travelled a long way off, from the law and order and regulatory days of 1947 and before. Administration was then far removed from the people, having very little to do with the national development, economic regeneration, social progress and people's well-being; its temper was authoritarian and its style was deeply formalistic. Its aim being preservation of status-quo, administration was not developmental and promotional. 1947 was the significant watershed, providing the final parting of the ways with the past not merely in the administrative ideology but also in its operational ways.

These new changes were reflected in atleast the following three dimensions:-

i) the purpose of the State has changed with the adoption of a new vision and mission of people's welfare;

ii) the functions of the State have registered fundamental growth and phenomenal explosion in terms of variety, complexity and scale, together with the large size of machinery and structure;

iii) the methodology of the State-operation has also undergone radical, transformation in terms of innovative practice, dynamic process, data-handling technology and leadership styles;

iv) the personnel in the system his also numerically expanded, in terms of categories, groups, specialities, etc.

But the old characteristic however, continue in that there has been no significant and radical change in the thinking and back-up action for reforming the system in the new functional context. There has been no new, novel and dynamic policy thrust in public management system in general and personnel system in particular.

The reality is that the days of negative, 'night-watchman' role performed earlier by the government are gone. The government, now has to play a more positive and pervasive part in shaping the citizen-life in all its multi-faceted aspects, more as an all round change-agent, accelerator of economic and social advancement, animator, if not the prime-mover, of total national development. Any modem government must harmonise the goals of the collective, communitarian welfare with the ideals of individual progress and enrichment of the quality of every life. General landscape of the new government is that it has to cater to the needs, demands and challenges of "the revolution of rising expectations" of the people who now, refuse to live under the shadow of poverty, hunger, illness, ignorance and squalor.

The Constitutional Policy

The personnel, in the context of the New Public Administration, as in India, have to be fine-tuned to the new ideology of the State and technology of dynamic, yet people oriented governance. They have to be enthused with the vibrant commitment towards the developmental objectives as enshrined in the basic charter of the State, that is, the Constitution of the country.

The Indian Constitution promulgated w.e.f. 26th January, 1950, makes eloquent pronouncement of the lofty ideals in its Preamble which assures justice, liberty, equality and fraternity to all its citizens; its section on Fundamental Rights makes provision for the individual safeguards against State authoritarianism and ensures Fundamental freedom for all citizens. The Directive Principles of State Policy enjoin upon the State the fundamental duty to create a promotive environment so that the citizens can lead a life of happiness, richness and fulness. This Constitutional culture has developed on the government a much wider rectangle of responsibility to shape the entire fabric of social and individual life in a more positive and constructive fashion.

Public Personnel in India

Against this changed ideological backdrop of the State, as a carrier of new values, the traditional 'folk-lore' administration in India has become development administration-"action-oriented, goal-oriented administrative system concerned with the achievement of definite programmatic goals, in which the most important component is the personnel. Public Personnel Administration similarly constitutes the central focus of Indian administrative system. If this vital sector is neglected, deficiencies would develop in the other sectors as well. As in human organism so in administrative organisation, vitality is a function of internal health and not derived from external cosmetics or superficial make-up. People in the administration must be efficient, effective, professionalised and well-motivated to accomplish the goals set for them.

This requires adoption of strategic policy for the induction, retention and optimal utilisation of personnel in the administrative system. The policy must cover all the aspects in the life of the human beings or personnel in government right from their birth in the bureaucracy to their separation from it.

Modern Personnel Functions

Some of the modern personnel functions of some significance may be noted, which would define in the ultimate analysis, the policy frame for personnel management: Survey of the contingent needs of the public services in the context of total development goals of the administration:

* Manpower planning
* Cadre management
* Job evaluation and position classification system
* Recruitment
* Positive recruitment
* Talent-hunting
* Selection techniques. Psychological tests
* Training and development programmes

* Career systems planning
* Compensation and remuneration adminisiration,
* Motivation and productivity, participative management principles
* Welfare programmes.
* Conduct, discipline and public service ethics
* Terminal benefits systems (Retirement benefits etc.)
* Developing personnel organisation and capability.

The Government of India has also undertaken to perform many of these functions as its new charter of activities. The awareness to look at the personnel from new angles, as input needing constant renewal has not come overnight. Initially, there was no planned policy-guide for handling personnel in the public organisations. There was on the contrary, vast army of persons at the lower echelons, particularly at the messengerial (Group 'D' or Class IV) and clerical (Group 'C' or Class III) levels who, mostly were denied opportunities of growth and were engaged in non-productive and routinistic functions. They were psychologically demotivated and highly discontented as promotions+in the civil service were beyond their easy reach; they were not suitably trained, and were left to fend for themselves; they constituted a kind of drainage on the efficiency of thee government. The middle levels consisting of Group 'B' (or Class II) and some segments of Group A (or Class I) were also not comfortably, certainly not ideally, placed in terms of decision-making, delegation of power and exercise of constructive authority. The general management at the Group 'B' level was devoid of any sense of positive responsibility and felt cut off from the mainstream of functional bureaucracy.

Post-Independence Studies for Formulation of Personnel Policy

The conditions in pre-Independence period were attributable to a lack of well-thought-out policy, and programming for the proper utilisation and motivation of public personnel. There was no plan for their career development; there was no uniform policy for objective performance appraisal and management of bureaucracy for result-oriented achievement. This paucity of policy has not only hindered transaction of developmental goals but also nearly crippled the personnel administration.

After Independence there had been several investigations undertaken into the personnel system, together with structural and methodological aspects of Public Administration in India. Upto mid-60s there have been atleast twelve such investigations conducted by different Committees and Commissions as also by some eminent experts. They may be mentioned as follows:

1) The Secretariat Reorganisation Committee 1947
2) The Central (First) Pay Commission 1946-47
3) Report on Reorganisation of the Machinery of the Govt., 1949
4) Report on Public Administration, 1951
5) Report on the Machinery of Govt.-Improvement of Efficiency, 1952
6) Public Administration in India-Report of a Survey, (Paul Appleby) 1953
7) The States Reorganisation Commission, 1955
8) The Report on the Public Services (Qualification for Recruitment) 1956
9) The Commission of Enquiry on Emoluments and Conditions of service of Central Government Employees (2nd Pay Commission) 1957
10) V.T. Krishnamachari's Report on Indian State Administrative Services etc. 1962
11) The Report of Committee on Prevention of Corruption, 1964 (Santhanam Committee)
12) Five Year Plans.

All these reports have made their contribution towards making the personnel system more effective, and to align with the challenges of new environment. Their recommendations have made impact on policy formulation with an eye to dynamise public personnel management. But obviously, all these were not enough. The system still needed a lot of changes.

Organisation for Personnel Policy

Apart from a lack of policy, there was also organisational deficiency to tackle the problems of personnel. There was no cohesive, centralised organisation in the Government of India from which the unified direction regarding personnel policies and programmes could flow. In the field of Central Government, with regard to personnel, the Ministries of Home Affairs (Services and Establishment Wings) and Finance (Establishment Division) ail along had joint management responsibilities, with Union Public Service Commission playing an important advisory role. The Establishment Officer to the Government of India, functioning under the Cabinet Secretary, was another official agent for performing some high level personnel-placement tasks. All this made for division of responsibility and resulted in negation of unified central direction. There was more of crisis-oriented personnel management and less of a centrally planned, positive or forward looking thrust in personnel programming. It had led inevitably to attending to mere 'maintenance' functions at the minimum level, leaving out the more significant 'growth' functions at the optimum level. The casualty was again the personnel.

Estimate Committee's Report (1966) on Personnel Agency

To plug this organisational loophole, the Estimates Committee (of the Third Lok Sabha) in its 93rd Report (April, 1966) observed that "the ever expanding role of the government, in a welfare state with its natural concomitant of a large civil service, calls for effective personnel control through a single agency." This unified agency should be under the control of the Cabinet Secretary and made responsible for regulating the terms and conditions in respect of services as a whole, replacing the earlier dual control of the Home Ministry and the Finance Ministry.

Administrative Reforms Commission on Personnel Organisation

To attend to the emerging problems in the field of administration, the systematic deficiencies of the public governance and to look at the various issues in Public Administration from a holistic angle, the Government of India constituted an Administrative Reforms Commission in 1966. The terms of reference were elaborate and comprehensive. The sectors of administration which it was asked to look into were also quite exhaustive. The Administrative Reforms Commission assisted by 20 Study Teams submitted 20 reports of which 5 reports dealt with the public personnel administration, namely:

1) Report on the M2-hinery of the Government of India and its procedures of work
2) Report on Public Sector Undertakings
3) Report on Personnel Administration
4) Report on Centre-State Relationships
5) Report on State Administration.

ARC'S Report on Personnel Administration

'Personnel' was also the exclusive subject matter of one report, namely, Report on Personnel Administration aided and advised by as many as 3 study teams, namely:

1) Patil Study Team on personnel Administration;
2) Thorat Study Team on Recruitment, Selection, UPSC/ State PSCs, and Training;
3) Nagarkatti Study Team on Promotion Policies, Conduct Rules, Discipline and Morale.

The Commission formulated its own recommendations on the various facets of personnel administration in India. This Report formulated important policies and programmes on the country's future personnel management system.

The Commission made specific policy suggestions related to:

Functionalism, Specialism and Staffing

A functional field must be carved out for the IAS, consisting of land revenue administration, exercise of magisterial functions and regulatory work in the states and in the fields other than those looked after by other services.

All posts in a functional area whether in the field or at headquarters or in the Secretariat should be staffed by members of the corresponding functional services or by functional officers not encadred in a service.

The posts at the level of Deputy Secretary or equivalent at the Central headquarters, which do not fall within a particular functional area, should be demarcated into eight areas of specialisms as follows:

i) Economic Administration

ii) Industrial Administration

iii) Agricultural and Rural Development Administration

iv) Social and Educational Administration

v) Personnel Administration

vi) Financial Administration

vii) Defence Administration and Internal Security

viii) Planning.

Senior management posts in functional areas should be filled by members of the respective functional services.

Senior management posts outside the functional areas should be filled by officers who have had experience as members of the policy and management pool in one of the eight specialisms. They should have completed not less than seventeen years of service.

Unified Grading Structure

The posts in the civil service should be grouped into grades so that all those which call for similar qualifications and similar difficulties and responsibilities are grouped in the same grade. The number of such grades may be between 20 and 25. All the Class I posts may be evaluated and assigned to, say 9 common pay scales. These nine grades or pay scales may be divided into three levels, namely junior, middle and senior. The progress of an officer of an established Class I service along with the grades within each level should be on the basis of proved performance. Promotions from the junior to the middle level and from the middle to the senior level should be by selection.

Cadre Management Planning

For all the services, advance projections should be made of the requirement of personnel for five years at a time. Mid-term appraisal also should, be made if circumstances warrant it and necessary correctives made on the basis of the appraisal. Such projections should be made by cadre management committees which should be constituted.

Recruitment

For the Indian Administrative Service/Indian Foreign Service and other non-technical Class I Services, recruitment should be made only through a single competitive examination, it being left to the candidates to express their order of preference for the different services. A Committee should he set up to go into the questions of devising speediers methods of recruitment, in general, of bringing down the proportion of candidates to posts, of reducing the expenditure on publicity, and of revising the syllabus of the examinations for the higher services.

The upper age limit for entrance to the competitive examination may be raised to 26.

In order to provide greater opportunities for the advancement of talented personnel who are not already in Class I:

a) The quota of vacancies in Class I to be filled by promotion may be increased up-to a maximum of 40 where the existing quota falls short of that percentage;

b) Every one who has completed 6 years of service in Government and is less than 35 year of age may be given one and only one chance to sit for the open competitive examination for Class I non-technical services, irrespective of the chances already taken, provided that he/she fulfils conditions relating to educational qualifications.

Training

Government should, with the assistance of experienced administrators and experts in training techniques, formulate a clear-cut and far sighted national policy on civil service training, setting out objectives and priorities and guidelines for preparation of training plans. Training for middle level management in the Secretariat (for Deputy Secretaries and other officers with equivalent status) should have the following three broad elements:

a) training in headquarters work;
b) special courses in each of the eight broad specialisms; and
c) sub-area specialism training.

Training in policy and planning should be provided as a part of training for all specialisms.

Performance Appraisal

At the end of each year, the official reported upon should submit a brief resume, not exceeding three hundred words, of the work done by him, bringing out any special achievement of his. The resume should be submitted to the reporting officer and should form a part of the confidential record. In giving his own assessment, the reporting officer should duly take note of the resume and after making his own comments and assessment, submit the entire record to the next 9 higher officer, namely, the reviewing officer. The reviewing officer should add his own comments, if any, and also do the grading.

Promotion

Half of the vacancies available for promotion of Class I1 officers to Class I, including All-India Services, may be filled up by the existing method and the other half on the basis of an examination. Class I1 officers may be allowed to Sit for this examination, provided that they have put in a prescribed minimum number of years of service, say, five, and have not been graded as 'not yet fit for promotion'.

Discipline

Provisions should be made in the rules for summary disposal of disciplinary cases in respect of any misdeed or other irregular acts arising from insubordination, contempt, and unbecoming conduct including intimidation or threat of violence.

Tribunals

Civil Service Tribunals should be set up to function as final appellate authorities in ' respect of orders inflicting major punishments of dismissal, removal from service and reduction in rank.

Voluntary Retirement

A civil servant may be allowed to retire voluntarily after he has complete fifteen years of service and given proportionate pension and gratuity.

Incentives

Incentives for timely completion of a specific project may be provided through suitable awards such as rolling cup or a shield. In individual cases, commendatory certificates may be issued.

These and other recommendations of the Report on Personnel Administration have far-reaching significance in terms of restructuring the new personnel policy and affecting almost all public services.

Department of Personnel

Personnel Policy

The Administrative Reforms Commission (ARC)'s recommendations envisaged careful handling of the new dynamic and forward-looking functions in the field of personnel. It required new policies in many areas and aspects. The old organisation for handling personnel matters was obviously inadequate to tackle the new personnel problems based on the recommendations of the Administrative Reforms Commission on the Central Personnel Agency. The Government set up in August, 1970, a new Department of Personnel. One of the Study Teams of the ARC, namely, Deshmukh Study Team on machinery of the Government of India and its Procedures of Work, had first made the suggestion that "the fashioning of an effective Central Personnel Agency and the allocation to it of all functions of an overall character in the field of personnel administration is one of the most important reforms required in the machinery of the Government of India." It was envisaged that progressive leads could flow out from the Department of Personnel if only the new departments were to induct into it persons from a variety of services including the technical and professional, so that the leadership of the agency in the matter of personnel rested on a solid foundation.

The organisational structure of the Department of Personnel was as follows:

* Policy and Planning Wing
* Training Wing
* All India Services Wing
* Establishment Wing
* Vigilance Wing
* E.O. s Wing.

It may be noted barring the Policy and Planning Wing, all the other Wings together with their functions existed in the Ministry of Home Affairs from which the Department of Personnel was carved out in August, 1970. The Policy and Planning Wing had been entrusted with the task of formulating and giving shape to the policy and planning activities in the field of personnel administration in the Government of India. This Wing also formed a base for a kind of 'perspective planning'-approach to personnel management and for all foundational-cum-applied research on overall aspects of public personnel administration. This charter of responsibilities could have been met only by staffing the Policy and Planning Wing with experts and professionals in personnel management. Also, it would have been better if certain amount of 'prioritisation ' was done at the beginning itself, as there was a potent risk of the 'routine' taking over the germinal and significant activities in the government. This was exactly what happened. Policy Planning Wing (PPW) was entrusted with the normal responsibility of handling the Administrative Reforms Commission's recommendations contained in the report on Personnel Administration as also the day-to-day routine activities like Cadre Reviews through all the usual hierarchies of the government. No proper methodology for handling research studies was in fact evolved. Later several other items of routine work were also added to the PPW which took away research-thrust from its activities. The PPW degenerated into another normal Wing of the government, doing mostly regular routine functions and not, as originally envisaged, futuristic personnel studies on major policy issues.

Training Division, no doubt, did quite a bit of leadership role in the area of training, and functioned as a clearing house for all training ideas and programmes. But it also had to attend to so many routine jobs that its main functions as an apex policy-maker on training lost their focus and consequently suffered considerably.

The other Wings/Divisions had nothing very new to offer; they continued to do in the new Department of Personnel what they were doing in the old Ministry of Home Affairs. In the matter of staffing, the same old policy of relying on the conventional sources like IAS and other Central Services was followed, with no change at all. Structurally, the same old hierarchy and procedurally, the same old work-ways and styles were continued. No worthwhile professional infiltration was in sight, even though administration was assumingly getting technical and science and technology were making deep dent into governmental programmes. The tragic gap surfaced, because of the total lack of concern for new personnel policy, interlinking all the new ventures

Department of Personnel as a Central Personnel Agency was a new structure-functional innovation in India on the Lines of Britain's Fulton Committee recommendation on establishment of Civil Service Department to which the personnel functions of the Treasury (counterpart of India's Ministry of Finance) as also those of Civil Service Commission (counterpart of India's UPSC) were transferred, in order to make it an integrated organisation for personnel administration. While British experiment was hailed by many as satisfactory, India's, however, was not considered to be very satisfactory and successful, as the later experience has proved. After the initial euphoria, it was seen that the Department was routinised, like any other Department of the government. None of the recommended measures relating to functional charter in the new areas, the dynamic thrust in procedural aspects of work, bold agenda of research, unconventional staffing patterns, cutting stranglehold of age-old bureaucratic hierarchy etc., were taken to make the new Department really effective. The leadership role of the Department was neglected and advantages of its direct working link with the Prime Minister through Cabinet Secretary were soon lost! Even so, some, though not many new policies.in the field of personnel were evolved at the initial stages of its existence, mainly on the basis of ARC'S recommendations.

These are:

Advisory Council on Personnel Administration

An Advisory Council on Personnel Administration, consisting of good mix of inside and outside experts, known professionals in the field, experienced Directors of Institutes of Management and Public Administration/National Academy etc. was set up, which was to function as a feederline of new ideas, developing research-base for radical policies and suggesting novel programmes. (After a two year tenure, however, the Council was disbanded!)

Premature Voluntary Retirement

The new scheme for Premature Voluntary Retirement with five years additional service benefit was adopted as a policy to weed out the dead woods or the inefficient personnel and those who are not comfortable in the government from functional and adjustmental points of view.

Administrative Tribunal

The Administrative Tribunal was another milestone in new policy experiments in the personnel. The civil servants all over the country have largely benefited from these Administrative Courts in terms of time, cost, harassment in alternative systems of grievance-handling.

Joint Consultative Machinery

Another important schematic innovation was Joint

Consultative Machinery and Compulsory Arbitration (based on 2nd Pay Commission's recommendations) for conflict management with the employees. The Staff Relations Policy had its fruition in this JCM experiment which has largely been successful in averting agitational methods to settle employer-employee disputes. But these few new policy schemes apart, the history of the public personnel administration here is a story not to be very eloquaent about.

The New Policy Perspective

Personnel policy is an integrated function which encompasses many aspects of the personnel management. In fact, there are inseparable inter-linkages as amongst the diverse personnel activities. Personnel management starts even before the actual employment or recruitment in the organisation. In fact, recruitment itself has to be moulded by the overall employment policy of the organisation. Whether there has to be a greater proportion of direct recruitment i.e. emphasis on 'catch them young' as a principle or there should be more reliance on age, experience and longevity by promoting the people already in the organisation to higher positions are matters of policy which management has to decide before-hand.

The long-term planning of cadre (if there is a 'cadre system' in the services) or determining individual positions (if there is a 'position classification system') have to be done in the beginning and also as a part of a policy of having the right person on the right job in the right time at the right cost. Even this salutary personnel principle is not followed in most of the organisations, though all pay lip service to this dictum.

The methodological issues of recruitment and selection processes-whether there should be positive recruitment, 'campus'-recruitment or other forms of aggressive lateral recruitment, also constitute matter of overall recruitment programmes. The employment policy must have to be linked up with training and development policy retentation policy, promotion policy, compensation policy, motivation policy, career management policy etc. Beside, there have to be well thought-out and positively articulated staff welfare policies and conflict management policy (i.e. Employer-Employee Relationship Policy). It is obvious that all these are basic building blocks of a comprehensive personnel policy.

Unfortunately, they are not framed in any systematic manner nor are they followed in any effective fashion. There is too much of casualness and adhocism in this regard. No serious attempt has been made to focus attention on the positive aspects of personnel growth and development of potentials. Looking into the 'human side of tomorrow' seems nobody's business. Talent hunting has been conspicuous by its absence. Careers for most are not managed by the senior management of the administration, on any scientific and objective basis with an eye on the future but they appear to manage themselves! Both rewards and punishment in the government and in other public organisations are tardily handled, no one can, under the rules, be sumptuously rewarded even if there is a high level of performance nor can any person by punished heavily for failure to achieve or even to perform. There is too much of safety, security and safeguard mechanisms in the government so-much so that there can be only 'hiring' but no 'firing', once one is in. Public organisations in India do not seem to have any commitment toward staff motivation nor do they work for the development of their own people, with the result that there is no semblance of succession policy' anywhere in the public administrative syster. The most common experience is the pervasive existence of a pernicious phenomenon called 'toplessness' in a large number of establishments. Vacancies, and consequential vacuum, often exist and persist for months at a stretch with concomitant adverse effect on efficiency.

Targets are fixed but never seem to be achieved and there is no disgrace attached to target-slippage because goal-consciousness and result-orientation are not taken to be basic to our personnel policy framework.

Structure of Organisation: Committee

A committee (some of which are titled instead as a "Commission", or other terms discussed below in Official and unofficial types) is a type of small deliberative assembly that is usually intended to remain subordinate to another, larger deliberative assembly—which when organized so that action on committee requires a vote by all its entitled members, is called the "Committee of the Whole". Committees often serve several different functions:

- Governance: in organizations considered too large for all the members to participate in decisions affecting the organization as a whole, a committee (such as a Board of Directors or "Executive Committee") is given the power to make decisions, spend money, or take actions. Some or all such powers may be limited or effectively unlimited. For example of the later case, the Board of directors can frequently enter into binding contracts and make decisions which once taken or made, can't be taken back or undone under the law.
- Coordination: individuals from different parts of an organization (for example, all senior vice presidents) might meet regularly to discuss developments in their areas, review projects that cut across organizational boundaries, talk about future options, etc. Where there is a large committee, it is common to have smaller committees with more specialized functions-for example, Boards of Directors of large corporations typically have an (ongoing) audit committee, finance committee, compensation committee, etc. Large academic conferences are usually organized by a co-ordinating committee drawn from the relevant professional body.
- Research and recommendations: committees are often formed to do research and make recommendations on a potential or planned project or change. For example, an organization considering a major capital investment might create a temporary working committee of several people to review options and make recommendations to upper management or the Board of Directors. Such committees are typically dissolved after issuing recommendations (often in the form of a final report).

- Project management: while it is generally considered poor management to give operational responsibility to a committee to actually manage a project, this is not unknown. The problem is that no single person can be held accountable for poor performance of the committee, particularly if the chairperson of the committee is seen as a facilitator.

Common Committee Procedures

- It is common for a chairperson to organize a committee meeting through an agenda, which is usually distributed in advance.
- The chairperson is responsible for running meetings: keeping the discussion on the appropriate subject, recognizing members (calling on them to speak) [often omitted in smaller committees], and calling for votes after a debate has taken place [formal voting is normally only done in committees involved in governance]. Governance committees often have formal processes (for example, they might follow Roberts Rules of Order); other types of committees typically operate informally, with the chairperson being responsible for deciding how formal the committee processes will be.
- Minutes, a record of the discussion and decisions of the meeting, are often taken by a person designated as the secretary of the committee; they may be legally obligatory (again, typically for governance committees, especially boards of directors).
- For committees that meet regularly, the minutes of the most recent meeting are often circulated to committee members before the next meeting, and are available to the membership of the whole.
- Committees may meet on a regular basis, often weekly or yearly, or meetings may be called irregularly as the need arises. During an emergency, a committee may meet more than once per day, or sit in permanent session, as, for example, ExComm (the President's Executive Committee) did during the Cuban Missile Crisis.

Subcommittees

A committee that is a subset of a larger committee is called a subcommittee.

Where the larger group has a name other than "committee"- for example, "Board" or "Commission", the smaller group(s) would usually be called committee(s), not subcommittee(s), and might go by an entirely different name, or substitute "Commission" for "Committee". For example in the sciences, the "International Commission on Stratigraphy" (ICS) a *standing working committee* is doing organizational work establishing uniform naming and benchmarks in the geologic record and timeline since 1974, all under the auspices of the International Union of Geological Sciences (IUGS). It is technically the "International Stratigraphy Committee" (ISC), which has limited executive committee powers to impanel other subcommittees (also called commissions) to resolve certain matters involving the Geologic time scale—its deliberations and those of its subcommittees must be adopted by the IUGS which meets in a committee-of-the-whole or Congress, every four years or so to deliberate on the subcommittee recommendations and officially adopt or not-adopt such.

From the foregoing, it can easily be seen subcommittees can generally be classified further by the adjectives: "Executive", "Standing", and "Working":

Executive Committees

A subcommittee which has well defined executive powers usually spelled out in the charter or by-laws and which meets frequently to manage the affairs and further the purposes of a organization or entity. These are commonly empanelled as well when an organization has a large Board of Directors such as an international labour union, large corporations (with thousands of stock holders) or national and international organizations. A Board of directors is itself a kind of Executive committee established by the charter and by-laws of the entity and elected by the overall franchised membership. For organizations where the Board of Directors is large-say 20 people or more-it is common to have an Executive Committee of the Board—a executive subcommittee of Board members, which is authorized to make some decisions on behalf of the entire Board.

Standing Committees

A committee established by an official and binding vote providing for its scope and powers. Most governmental legislative subcommittees are standing committees, which by another name is a permanent committee. Standing committees meet on a regular or irregular basis dependent upon their enabling act, and retain any power or oversight claims originally given them until subsequent official actions of the committee of the whole (changes to law or by-laws) disbands the committee.

Working Committees

An ad hoc committee established to accomplish a particular task or to oversee an ongoing area in need of control or oversight. Many are research or co-ordination committees in type or purpose, and can be temporary. Some are a sub-group of a larger society with a particular area of interest which decides to meet and discuss matters pertaining to their interests. For example a group of astronomers might get together *ad hoc* to discuss how to get the larger society to address near earth objects; A subgroup of engineers and scientists of a large project's development team could meet ad hoc to solve some particular issue with offsetting considerations and trade-offs. The term when used officially, generally means a group with specific duties and related authority, so when encountered in official contexts subsumes all other official types of committees. The International Commission on Stratigraphy and its subcommittees (commissions in name) are working committees that meet both far more regularly and more frequently both in deliberation and co-ordination furthering the needs of the IUGS (which regularly schedules meetings only every fourth year) and the larger scientific community. They fulfil a basic need.

A Basic Need

Committees are a necessary aspect of organizations of any significant size (say, more than 15 or 20 people). They keep the number of participants manageable; with larger groups, either many people do not get to speak (and feel left out), or discussions are quite lengthy (and many participants find them duplicative and often boring).

Cross-field Reasons

Committees are a way to formally draw together people of relevant expertise from different parts of an organization who otherwise would not have a good way to share information and coordinate actions. They may have the advantage of widening viewpoints and sharing out responsibilities. They can also be empaneled with experts to recommend actions by the committee of the whole in matters that require specialized knowledge or technical judgment. A "Defence" or "Banking" subcommittee in legislative bodies or the many International science commissions such as the ICS mentioned above, or a local "board of health" are or may be such.

Disadvantages

Their disadvantages appear in the possibilities for procrastination, undesirable compromises in order to build consensus, and group think, where (valid) objections or disconfirming evidence is either not voiced or is ignored. Moreover, the need to schedule a meeting, get enough committee members together to have a quorum, and debate until a majority agrees on a course of action, can result in undesirable delays in taking action. (A common joke, in organizations, is that when someone doesn't want to make an unpopular decision, he/she creates a committee to study the question.)

Conference Committee

Standing Committees

A standing committee is a subunit of a political or deliberative body established in a permanent fashion to aid the parent assembly in accomplishing its duties. A standing committee is usually granted jurisdiction over a particular area of legislation by the parent body. Under the laws of the United States of America, a standing committee is a Congressional committee permanently authorized by United States House of Representatives and United States Senate rules. The Legislative Reorganization Act of 1946 greatly reduced the number of committees, and set up the legislative committee structure still in use today, as modified by authorized changes via the orderly mechanism of rules changes.

Standing Committees in Legislatures

The phrase is used in the legislatures of the following countries:

- Australia: see Australian House of Representatives committees and Australian Senate committees
- Canada: see Standing committee (Canada)
- China: see Standing Committee of the National People's Congress
- India
- United Kingdom: see Public bill committee
- United States: see Standing committee (United States Congress).

Parliamentary Committees

In the parliamentary procedure take part:

- Fiscal committee, if the bill contains an appropriation or has financial implications for the state or federation.
- Policy committee. Appropriate committee to the subject matter.
- Rules committee. The rules committee of the House assigns each bill to a policy committee.

Planning Commission (India)

The Planning Commission is an institution in the Government of India, which formulates India's Five-Year Plans, among other functions.

History

Rudimentary economic planning, deriving the sovereign authority of the state, first began in India in 1930s under the

British Raj, and the colonial government of India formally established a planning board that functioned from 1944 to 1946. Private industrialists and economist formulated at least three development plans in 1944.

After India gained independence, a formal model of planning was adopted, and the planning commission, reporting directly to the Prime Minister of India was established. Accordingly, the Planning Commission was set up on 15 March 1950, with Prime Minister Jawaharlal Nehru as the chairman. Planing Commission though is a non statutory as well extra constitutional body, i.e has been brought by an executive order.

The first Five-year Plan was launched in 1951 and two subsequent five-year plans were formulated till 1965, when there was a break because of the Indo-Pakistan Conflict. Two successive years of drought, devaluation of the currency, a general rise in prices and erosion of resources disrupted the planning process and after three Annual Plans between 1966 and 1969, the fourth Five-year plan was started in 1969.

The Eighth Plan could not take off in 1990 due to the fast changing political situation at the Centre and the years 1990-91 and 1991-92 were treated as Annual Plans. The Eighth Plan was finally launched in 1992 after the initiation of structural adjustment policies.

For the first eight Plans the emphasis was on a growing public sector with massive investments in basic and heavy industries, but since the launch of the Ninth Plan in 1997, the emphasis on the public sector has become less pronounced and the current thinking on planning in the country, in general, is that it should increasingly be of an indicative nature.

Organisation

The composition of the Commission has undergone a lot of change since its inception. With the Prime Minister as the ex-officio Chairman, the committee has a nominated Deputy Chairman, who is given the rank of a full Cabinet Minister. Mr. Montek Singh Ahluwalia is presently the Deputy Chairman of the Commission.

Cabinet Ministers with certain important portfolios act as part-time members of the Commission, while the full-time members are experts of various fields like Economics, Industry, Science and General Administration.

The Commission works through its various divisions, of which there are three kind:

General Planning Divisions.

Programme Administration Divisions.

The majority of experts in the Commission are economists, making the Commission the biggest employer of the Indian Economic Services.

Functions

- Assessment of resources of the country
- Formulation of Five-Year Plans for effective use of these resources
- Determination of priorities, and allocation of resources for the Plans
- Determination of requisite machinery for successful implementation of the Plans
- Periodical appraisal of the progress of the Plan.

To formulate plans for the most effective and balanced utilization of country's resources.

To indicate the factors which are hampering economic development.

5

Public Relations and Policy

Public relations and publicity are not synonymous, but many PR campaigns include provisions for publicity. Publicity is the spreading of information to gain public awareness for a product, person, service, cause or organization, and can be seen as a result of effective PR planning.

More recently in public relations, professionals are using technology as their main tool to get their messages to target audiences. With the creation of social networks, blogs, and even internet radio public relations professionals are able to send direct messages through these mediums that attract the target audiences. Methods used to find out what is appealing to target audiences include the use of surveys, conducting research or even focus groups. Tactics are the ways to attract target audiences by using the information gathered about that audience and directing a message to them using tools such as social media or other technology.

Tools

There are various tools that can be used in the practice of PR. Traditional tools include press releases and media kits which are sent out to generate positive press on behalf of the organization. Other widely-used tools include brochures, newsletters and annual reports.

Increasingly, companies are utilizing interactive social media, such as blogs, Twitter and Facebook, as tools in their PR campaigns. Unlike the traditional tools which allowed for only one-way communication, social media allows the organization to engage in two-way communication, and receive immediate feedback from their various stakeholders and publics.

Publics Targeting

A fundamental technique used in public relations is to identify the target audience, and to tailor every message to appeal to that audience. It can be a general, nationwide or worldwide audience, but it is more often a segment of a population. A good elevator pitch can help tailor messaging to each target audience. Marketers often refer to economy-driven "demographics," such as "black males 18-49," but in public relations an audience is more fluid, being whoever someone wants to reach. For example, recent political audiences include "soccer moms" and "NASCAR dads." There is also a psychographic grouping based on fitness level, eating preferences, "adrenaline junkies," etc...

In addition to audiences, there are usually stakeholders, people who have a stake in a given issue. All audiences are stakeholders (or presumptive stakeholders), but not all stakeholders are audiences. For example, if a charity commissions a PR agency to create an advertising campaign to raise money to find a cure for a disease, the charity and the people with the disease are stakeholders, but the audience is anyone who is likely to donate money.

Sometimes the interests of differing audiences and stakeholders common to a PR effort necessitate the creation of several distinct but complementary messages. This is not always easy to do, and sometimes – especially in politics – a spokesperson or client says something to one audience that angers another audience or group of stakeholders.

Lobby Groups

Lobby groups are established to influence government policy, corporate policy, or public opinion. An example of this is the American Israel Public Affairs Committee, AIPAC, which influences American foreign policy. Such groups claim to represent a particular interest and in fact are dedicated to doing so. When a lobby group hides its true purpose and support base, it is known as a front group. Moreover, governments may also lobby public relations firms in order to sway public opinion. A well illustrated example of this is the way civil war in Yugoslavia was portrayed. Governments of newly succeeded republics of Croatia and Bosnia invested heavily with American PR firms, so that the PR firms would give them a positive war image in the US.

Spin

In PR, "spin" is sometimes a pejorative term signifying a heavily biased portrayal in one's own favour of an event or situation. While traditional public relations may also rely on creative presentation of the facts, "spin" often, though not always, implies disingenuous, deceptive and/or highly manipulative tactics. Politicians are often accused of spin by commentators and political opponents when they produce a counterargument or position.

The techniques of spin include selectively presenting facts and quotes that support one's position (cherry picking), the so-called "non-denial," phrasing in a way that assumes unproven truths, euphemisms for drawing attention away fr m items considered distasteful, and ambiguity in public statements. Another spin technique involves careful choice of timing in the release of certain news so it can take advantage of prominent events in the news. A famous reference to this practice occurred when British Government press officer Jo Moore used the phrase *It's now a very good day to get out anything we want to bury*, (widely paraphrased or misquoted as "It's a good day to bury bad news"), in an email sent on September 11, 2001. The furor caused when this email was reported in the press eventually caused her to resign.

Spin Doctors

Skilled practitioners of spin are sometimes called "spin doctors," despite the negative connotation associated with the term. Perhaps the best-known person in the UK often described as a "spin doctor" is Alastair Campbell, who was involved with Tony Blair's public relations between 1994 and 2003, and also played a controversial role as press relations officer to the British and Irish Lions rugby union side during their 2005 tour of New Zealand.

State-run media in many countries also engage in spin by selectively allowing news stories that are favourable to the government while censoring anything that could be considered critical. They may also use propaganda to indoctrinate or actively influence citizens' opinions. Privately run media also uses the same techniques of 'issue' versus 'non-issue' to spin its particular political viewpoints.

Meet and Greet

Many businesses and organizations will use a Meet and Greet as a method of introducing two or more parties to each other in a comfortable setting. These will generally involve some sort of incentive, usually food catered from restaurants, to encourage employees or members to participate.

There are opposing schools of thought as to how the specific mechanics of a Meet and Greet operate. The Gardiner school of thought states that unless specified as an informal event, all parties should arrive promptly at the time at which the event is scheduled to start. The Kolanowski school of thought, however, states that parties may arrive at any time after the event begins, in order to provide a more relaxed interaction environment.

Other

- Publicity events, pseudo-events, photo ops or publicity stunts.
- Talk show circuit. A PR spokesperson (or his/her client) "does the circuit" by being interviewed on television and radio talk shows with audiences that the client wishes to reach.
- Books and other writings.
- Blogs.
- After a PR practitioner has been working in the field for a while, he or she accumulates a list of contacts in

the media and elsewhere in the public affairs sphere. This "Rolodex" becomes a prized asset, and job announcements sometimes even ask for candidates with an existing Rolodex, especially those in the media relations area of PR.

- Direct communication (carrying messages directly to constituents, rather than through the mass media) with, e.g., newsletters – in print and e-letters.
- Collateral literature, traditionally in print and now predominantly as web sites.
- Speeches to constituent groups and professional organizations; receptions; seminars, and other events; personal appearances.
- The slang term for a PR practitioner or publicist is a "flack" (sometimes spelled "flak").
- A Desk Visit is where the PR person literally takes their product to the desk of the journalist in order to show them what they are promoting.
- Astroturfing is the act of PR agencies placing blog and online forum messages for their clients, in the guise of a normal "grassroots" user or comment.

Politics and Civil Society

Defining the Opponent

The tactic known as "defining one's opponent" is used in political campaigns. Opponents can be candidates, organizations and other groups of people.

In the 2004 US presidential campaign, Howard Dean defined John Kerry as a "flip-flopper," which was widely reported and repeated by the media, particularly the conservative media. Similarly, George H.W. Bush characterized Michael Dukakis as weak on crime (the Willie Horton ad) and hopelessly liberal ("a card-carrying member of the ACLU"). In 1996, President Bill Clinton seized upon opponent Bob Dole's promise to take America back to a simpler time, promising in contrast to "build a bridge to the 21st century." This painted Dole as a person who was somehow opposed to progress. In the debate over abortion, self-titled pro-choice groups, by virtue of their name, defined their opponents as "anti-choice", while self-titled pro-life groups refer to their opponents as "pro-abortion" or "anti-life".

Managing Language

If a politician or organization can use an apt phrase in relation to an issue in interviews or news releases, the news media will often repeat it verbatim, without questioning its aptness. This perpetuates both the message and whatever preconceptions might underlie it. Often, something that sounds innocuous can stand in for something greater; a "culture of life" sounds like general goodwill to most people, but will evoke opposition to abortion for many pro-life advocates. The phrase "States' rights" was used as a code for anti-civil rights legislation in the United States in the 1960s, and allegedly in the 1970s and 1980s.

Conveying the Message

The method of a message's communication can be as important as the message itself. Direct mail, robocalling, advertising and public speaking are used depending upon the intended audience and the message that is conveyed. Press releases are also used, but since many newspapers are folding, they have become a less reliable way of communicating, and other methods have become more popular.

Arts organizations have begun to rely more on their own websites and have developed a variety of unique approaches to publicity and public relations, on and off the web.

The country of Israel has recently employed a series of Web 2.0 initiatives, including a blog, MySpace page, YouTube channel, Facebook page and a political blog to reach different audiences. The Israeli Ministry of Foreign Affairs started the country's video blog as well as its political blog.

The Foreign Ministry held the first microblogging press conference via Twitter about its war with Hamas, with Consul David Saranga answering live questions from a worldwide public in common text-messaging abbreviations. The questions and answers were later posted on Israel Politik, the country's official political blog.

Front Groups

One of the most controversial practices in public relations is the use of front groups – organizations that purport to serve a public cause while actually serving the interests of a client whose sponsorship may be obscured or concealed. Critics of the public relations industry, such as PR Watch, have contended that Public Relations involves a "multi-billion dollar propaganda-for-hire industry" that "concoct[s] and spin[s] the news, organize[s] phoney 'grassroots' front groups, sp[ies] on citizens, and conspire[s] with lobbyists and politicians to thwart democracy."

Instances of the use of front groups as a PR technique have been documented in many industries. Coal mining corporations have created environmental groups that contend that increased CO_2 emissions and global warming will contribute to plant growth and will be beneficial, trade groups for bars have created and funded citizens' groups to attack anti-alcohol groups, tobacco companies have created and funded citizens' groups to advocate for tort reform and to attack personal injury lawyers, while trial lawyers have created "consumer advocacy" front groups to oppose tort reform.

Message Discipline

Message discipline is the concept that politicians and other public policy advocates should talk about what is relevant to achieve their aims, and not allow themselves to be sidetracked either by their own thoughts or the questions of press or audience.

When a politician repeats the same thing over and over, or uses a question on one subject as a launching pad to talk about a different subject, he or she is said to be exercising message discipline. Message discipline is a difficult thing for politicians or other quotable people to achieve, because it may involve a subordination of one's personal opinions, or a subordination of one's desire to say what others want to hear.

Propaganda

Propaganda is a form of communication that is aimed at influencing the attitude of a community toward some cause or position. As opposed to impartially providing information, propaganda in its most basic sense, presents information primarily to influence an audience. Propaganda often presents facts selectively (thus possibly lying by omission) to encourage a particular synthesis, or uses loaded messages to produce an emotional rather than rational response to the information presented. The desired result is a change of the attitude toward the subject in the target audience to further a political agenda.

> *"Propaganda is neutrally defined as a systematic form of purposeful persuasion that attempts to influence the emotions, attitudes, opinions, and actions of specified target audiences for ideological, political or commercial purposes through the controlled transmission of one-sided messages (which may or may not be factual) via mass and direct media channels."*
>
> *— Richard Alan Nelson, A Chronology and Glossary of Propaganda in the United States.*

Etymology

The English term is an 18th century coinage, from the Latin feminine gerund of *propagare* "to propagate", originally in *Congregatio de Propaganda Fide* "Congregation for Propagating the Faith", a committee of cardinals established 1622 by Gregory XV. In its turn, the word *propagare* is related to the word *propages' ', "a slip, a cutting of a vine" and refers to the gardener's practice to disseminate plants by planting shoots.*

The term is not pejorative in origin and its political sense dates back to World War I.

Types

Defining propaganda has always been a problem. Garth Jowett and Victoria O'Donnell have provided a concise, workable definition of the term: "Propaganda is the deliberate, systematic attempt to shape perceptions, manipulate cognitions, and direct behaviour to achieve a response that furthers the desired intent of the propagandist." This definition focuses on the communicative process involved—more precisely, on the purpose of the process, and allows "propaganda" to be considered as a neutral activity, which can be seen as positive or negative behaviour depending on the perspective of the viewer.

Propaganda is generally an appeal to emotion, not intellect. It shares techniques with advertising and public relations, each of which can be thought of as propaganda that promotes a commercial product or shapes the perception of an organization, person or brand, though in post-World War II usage the word "propaganda" more typically refers to political or nationalist uses of these techniques or to the promotion of a set of ideas, since the term had gained a pejorative meaning, which commercial and government entities could not accept. The refusal phenomenon was eventually to be seen in politics itself by the substitution of "political marketing" and other designations for "political propaganda". Propaganda was often used to influence opinions and beliefs on religious issues, particularly during the split between the Roman Catholic Church and the Protestant churches. Propaganda has become more common in political contexts, in particular to refer to certain efforts sponsored by governments, political groups, but also often covert interests. In the early 20th century, propaganda was exemplified in the form of party slogans. Also in the early 20th century the term propaganda was used by the founders of the nascent public relations industry to describe their activities. This usage died out around the time of World War II, as the industry started to avoid the word, given the pejorative connotation it had acquired.

Literally translated from the Latin gerundive as "things that must be disseminated", in some cultures the term is neutral or even positive, while in others the term has acquired a strong negative connotation. The connotations of the term "propaganda" can also vary over time. For example, in Portuguese and some Spanish language speaking countries, particularly in the Southern Cone, the word "propaganda" usually refers to the most common manipulative media — "advertising".

In English, "propaganda" was originally a neutral term used to describe the dissemination of information in favour of any given cause. During the 20th century, however, the term acquired a thoroughly negative meaning in western countries, representing the intentional dissemination of often false, but certainly "compelling" claims to support or justify political actions or ideologies. This redefinition arose because both the Soviet Union and Germany's government under Hitler admitted explicitly to using propaganda favouring, respectively, communism and Nazism, in all forms of public expression. As these ideologies were repugnant to liberal western societies, the negative feelings toward them came to be projected into the word "propaganda" itself.

Propaganda is neutrally defined as a systematic form of purposeful persuasion that attempts to influence the emotions, attitudes, opinions, and actions of specified target audiences for ideological, political or commercial purposes through the controlled transmission of one-sided messages (which may or may not be factual) via mass and direct media channels. A propaganda organization employs propagandists who engage in propagandism—the applied creation and distribution of such forms of persuasion.

—Richard Alan Nelson, A Chronology and Glossary of Propaganda in the United States, 1996

Roderick Hindery argues that propaganda exists on the political left, and right, and in mainstream centrist parties. Hindery further argues that debates about most social issues can be productively revisited in the context of asking "what is or is not propaganda?" Not to be overlooked is the link between propaganda, indoctrination, and terrorism/counterterrorism. He argues that threats to destroy are often as socially disruptive as physical devastation itself.

Propaganda also has much in common with public information campaigns by governments, which are intended to encourage or discourage certain forms of behaviour (such as wearing seat belts, not smoking, not littering and so forth). Again, the emphasis is more political in propaganda. Propaganda can take the form of leaflets, posters, TV and radio broadcasts and can also extend to any other medium. In the case of the United States, there is also an important legal (imposed by law) distinction between advertising (a type of overt propaganda) and what the Government Accountability Office (GAO), an arm of the United States Congress, refers to as "covert propaganda".

Journalistic theory generally holds that news items should be objective, giving the reader an accurate background and analysis of the subject at hand. On the other hand, advertisements evolved from the traditional commercial advertisements to include also a new type in the form of paid articles or broadcasts disguised as news. These generally present an issue in a very subjective and often misleading light, primarily meant to persuade rather than inform. Normally they use only subtle propaganda techniques and not the more obvious ones used in traditional commercial advertisements. If the reader believes that a paid advertisement is in fact a news item, the message the advertiser is trying to communicate will be more easily "believed" or "internalized".

Such advertisements are considered obvious examples of "covert" propaganda because they take on the appearance of objective information rather than the appearance of propaganda, which is misleading. Federal law specifically mandates that any advertisement appearing in the format of a news item must state that the item is in fact a paid advertisement.

The propagandist seeks to change the way people understand an issue or situation for the purpose of changing their actions and expectations in ways that are desirable to the interest group. Propaganda, in this sense, serves as a corollary to censorship in which the same purpose is achieved, not by filling people's minds with approved information, but by preventing people from being confronted with opposing points of view. What sets propaganda apart from other forms of advocacy is the willingness of the propagandist to change people's understanding through deception and confusion rather than persuasion and understanding. The leaders of an organization know the information to be one sided or untrue, but this may not be true for the rank and file members who help to disseminate the propaganda.

More in line with the religious roots of the term, it is also used widely in the debates about new religious movements (NRMs), both by people who defend them and by people who oppose them. The latter pejoratively call these NRMs cults. Anti-cult activists and countercult activists accuse the leaders of what they consider cults of using propaganda extensively to recruit followers and keep them. Some social scientists, such as the late Jeffrey Hadden, and CESNUR affiliated scholars accuse ex-members of "cults" who became vocal critics and the anti-cult movement of making these unusual religious movements look bad without sufficient reasons. Propaganda is a powerful weapon in war; it is used to dehumanize and create hatred toward a supposed enemy, either internal or external, by creating a false image in the mind. This can be done by using derogatory or racist terms, avoiding some words or by making allegations of enemy atrocities. Most propaganda wars require the home population to feel the enemy has inflicted an injustice, which may be fictitious or may be based on facts. The home population must also decide that the cause of their nation is just.

Propaganda is also one of the methods used in psychological warfare, which may also involve false flag operations. The term propaganda may also refer to false information meant to reinforce the mindsets of people who already believe as the propagandist wishes. The assumption is that, if people believe something false, they will constantly be assailed by doubts. Since these doubts are unpleasant, people will be eager to have them extinguished, and are therefore receptive to the reassurances of those in power. For this reason propaganda is often addressed to people who are already sympathetic to the agenda. This process of reinforcement uses an individual's predisposition to self-select "agreeable" information sources as a mechanism for maintaining control.

Propaganda can be classified according to the source and nature of the message. White propaganda generally comes from an openly identified source, and is characterized by gentler methods of persuasion, such as standard public relations techniques and one-sided presentation of an argument. Black propaganda is identified as being from one source, but is in fact from another. This is most commonly to disguise the true origins of the propaganda, be it from an enemy country or from an organization with a negative public image. Grey propaganda is propaganda without any identifiable source or author. A major application of grey propaganda is making enemies believe falsehoods using straw arguments: As phase one, to make someone believe "A", one releases as grey propaganda "B", the opposite of "A". In phase two, "B" is discredited using some strawman. The enemy will then assume "A" to be true.

In scale, these different types of propaganda can also be defined by the potential of true and correct information to compete with the propaganda.

For example, opposition to white propaganda is often readily found and may slightly discredit the propaganda source. Opposition to grey propaganda, when revealed (often by an inside source), may create some level of public outcry. Opposition to black propaganda is often unavailable and may be dangerous to reveal, because public cognizance of black propaganda tactics and sources would undermine or backfire the very campaign the black propagandist supported.

Propaganda may be administered in insidious ways. For instance, disparaging dis-information about the history of certain groups or foreign countries may be encouraged or tolerated in the educational system. Since few people actually double-check what they learn at school, such dis-information will be repeated by journalists as well as parents, thus reinforcing the idea that the dis-information item is really a "well-known fact", even though no one repeating the myth is able to point to an authoritative source.

The dis-information is then recycled in the media and in the educational system, without the need for direct governmental intervention on the media. Such permeating propaganda may be used for political goals: by giving citizens a false impression of the quality or policies of their country, they may be incited to reject certain proposals or certain remarks or ignore the experience of others.

Techniques

Common media for transmitting propaganda messages include news reports, government reports, historical revision, junk science, books, leaflets, movies, radio, television, and posters. Less common nowadays are letterpost envelopes examples of which of survive from the time of the American Civil War. (Connecticut Historical Society; Civil War Collections; Covers.) In principle any thing that appears on a poster can be produced on a reduced scale on a pocket-style envelope with corresponding proportions to the poster. The case of radio and television, propaganda can exist on news, current-affairs or talk-show segments, as advertising or public-service announce "spots" or as long-running advertorials. Propaganda campaigns often follow a strategic transmission pattern to indoctrinate the target group. This may begin with a simple transmission such as a leaflet dropped from a plane or an advertisement. Generally these messages will contain directions on how to obtain more information, via a web site, hot line, radio program, et cetera (as it is seen also for selling purposes among other goals). The strategy intends to initiate the individual from information recipient to information seeker through reinforcement, and then from information seeker to opinion leader through indoctrination. A number of techniques based in social psychological research are used to generate propaganda. Many of these same techniques can be found under logical fallacies, since propagandists use arguments that, while sometimes convincing, are not necessarily valid. Some time has been spent analysing the means by which the propaganda messages are transmitted. That work is important but it is clear that information dissemination strategies become propaganda strategies only when coupled with *propagandistic messages*. Identifying these messages is a necessary prerequisite to study the methods by which those messages are spread. Below are a number of techniques for generating propaganda:

Ad hominem

A Latin phrase that has come to mean attacking one's opponent, as opposed to attacking their arguments.

Ad Nauseam

This argument approach uses tireless repetition of an idea. An idea, especially a simple slogan, that is repeated enough times, may begin to be taken as the truth. This approach works best when media sources are limited and controlled by the propagator.

Appeal to Authority

Appeals to authority cite prominent figures to support a position, idea, argument, or course of action.

Appeal to Fear

Appeals to fear and seeks to build support by instilling anxieties and panic in the general population, for example, Joseph Goebbels exploited Theodore Kaufman's *Germany Must Perish!* to claim that the Allies sought the extermination of the German people.

Appeal to Prejudice

Using loaded or emotive terms to attach value or moral goodness to believing the proposition. Used in biased or misleading ways.

Bandwagon

Bandwagon and "inevitable-victory" appeals attempt to persuade the target audience to join in and take the course of action that "everyone else is taking".

Inevitable victory: invites those not already on the bandwagon to join those already on the road to certain victory. Those already or at least partially on the bandwagon are reassured that staying aboard is their best course of action. Join the crowd: This technique reinforces people's natural desire to be on the winning side. This technique is used to convince the audience that a program is an expression of an irresistible mass movement and that it is in their best interest to join.

Beautiful People

The type of propaganda that deals with famous people or depicts attractive, happy people. This makes other people think that if they buy a product or follow a certain ideology, they too will be happy or successful.

Big Lie

The repeated articulation of a complex of events that justify subsequent action. The descriptions of these events have elements of truth, and the "big lie" generalizations merge and eventually supplant the public's accurate perception of the underlying events. After World War I the German Stab in the back explanation of the cause of their defeat became a justification for Nazi re-militarization and revanchist aggression.

Black-and-white Fallacy

Presenting only two choices, with the product or idea being propagated as the better choice. (e.g., George W. Bush: "Either you are with us or with the terrorists.")

Classical Conditioning

All vertebrates including people respond to classical conditioning. That is, if object A is always present when object B is present and object B causes a negative physical reaction (e.g., disgust, pleasure) then we will when presented with object A when object B is not present, we will experience the same feelings.

Cognitive Dissonance

People desire to be consistent. Suppose a pollster finds that a certain group of people hates his candidate for senator but love actor A. They use actor A's endorsement of their candidate to change people's minds because people cannot tolerate inconsistency. They are forced to either to disklike the actor or like the candidate.

Common Man

The "plain folks" or "common man" approach attempts to convince the audience that the propagandist's positions reflect the common sense of the people. It is designed to win the confidence of the audience by communicating in the common manner and style of the target audience. Propagandists use ordinary language and mannerisms (and clothe their message in face-to-face and audiovisual communications) in attempting to identify their point of view with that of the average person. For example, a propaganda leaflet may make an argument on a macroeconomic issue, such as unemployment insurance benefits, using everyday terms: "Given that the country has little money during this recession, we should stop paying unemployment benefits to those who do not work, because that is like maxing out all your credit cards during a tight period, when you should be tightening your belt."

Demonizing the Enemy

Making individuals from the opposing nation, from a different ethnic group, or those who support the opposing viewpoint appear to be subhuman (e.g., the Vietnam War-era term "gooks" for National Front for the Liberation of South Vietnam aka Vietcong, or "VC", soldiers), worthless, or immoral, through suggestion or false accusations.

Direct order

This technique hopes to simplify the decision making process by using images and words to tell the audience exactly what actions to take, eliminating any other possible choices. Authority figures can be used to give the order, overlapping it with the Appeal to authority technique, but not necessarily. The Uncle Sam "I want you" image is an example of this technique.

Dis-information

The creation or deletion of information from public records, in the purpose of making a false record of an event or the actions of a person or organization, including outright forgery of photographs, motion pictures, broadcasts, and sound recordings as well as printed documents.

Door-in-the-Face Technique

Is used to increase a person's lattitudes of acceptance. For example, if a salesperson wants to sell an item for $100 but the public would only be willing to pay $50 for the item, the salesman first offers the product at a much higher price (e.g., $500). Few buy the item at this price but offering the price at a much higher values makes it seem that a price of a $100 is a good prices when previously, people felt the price of a $100 was too high.

Euphoria

The use of an event that generates euphoria or happiness, or using an appealing event to boost morale. Euphoria can be created by declaring a holiday, making luxury items available, or mounting a military parade with marching bands and patriotic messages.

Flag-waving

An attempt to justify an action on the grounds that doing so will make one more patriotic, or in some way benefit a group, country, or idea. The feeling of patriotism this technique attempts to inspire may not necessarily diminish or entirely omit one's capability for rational examination of the matter in question.

Glittering Generalities

Glittering generalities are emotionally appealing words applied to a product or idea, but which present no concrete argument or analysis. A famous example is the campaign slogan "Ford has a better idea!" This technique has also been referred to as the PT Barnum effect.

Half-truth

A half-truth is a deceptive statement, which may come in several forms and includes some element of truth. The statement might be partly true, the statement may be totally true but only part of the whole truth, or it may utilize some deceptive element, such as improper punctuation, or double meaning, especially if the intent is to deceive, evade, blame or misrepresent the truth.

Obfuscation, Intentional Vagueness, Confusion

Generalities are deliberately vague so that the audience may supply its own interpretations. The intention is to move the audience by use of undefined phrases, without analysing their validity or attempting to determine their reasonableness or application. The intent is to cause people to draw their own interpretations rather than simply being presented with an explicit idea. In trying to "figure out" the propaganda, the audience forgoes judgment of the ideas presented. Their validity, reasonableness and application may still be considered.

Labelling

A Euphemism is used when the propagandist attempts to increase the perceived quality, credibility, or credence of a particular ideal. A Dysphemism is used when the intent of the propagandist is to discredit, diminish the perceived quality, or hurt the perceived righteousness of the Mark.

By creating a "label" or "category" or "faction" of a population, it is much easier to make an example of these larger bodies, because they can uplift or defame the Mark without actually incurring legal-defamation.

Example: "Liberal" is a dysphemism intended to diminish the perceived credibility of a particular Mark. By taking a displeasing argument presented by a Mark, the propagandist can quote that person, and then attack "liberals" in an attempt to both (1) create a political battle-ax of unaccountable aggression and (2) diminish the quality of the Mark. If the propagandist uses the label on too-many perceivably credible individuals, muddying up the word can be done by broadcasting bad-examples of "liberals" into the media. Labelling can be thought of as a sub-set of Guilt by association, another logical fallacy.

Latitudes of Acceptance

If a person's message is outside the bounds of acceptance for an individual and group, most techniques will engender psychological reactance (simply hearing the argument will make the message even less acceptable. There are two techniques for increasing the bounds of acceptance. First, one can take a more even extreme position that will make more moderate positions seem more acceptable. This is similar to the Door-in-the-Face technique. Alternatively, one can moderate one's own position to the edge of the attitude of acceptance and then over time slowly move to the position that was previously.

Lying and Deception

Lying and Deception can be the basis of many propaganda techniques including Ad Homimen arguments, Big-Lie, Defamation, Door-in-the-Face, Half-truth, Name-calling or any other technique that is based on dishonesty or deception. For example, in politics have found that politicians frequently stretch or break the truth.

Name-calling

Propagandists use the *name-calling technique* to incite fears and arouse prejudices in their hearers in the intent that the bad names will cause hearers to construct a negative opinion about a group or set of beliefs or ideas that the propagandist would wish hearers to denounce. The method is intended to provoke conclusions about a matter apart from impartial examinations of facts. Name-calling is thus a substitute for rational, fact-based arguments against the an idea or belief on its own merits.

Obtain Disapproval or Reductio ad Hitlerum

This technique is used to persuade a target audience to disapprove of an action or idea by suggesting that the idea is popular with groups hated, feared, or held in contempt by the target audience.

Thus if a group that supports a certain policy is led to believe that undesirable, subversive, or contemptible people support the same policy, then the members of the group may decide to change their original position. This is a form of bad logic, where a is said to include X, and b is said to include X, therefore, a = b.

Oversimplification

Favourable generalities are used to provide simple answers to complex social, political, economic, or military problems.

Quotes out of Context

Selectively editing quotes to change meanings—political documentaries designed to discredit an opponent or an opposing political viewpoint often make use of this technique.

Foot-in-the-door Technique

Often used by recruiters and salesman. For example, a member of the opposite sex walks up to the victim and pins a flower or gives a small gift to the victim. The victim says thanks and now they have incurred a psychological debt to the perpetrator. The person eventually asks for a larger favour (e.g., a donation or to buy something far more expensive). The unwritten social contract between the victim and perpetrator causes the victim to feel obligated to reciprocate by agreeing to do the larger favour or buy the more expensive gift.

Operant Conditioning

Operant conditioning involves learning through imitation. For example, watching an appealing people buy products or endorse positions teaches a person to buy the product or endorse the position. Operant conditioning is the underlying principle behind the Ad Nauseam, Slogan and other repetition public relations campaigns.

Rationalization

Individuals or groups may use favourable generalities to rationalize questionable acts or beliefs. Vague and pleasant phrases are often used to justify such actions or beliefs.

Red Herring

Presenting data or issues that, while compelling, are irrelevant to the argument at hand, and then claiming that it validates the argument.

Scapegoating

Assigning blame to an individual or group, thus alleviating feelings of guilt from responsible parties and/or distracting attention from the need to fix the problem for which blame is being assigned.

Slogans

A slogan is a brief, striking phrase that may include labelling and stereotyping. Although slogans may be enlisted to support reasoned ideas, in practice they tend to act only as emotional appeals. Opponents of the US's invasion and occupation of Iraq use the slogan "blood for oil" to suggest that the invasion and its human losses was done to access Iraq's oil riches. On the other hand, "hawks" who argue that the US should continue to fight in Iraq use the slogan "cut and run" to suggest that it would be cowardly or weak to withdraw from Iraq. Similarly, the names of the military campaigns, such as "enduring freedom" or "just cause", may also be regarded to be slogans, devised to influence people.

Stereotyping

This technique attempts to arouse prejudices in an audience by labelling the object of the propaganda campaign as something the target audience fears, hates, loathes, or finds undesirable. For instance, reporting on a foreign country or social group may focus on the stereotypical traits that the reader expects, even though they are far from being representative of the whole country or group; such reporting often focuses on the anecdotal. In graphic propaganda, including war posters, this might include portraying enemies with stereotyped racial features.

Straw Man

A straw man argument is an informal fallacy based on misrepresentation of an opponent's position. To "attack a straw man" is to create the illusion of having refuted a proposition by substituting a superficially similar proposition (the "straw man"), and refuting it, without ever having actually refuted the original position.

Testimonial

Testimonials are quotations, in or out of context, especially cited to support or reject a given policy, action, program, or personality. The reputation or the role (expert, respected public figure, etc.) of the individual giving the statement is exploited. The testimonial places the official sanction of a respected person or authority on a propaganda message. This is done in an effort to cause the target audience to identify itself with the authority or to accept the authority's opinions and beliefs as its own.

Third Party Technique

Invented by the father of spin (Bernays used third party sources to argue his clients cases. For example, the tobacco industry formed "scientific institutes" in an attempt to discredit evidence that tobacco causes cancer.

Transfer

Also known as association, this is a technique that involves projecting the positive or negative qualities of one person, entity, object, or value onto another to make the second more acceptable or to discredit it. It evokes an emotional response, which stimulates the target to identify with recognized authorities. Often highly visual, this technique often utilizes symbols superimposed over other visual images. These symbols may be used in place of words; for example, placing swastikas on or around a picture of an opponent to associate the opponent with Naziism.

Unstated Assumption

This technique is used when the propaganda concept that the propagandist intends to transmit would seem less credible if explicitly stated. The concept is instead repeatedly assumed or implied.

Virtue Words

These are words in the value system of the target audience that produce a positive image when attached to a person or issue. Peace, happiness, security, wise leadership, freedom, "The Truth", etc. are virtue words. In countries such as the U.S. religiosity is seen as a virtue, making associations to this quality affectively beneficial.

Models

Herman and Chomsky's Propaganda Model

The propaganda model is a theory advanced by Edward S. Herman and Noam Chomsky that alleges systemic biases in the mass media and seeks to explain them in terms of structural economic causes.

The 20th century has been characterized by three developments of great political importance: the growth of democracy, the growth of corporate power, and the growth of corporate propaganda as a means of protecting corporate power against democracy.

First presented in their 1988 book *Manufacturing Consent: the Political Economy of the Mass Media*, the propaganda model views the private media as businesses selling a product — readers and audiences (rather than news) — to other businesses (advertisers) and relying primarily on government and corporate information and propaganda. The theory postulates five general classes of "filters" that determine the type of news that is presented in news media: Ownership of the medium, the medium's Funding, Sourcing of the news, Flak, and Anti-communist ideology.

The first three (ownership, funding, and sourcing) are generally regarded by the authors as being the most important. Although the model was based mainly on the characterization of United States media, Chomsky and Herman believe the theory is equally applicable to any country that shares the basic economic structure and organizing principles the model postulates as the cause of media biases. After the disintegration of the Soviet Union, Chomsky stated that the new filter replacing communism would be terrorism and Islam.

Ross' Epistemic Merit Model

The epistemic merit model is a method for understanding propaganda conceived by Sheerly Tuttle Ross and detailed in her 2002 article for the *Journal of Aesthetic Education* entitled "Understanding Propaganda: The Epistemic Merit Model and Its Application to Art".

Ross developed the Epistemic merit model due to concern about narrow, misleading definitions of propaganda. She contrasted her model with the ideas of Pope Gregory XV, the Institute for Propaganda Analysis, Alfred Lee, F.C. Bartlett, and Hans Speier. Insisting that each of their respective discussions of propaganda are too narrow, Ross proposed her own definition.

To appropriately discuss propaganda, Ross argues that one must consider a threefold communication model: that of Sender-Message-Receiver. "That is... propaganda involve[s]... the one who is persuading (Sender) [who is] doing so intentionally, [the] target for such persuasion (Receiver) and [the] means of reaching that target (Message)." There are four conditions for a message to be considered propaganda. Propaganda involves the intention to persuade. As well, propaganda is sent on behalf of a sociopolitical institution, organization, or cause. Next, the recipient of propaganda is a socially significant group of people. Finally, propaganda is an epistemic struggle to challenge other thoughts. Ross claims that it is misleading to say that propaganda is simply false, or that it is conditional to a lie, since often the propagandist believes in what he/she is propagandizing. In other words, it is not necessarily a lie if the person who creates the propaganda is trying to persuade you of a view that they actually hold. "The aim of the propagandist is to create the semblance of credibility." This means that they appeal to an epistemology that is weak or defective.

False statements, bad arguments, immoral commands as well as inapt metaphors (and other literary tropes) are the sorts of things that are epistemically defective... Not only does epistemic defectiveness more accurately describe how propaganda endeavors to function... since many messages are in forms such as commands that do not admit to truth-values, [but it] also accounts for the role context plays in the workings of propaganda. Throughout history those who have wished to persuade have used art to get their message out. This can be accomplished by hiring artists for the express aim of propagandizing or by investing new meanings to a previously non-political work. Therefore, Ross states, it is important to consider "the conditions of its making [and] the conditions of its use."

History

Ancient Propaganda

Propaganda has been a human activity as far back as reliable recorded evidence exists. The Behistun Inscription (c.

515 BC) detailing the rise of Darius I to the Persian throne, can be seen as an early example of propaganda. The *Arthashastra* written by Chanakya (c. 350-283 BC), a professor of political science at Takshashila University and a prime minister of the Maurya Empire in ancient India, discusses propaganda in detail, such as how to spread propaganda and how to apply it in warfare.

His student Chandragupta Maurya (c. 340-293 BC), founder of the Maurya Empire, employed these methods during his rise to power. The writings of Romans such as Livy (c. 59 BC-17 AD) are considered masterpieces of pro-Roman propaganda. Another example of early propaganda would be the 12th century work *The War of the Irish with the Foreigners*, written by the Dal gCais to portray themselves as legitimate rulers of Ireland.

Propaganda During the Reformation

Propaganda during the Reformation, helped by the spread of the printing press throughout Europe, and in particular within Germany, caused new ideas, thoughts, and doctrine to be made available to the public in ways that had never been seen before the sixteenth century. The printing press was invented in approximately 1450 and quickly spread to other major cities around Europe; by the time the Reformation was underway in 1517 there were printing centers in over 200 of the major European cities. These centers became the primary producers of both Reformation works by the Protestant Reformers and anti-Reformation works put forth by the Roman Catholics.

19th and 20th Centuries

With the beginnings of the mass media in the 19th century, war rape was sometimes used as propaganda by European colonialists to justify the colonization of places they had conquered. The most notable example was perhaps during the Indian Rebellion of 1857, known as "India's First War of Independence" to the Indians and as the "Sepoy Mutiny" to the British, where Indian sepoys rebelled against the British East India Company's rule in India. While incidents of rape committed by Indian rebels against English women or girls were generally uncommon during the rebellion, this was exaggerated to great effect by the British media to justify continued British colonialism in the Indian subcontinent. At the time, British newspapers had printed various accounts about English women and girls being raped by the Indian rebels, but with little physical evidence to support these stories. It was later found that some of these accounts were false stories created to paint the native people of India as savages who need to be civilized by British colonialists, a mission sometimes known as "The White Man's Burden". One such account published by *The Times*, regarding an incident where 48 English girls as young as 10–14 were supposedly raped by the Indian rebels in Delhi, was criticized as a false propaganda story by Karl Marx, who pointed out that the story was reported by a clergyman in Bangalore, far from the events of the rebellion. Gabriel Tarde's *Laws of Imitation* (1890) and Gustave Le Bon's *The Crowd: A Study of the Popular Mind* (1897) were two of the first codifications of propaganda techniques, which influenced many writers afterward, including Sigmund Freud. Hitler's *Mein Kampf* is heavily influenced by Le Bon's theories. Journalist Walter Lippmann, in *Public Opinion* (1922) also worked on the subject, as well as the American advertising pioneer Edward Bernays, a nephew of Freud, early in the 20th century.

During World War I, Lippmann and Bernays were hired by then United States President, Woodrow Wilson, to participate in the Creel Commission, the mission of which was to sway popular opinion in favour of entering the war, on the side of the United Kingdom. The Creel Commission provided themes for speeches by "four-minute men" at public functions, and also encouraged censorship of the American press. The Commission was so unpopular that after the war, Congress closed it down without providing funding to organize and archive its papers.

The war propaganda campaign of Lippmann and Bernays produced within six months such an intense anti-German hysteria as to permanently impress American business (and Adolf Hitler, among others) with the potential of large-scale propaganda to control public opinion. Bernays coined the terms "group mind" and "engineering consent", important concepts in practical propaganda work. The file Century of the Self by Adam Curtis documents the immense influence of these ideas on public relations and politics throughout the last century.

The current public relations industry is a direct outgrowth of Lippmann's and Bernays' work and is still used extensively by the United States government. For the first half of the 20th century Bernays and Lippmann themselves ran a very successful public relations firm. World War II saw continued use of propaganda as a weapon of war, both by Hitler's propagandist Joseph Goebbels and the British Political Warfare Executive, as well as the United States Office of War Information.

In the early 2000s, the United States government developed and freely distributed a video game known as *America's Army*. The stated intention of the game is to encourage players to become interested in joining the U.S. Army.

Russian Revolution

Russian revolutionaries of the 19th and 20th centuries distinguished two different aspects covered by the English term *propaganda*. Their terminology included two terms: Russian: agitatsiya, or *agitation*, (agitprop is not, however, limited to the Soviet Union, as it was considered, before the October Revolution, to be one of the fundamental activities of any Marxist activist; this importance of agit-prop in Marxist theory may also be observed today in Trotskyist circles, who insist on the importance of leaflet distribution).

Soviet *propaganda* meant dissemination of revolutionary ideas, teachings of Marxism, and theoretical and practical knowledge of Marxist economics, while *agitation* meant forming favourable public opinion and stirring up political unrest. These activities did not carry negative connotations (as they usually do in English) and were encouraged. Expanding dimensions of state propaganda, the Bolsheviks actively used transportation such as trains, aircraft and other means.

Joseph Stalin's regime built the largest fixed-wing aircraft of the 1930s, Tupolev ANT-20, exclusively for this purpose. Named after the famous Soviet writer Maxim Gorky who had recently returned from fascist Italy, it was equipped with a powerful radio set called "Voice from the sky", printing and leaflet-dropping machinery, radio stations, photographic laboratory, film projector with sound for showing movies in flight, library, etc. The aircraft could be disassembled and transported by railroad if needed. The giant aircraft set a number of world records.

Nazi Germany

Most propaganda in Germany was produced by the Ministry of Public Enlightenment and Propaganda. Joseph Goebbels was placed in charge of this ministry shortly after Hitler took power in 1933. All journalists, writers, and artists were required to register with one of the Ministry's subordinate chambers for the press, fine arts, music, theatre, film, literature, or radio.

The Nazis believed in propaganda as a vital tool in achieving their goals. Adolf Hitler, Germany's Fuhrer, was impressed by the power of Allied propaganda during World War I and believed that it had been a primary cause of the collapse of morale and revolts in the German home front and Navy in 1918. Hitler would meet nearly every day with Goebbels to discuss the news and Goebbels would obtain Hitler's thoughts on the subject; Goebbels would then meet with senior Ministry officials and pass down the official Party line on world events. Broadcasters and journalists required prior approval before their works were disseminated. Along with posters, the Nazis produced a number of films and books to spread their beliefs.

Cold War Propaganda

Poster showing the increase of agricultural production in the German Democratic Republic from 1981 to 1983 and 1986

The United States and the Soviet Union both used propaganda extensively during the Cold War. Both sides used film, television, and radio programming to influence their own citizens, each other, and Third World nations. The United States Information Agency operated the Voice of America as an official government station. Radio Free Europe and Radio Liberty, which were, in part, supported by the Central Intelligence Agency, provided grey propaganda in news and entertainment programs to Eastern Europe and the Soviet Union respectively. The Soviet Union's official government station, Radio Moscow, broadcast white propaganda, while Radio Peace and Freedom broadcast grey propaganda. Both sides also broadcast black propaganda programs in periods of special crises.

In 1948, the United Kingdom's Foreign Office created the IRD, which took over from wartime and slightly post-war departments such as the Ministry of Information and dispensed propaganda via various media such as the BBC and publishing.

The ideological and border dispute between the Soviet Union and People's Republic of China resulted in a number of cross-border operations. One technique developed during this period was the "backwards transmission", in which the radio program was recorded and played backwards over the air. (This was done so that messages meant to be received by the other government could be heard, while the average listener could not understand the content of the program.)

When describing life in capitalist countries, in the US in particular, propaganda focused on social issues such as poverty and anti-union action by the government. Workers in capitalist countries were portrayed as "ideologically close". Propaganda claimed rich people from the US derived their income from weapons manufacturing, and claimed that there was substantial racism or neo-fascism in the US.

When describing life in Communist countries, western propaganda sought to depict an image of a citizenry held captive by governments that brainwash them. The West also created a fear of the East, by depicting an aggressive Soviet Union. In the Americas, Cuba served as a major source and a target of propaganda from both black and white stations operated by the CIA and Cuban exile groups. Radio Habana Cuba, in turn, broadcast original programming, relayed Radio Moscow, and broadcast *The Voice of Vietnam* as well as alleged confessions from the crew of the *USS Pueblo*.

George Orwell's novels *Animal Farm* and *Nineteen Eighty-Four* are virtual textbooks on the use of propaganda. Though not set in the Soviet Union, these books are about totalitarian regimes that constantly corrupt language for political purposes. These novels were, ironically, used for explicit propaganda. The CIA, for example, secretly commissioned an animated film adaptation of *Animal Farm* in the 1950s with small changes to the original story to suit its own needs.

Revolution in Central and Eastern Europe

During the democratic revolutions of 1989 in Central and Eastern Europe the propaganda poster was an important weapon in the hand of the opposition. Printed and hand-made political posters appeared on the Berlin Wall, on the statue of St. Wenceslas in Prague and around the unmarked grave of Imre Nagy in Budapest and the role of them was important for the democratic change.

Yugoslav Wars

During the Yugoslav wars propaganda was used as a military strategy by governments of Federal Republic of Yugoslavia and Croatia.

Propaganda was used to create fear and hatred and particularly incite the Serb population against the other ethnicities (Bosniaks, Croats, Albanians and other non-Serbs). Serb media made a great effort in justifying, revising or denying mass war crimes committed by Serb forces during the Yugoslav wars on Bosniaks and other non-Serbs. According to the ICTY verdicts against Serb political and military leaders, during the Bosnian war, the propaganda was a part of the Strategic Plan by Serb leadership, aimed at linking Serb-populated areas in Bosnia and Herzegovina together, gaining control over these areas and creating a separate Serb state, from which most non-Serbs would be permanently removed. The Serb leadership was aware that the Strategic Plan could only be implemented by the use of force and fear, thus by the commission of war crimes.

Croats also used propaganda against Serbs throughout and against Bosniaks during the 1992–1994 Croat-Bosniak war, which was part of the larger Bosnian War. During Lasva Valley ethnic cleansing Croat forces seized the television broadcasting stations (for example at Skradno) and created its own local radio and television to carry propaganda, seized the public institutions, raised the Croatian flag over public institution buildings, and imposed the Croatian Dinar as the unit of currency. During this time, Busovaea's Bosniaks were forced to sign an act of allegiance to the Croat authorities, fell victim to numerous attacks on shops and businesses and, gradually, left the area out of fear that they would be the victims of mass crimes. According to ICTY Trial Chambers in *Blaskic case* Croat authorities created a radio station in Kiseljak to broadcast nationalist propaganda.

A similar pattern was applied in Mostar and Gornji Vakuf (where Croats created a radio station called *Radio Uskoplje*). Local propaganda efforts in parts of Bosnia and Herzegovina controlled by the Croats, were supported by Croatian daily newspapers such as Vecernji list and Croatian Radiotelevision, especially by controversial reporters Dijana Culjak and Smiljko Sagolj who are still blamed by the families of Bosniak victims in *Vranica case* for inciting massacre of Bosnian POWs in Mostar, when broadcasting a report about alleged terrorists arrested by Croats who victimized Croat civilians. The bodies of Bosnian POWs were later found in Goranci mass grave. Croatian Radiotelevision presented Croat attack on Mostar, as a Bosnian Muslim attack on Croats in alliance with the Serbs. According to ICTY, in the early hours of May 9, 1993, the Croatian Defence Council (HVO) attacked Mostar using artillery, mortars, heavy weapons and small arms. The HVO controlled all roads leading into Mostar and international organisations were denied access. Radio Mostar announced that all Bosniaks should hang out a white flag from their windows. The HVO attack had been well prepared and planned.

During the ICTY trials against Croat war leaders, many Croatian journalists participated as the defence witnesses trying to relativise war crimes committed by Croatian troops against non-Croat civilians (Bosniaks in Bosnia and Herzegovina and Serbs in Croatia).

During the trial against general Tihomir Blaskic (later convicted of war crimes), Ivica Mlivoncie, Croatian columnist in Slobodna Dalmacija, tried to defend general Blaskic presenting number of claims in his book *Zlocin s pecatom* about alleged *genocide against Croats* (most of it unproven or false), which was considered by the Trial Chambers as irrelevant for the case. After the conviction, he continued to write in *Slobodna Dalmacija* against the ICTY presenting it *as the court against Croats*, with chauvinistic claims that the ICTY cannot be unbiased because *it is financed by Saudi Arabia (Muslims).*

Afghan War

In the 2001 invasion of Afghanistan, psychological operations tactics were employed to demoralize the Taliban and to win the sympathies of the Afghan population. At least six EC-130E Commando Solo aircraft were used to jam local radio transmissions and transmit replacement propaganda messages. Leaflets were also dropped throughout Afghanistan, offering rewards for Osama bin Laden and other individuals, portraying Americans as friends of Afghanistan and emphasizing various negative aspects of the Taliban. Another shows a picture of Mohammed Omar in a set of crosshairs with the words "We are watching." This technique has been shown to be rather ineffective in terms of long term opinions change given current political and social conditions in Afghanistan.

The US Air Force can use cluster bombs to deliver leaflets. The LBU-30 clusterbomb is designed to allow an aircraft to deliver leaflets to a target area while minimizing wind drift.

Iraq War

The United States and Iraq both contributed to the use of propaganda and like strategy during the Iraq War. With the growing discomfort in the hearts of the American and Iraqi people, there needed to be a way to gain the support of the on-going war. The United States established campaigns towards the American people on the justifications of the war while using similar tactics to bring down Saddam Hussein's regime in Iraq. By looking at the ways America and Iraq used propaganda to benefit their individual views it is clear that both sides had similar ideas on how to gain the support needed to win the war.

Iraqi Propaganda

The Iraqi insurgency had a plan, and that was to gain as much support as possible by using violence as their propaganda tool. By using the inspiration of the Vietcong, the insurgents were using rapid movement to keep the coalition off-balance. By using low-technology strategies to convey their messages, they were able to gain support. Graffiti slogans were used on walls and houses praising the virtues of many group leaders while condemning the Iraqi government. Others used flyers, leaflets, articles and self published newspapers and magazines to get the point across.

Low-tech methods were most common in Iraqi propaganda however, they were also proficient in high-tech methods. The insurgents would produce CDs and DVDs and distribute them in communities that the Iraq and the U.S. Government were trying to influence. The insurgents designed advertisements that cost a fraction of what the U.S. was spending on their ads aimed at the same people in Iraq with much more success. In addition, the Iraqis also created and established an Arabic language television station to transmit information to the people of Iraq about the rumors and lies that the Americans were spreading about the war.

American Propaganda in Iraq

For the U.S. to achieve their aim of a moderate, pro-western Iraq, the U.S. authorities have been careful to avoid conflict with Islamic culture that would produce passionate reaction from the Iraqis. As a result, differentiating between "good" and "bad" Islams has proved challenging for the U.S. The U.S. implemented something called "Black Propaganda" by creating false radio personalities that would disseminate pro-American information but supposedly run by the supporters of Saddam Hussein. One radio station used was Radio Tikrit. Another example of America's attempt with Black Propaganda is that the U.S. paid Iraqis to publish articles written by American troops in their newspapers under the idea that they are unbiased and real accounts; this was brought forth by the *New York Times* in 2005. The article stated that it was the Lincoln Group who had been hired by the U.S. government to create the propaganda, however their names were later cleared from any wrong doing.

The U.S. was more successful with the "Voice of America" campaign, which is an old Cold War tactic that exploited people's desire for information. While the information they gave out to the Iraqis was truthful, they were in a high degree of competition with the opposing forces after the censorship of the Iraqi media was lifted with the removal of Saddam from power. If the U.S. had wished to be more successful with their news media they could have followed Hussein's lead and prohibited Satellite TV and popular access to the internet directly after the Fall of Hussein.

In addition to the employment of Black Propaganda and other types of mass communication attempts in Iraq, the U.S. also used many different leaflets that were pro-western in nature. Some of which read that the no-fly zones were for the safety of Iraqis and others attempt to persuade Iraqis to become civil servants for the post-Saddam era in Iraq.

In November 2005, the *Chicago Tribune* and the *Los Angeles Times*, alleged that the United States military had manipulated news reported in Iraqi media in an effort to cast a favourable light on its actions while demoralizing the insurgency. Lt. Col. Barry Johnson, a military spokesman in Iraq, said the program is "an important part of countering misinformation in the news by insurgents", while a spokesman for former Defence Secretary Donald H. Rumsfeld said the allegations of manipulation were troubling if true. The Department of Defence has confirmed the existence of the program. *The New York Times* published an article about how the Pentagon has started to use contractors with little experience in journalism or public relations to plant articles in the Iraqi press.

These articles are usually written by US soldiers without attribution or are attributed to a non-existent organization called the "International Information Center." Planting propaganda stories in newspapers was done by both the Allies and Central Powers in the First World War and the Axis and Allies in the Second; this is the latest version of this technique.

Propaganda Aimed at Americans

Media such as daily news coverage, advertisements, videos, pictures, polls, and various others are indirectly controlled by the news media. The country has strayed from its popular form of mass advertising media and focused more on its biased coverage found in the news. This is seen as a credible source, allowing information on the current situation to be known to the general public. As noted in the book *Selling Intervention & War* by Jon Western, the president is "selling the war" to the public.

People had their initial reactions to the War on Terror, but with more biased and persuading information, Iraq as a whole has been negatively targeted.. America's goal was to remove Saddam Hussein's power in Iraq with allegations of possible weapons of mass destruction related to Osama Bin Laden. Video and picture coverage in the news has shown shocking and disturbing images of torture and other evils being done under the Iraqi Government.

This is one way United States media is fabricating the enemy. By providing purely negative and exaggerated alleged evidence on the situation, Americans are provided with the generally accepted opinion of hatred towards the evil in Iraq. While torture and mass murder of the civilian population was common in Iraq, there were positive positions. The Iraqi government's strong military position was able to keep terrorists under control, a position that changed quickly after that fall of the regime.

North Korea

Every year, a state-owned publishing house releases several cartoons (called geurim-chaek in North Korea), many of which are smuggled across the Chinese border and, sometimes, end up in university libraries in the United States. The books are designed to instill the Juche philosophy of Kim Il-sung (the 'father' of North Korea)—radical self-reliance of the state. The plots mostly feature scheming capitalists from the United States and Japan who create dilemmas for naive North Korean characters.

War in Somalia

Of all the potential targets for propaganda, children are the most vulnerable because they are the most unprepared for the critical reasoning and contextual comprehension required to determine whether a message is propaganda or not. Children's vulnerability to propaganda is rooted in developmental psychology. The attention children give their environment during development, due to the process of developing their understanding of the world, will cause them to absorb propaganda indiscriminately. Also, children are highly imitative: studies by Albert Bandura, Dorothea Ross and Sheila A. Ross in the 1960s indicated that children are susceptible to filmed representations of behaviour. Therefore television is of particular interest in regard to children's vulnerability to propaganda.

Another vulnerability of children is the theoretical influence that their peers have over their behaviour. According to Judith Rich Harris's group-socialization theory, children learn the majority of what they do not receive paternally, through genes, from their peer groups. The implication then is that if peer-groups can be indoctrinated through propaganda at a young age to hold certain beliefs, the group will self-regulate the indoctrination, since new members to the group will adapt their beliefs to fit the group's.

To a degree, socialization, formal education, and standardized television programming can be seen as using propaganda for the purpose of indoctrination. The use of propaganda in schools was highly prevalent during the 1930s and 1940s in Germany, as well as in Stalinist Russia.

Anti-Semitic Propaganda for Children

In Nazi Germany, the education system was thoroughly co-opted to indoctrinate the German youth with anti-Semitic ideology. This was accomplished through the National Socialist Teachers League, of which 97% of all German teachers were members in 1937. It encouraged the teaching of "racial theory." Picture books for children such as *Don't Trust A Fox in A Green Meadow Or the Word of A Jew*, The *Poisonous Mushroom*, and *The Poodle-Pug-Dachshund-Pincher* were widely circulated (over 100,000 copies of *Don't Trust A Fox* were circulated during the late 1930s) and contained depictions of Jews as devils, child molesters, and other morally charged figures. Slogans such as "Judas the Jew betrayed Jesus the German to the Jews" were recited in class. The following is an example of a propagandistic math problem recommended by the National Socialist Essence of Education:

The Jews are aliens in Germany—in 1933 there were 66,606,000 inhabitants in the German Reich, of whom 499,682 (.75%) were Jews.

Tomorrow's Pioneers is a children's program, broadcast since April 13, 2007 on the official Palestinian Hamas television station, Al-Aqsa TV. The program deals with many life aspects Palestinan children face. Assoud, a Bugs Bunny-like rabbit character whose hiname means lion was introduced after his brother, the previous co-host, Nahoul died of illness.

In explaining why he is called Assoud (lion), when Arnoub (rabbit) would be more appropriate, Assoud explains that "A rabbit is a term for a bad person and coward. And I, Assoud, will finish off the Jews and eat them." Before Nahoul's death, Assoud lived in Lebanon; he returned "in order to return to the homeland and liberate it." Assoud has hinted in episode 113 that he will be replaced by a tiger when he is martyred.

6

Personnel Administration

Personnel administration is more commonly called human resources (HR) management. People are considered the most important resource a business has. HR or personnel administration refers to the areas of recruiting, selecting, assessing, developing and retaining employees. Organization is a large part of personnel administration.

Employees must be organized in a way that gets the work done. As long as employees are striving to be efficient in completing their employment responsibilities, companies usually work at retaining them. Keeping good employees saves the time and expense of replacing them. Laws pertaining to wrongful dismissal of employees must also be adhered to or a business could find itself in a lawsuit. The human resources department of a company instructs managers on proper conduct toward employees. Recruiting and selecting successful employees at the start is a main objective of personnel administration.

In many companies today, HR staff will conduct initial telephone interviews for advertised jobs to try to weed out unsuitable job applicants. A manager then has a lower number of higher qualified applicants to interview for the advertised position. Once employees are hired, they may take part in training programs that have been developed or approved by HR personnel. During their employment, employees may be evaluated by managers who use assessment forms created by the company's personnel administration. Most companies use assessment forms during employees' performance reviews. A performance review allows a manager to evaluate an employee's overall job performance and suggest any improvements. Performance reviews are often conducted before a raise in pay is considered.

Personnel administration handles issues in the workplace such as violence, discrimination or sexual harassment complaints. The personnel department must work within the law — therefore an understanding of laws pertaining to conduct in the workplace is important. Correct procedures and actions must be followed by the company or it could face legal consequences if employees take the matter to court. Following laws that apply to safe working conditions, minimum wage and overtime work is also crucial for personnel administration to focus on. The personnel department must always keep thorough records of all employees.

The scope of personnel administration is quite wide. It includes all activities which help the management in getting the work done by the labour force in the best manner possible to accomplish the organizational objectives. The main objective in any organization is the optimum utilization of available resources. Personnel administration is primarily concerned with the organization of men; therefore, the main objective may be summarized as to utilize the available human resources in a way so as to get the work done effectively to the maximum satisfaction of the individual worker to seek their cooperation in accomplishing the general goals of the organization.

The objectives of personnel administration can be classified into General objectives and specific objectives.

General Objectives

Maximum individual development – the employer should always be careful in developing the personality of each individual. If an act of the employer can adversely affect the personality of the individual, he should avoid it. Employer should establish and support such human values that may have social recognition and importance. They should always be regarded as partners and given due importance. The objective of Personnel administration as a bridge between the management and the employees is to keep the management apprised of positive accomplishments and warning signals in the personnel practices. If the human assets of an organization are being misused in the process of profit maximization, it is definitely a short term achievement, because in the long run, the adverse effects felt by the work force will translate into lesser profits for the organization.

Desirable working relationship between employer and employee – it is the major objective of personnel administration to achieve a desirable working relationship between the employer and the employees so that they may cooperate with the management. Both of them must rely on each other. The personnel administrator should get it realized to the top management that personnel should be given fair and equitable treatment and on the other hand, convey to the workers that they should cooperate in achieving the goals of the management. The basic responsibility for the personnel lies with the supervisors although the administrator supplies tools such as policy, record keeping, control and advice. His objective is therefore to ensure that the line supervisor is aware of his personnel responsibilities and carries them out responsibly. Simultaneously he should also ensure ethical conduct amongst all personnel and on the part of each supervisor towards each employee for whom he is responsible.

Specialized services – The administrator provides the tools such as record keeping, policy making, controlling and advising. Although not directly responsible for the personnel, who lie with the line supervisor, he may examine causes for non-efficiency or non-effectiveness, suggest remedial measure, perform research into proposed personnel procedures, handle negotiations with a government agency, etc. The basic objective here is to provide assistance to the line supervisor whilst simultaneously ensuring that the line supervisor meets his responsibilities to the personnel.

Molding of human resources – Human beings is the most important resource and the only active factor which engages all other factors of production. Therefore, the administrator should emphasize the effective utilization of human resources as compared to physical resources so that production and productivity is optimized. Other factors of production will be ineffective without effective molding of human resources.

Specific Objectives

1. Selection of the right type and number of persons
2. Proper orientation and introduction of new employees to their jobs
3. Organisation of suitable training facilities
4. Provision of better working conditions and facilities.
5. Provision of sound, fair and effective wage and salary administration and incentives.
6. Good industrial relations with representative trade unions
7. Personnel research

Duties of Personnel Staff

In a dynamic working environment, the boundaries of any role cannot be clearly defined. However, the duties of Personnel staff may be described as under:-

1. As a Service Provider – providing information on market statistics of personnel availability, pay rates, etc. Interpret the complex laws and legislations. Employment and placement programs, employee compensation programs, training and development programs, labour relations could be stated to be the duty as a service provider. It must be noted that there will often be an overlap between the different roles that a Personnel staff may assume
2. As a facilitator – advises the supervisors on employee problems, facilitates training and development, and when performance appraisals are done. One of the responsibilities of Personnel staff is also to ensure that other managers who undertake such activities are well equipped to do so.

3. as a consultant – to help the supervisors resolve problems due to lack of motivation, lack of training, grievances, etc.
4. As an auditor – to ensure that all members of the management perform their respective roles, to determine whether personnel policies and procedures are being administered uniformly by supervisors.

Bureaucracy and Administration

Bureaucracy is the combined organizational structure, procedures, protocols, and set of regulations in place to manage activity, usually in large organizations. As opposed to adhocracy, it is often represented by standardized procedure (rule-following) that guides the execution of most or all processes within the body; formal division of powers; hierarchy; and relationships, intended to anticipate needs and improve efficiency. A bureaucracy traditionally does not create policy but, rather, enacts it. Law, policy, and regulation normally originates from a leadership, which creates the bureaucracy to implement them. In practice, the interpretation and execution of policy, etc. can lead to informal influence-but not necessarily. A bureaucracy is directly responsible to the leadership that creates it, such as a government executive or board of directors. Conversely, the leadership is usually responsible to an electorate, shareholders, membership or whoever is intended to benefit. As a matter of practicality, the bureaucracy is where the individual will interface with an organization such as a government etc., rather than directly with its leadership. Generally, larger organizations result in a greater distancing of the individual from the leadership, which can be consequential or intentional by design.

Definition

Bureaucracy is a concept in sociology and political science referring to the way that the administrative execution and enforcement of legal rules are socially organized. Four structural concepts are central to any definition of bureaucracy:

1. a well-defined division of administrative labour among persons and offices,

2. a personnel system with consistent patterns of recruitment and stable linear careers,
3. a hierarchy among offices, such that the authority and status are differentially distributed among actors, and
4. formal and informal networks that connect organizational actors to one another through flows of information and patterns of cooperation.

Examples of everyday bureaucracies include governments, armed forces, corporations, non-governmental organizations (NGOs), intergovernmental organizations (IGOs), hospitals, courts, ministries, social clubs, sports leagues, professional associations and academic institutions.

Origins

While the concept as such existed at least from the early forms of nationhood in ancient times, the word "bureaucracy" itself stems from the word "bureau", used from the early 18th century in Western Europe not just to refer to a writing desk, but to an office, i.e., a workplace, where officials worked. The original French meaning of the word *bureau* was the baize used to cover desks. The term bureaucracy came into use shortly before the French Revolution of 1789, and from there rapidly spread to other countries. The Greek suffix-*kratia* or *kratos*- means "power" or "rule".

Development

Perhaps the early example of a bureaucrat is the scribe, who first arose as a professional on the early cities of Sumer. The Sumerian script was so complicated that it required specialists who had trained for their entire lives in the discipline of writing to manipulate it. These scribes could wield significant power, as they had a total monopoly on the keeping of records and creation of inscriptions on monuments to kings.

In later, larger empires like Achaemenid Persia, bureaucracies quickly expanded as government expanded and increased its functions. In the Persian Empire, the central government was divided into administrative provinces led by satraps. The satraps were appointed by the Shah to control the provinces. In addition, a general and a royal secretary were stationed in each province to supervise troop recruitment and keep records, respectively. The Achaemenid Great Kings also sent royal inspectors to tour the empire and report on local conditions.

The most modernesque of all ancient bureaucracies, however, was the Chinese bureaucracy. During the chaos of the Spring and Autumn Period and the Warring States Period, Confucius recognized the need for a stable system of administrators to lend good governance even when the leaders were inept. Chinese bureaucracy, first implemented during the Qin dynasty but under more Confucian lines under the Han, calls for the appointment of bureaucratic positions based on merit via a system of examinations. Although the power of the Chinese bureaucrats waxed and waned throughout China's long history, the imperial examination system lasted as late as 1905, and modern China still employs a formidable bureaucracy in its daily workings.

Modern bureaucracies arose as the government of states grew larger during the modern period, and especially following the Industrial Revolution. As the authors David Osborne and Ted Gaebler point out

"It is hard to imagine today, but a hundred years ago bureaucracy meant something positive. It connoted a rational, efficient method of organization – something to take the place of the arbitrary exercise of power by authoritarian regimes. Bureaucracy brought the same logic to government work that the assembly line brought to the factory. With the hierarchical authority and functional a specialization, they made possible the efficient undertaking of large complex tasks."

Tax collectors, perhaps the most disliked of all bureaucrats, became increasingly necessary as states began to take in more and more revenue, while the role of administrators increased as the functions of government multiplied. Along with this expansion, though, came the recognition of the corruption and nepotism often inherent within the managerial system, leading to civil service reform on a large scale in many countries towards the end of the 19th century.

Types of Bureaucratic Agencies

Examining different agencies from a management point of view, they differ in two main ways: whether or not the activities of the operators can be observed, and whether the results of those activities can be observed. The first factor deals with outputs, or what the agency does on a day to day basis. The second factor deals with outcomes, or the overall results of agency work. The extreme cases where outputs and outcomes are either simple or difficult to observe yields four different kinds of agencies: production, procedural, craft, and coping.

- Production organizations are those in which both outputs and outcomes are observable. Examples include the Social Security Administration, United States Postal Service, and IRS. In production organizations, managers can observe the outputs of officials, and can (for example in the IRS) measure the amount of money collected in taxes, and estimate with accuracy how much more tax money will be produced by increasing the level of auditing activity.
- Procedural organizations are those where outputs can be observed, but outcomes are unclear or not observable. Examples include the Occupational Safety and Health Administration, and the United States armed forces during peace time. OSHA may observe the actions of health inspectors, but may not be able to measure how these individual actions add up to improved safety and health in the workplace. In the armed forces during peacetime, all aspects of training and deployment can be observed, but it cannot be measured how these activities deter aggression, or prepare for a future (unknown) conflict.
- Craft organizations are those where outputs are hard to observe, but outcomes are fairly easy to evaluate. Examples include the armed services at war, who may operate under a fog of war, but whose battle outcomes can be easily measured. Another example is the United States Department of Labour and their "Wage and Hour Division". While the outputs of individual

inspectors in the field are difficult to measure, overall outcomes of negotiated compliance agreements and referrals to federal attorneys for legal action are easily measurable.

- Coping organizations are those where neither outputs nor outcomes are observable. Typical examples include Police Departments, and the United States Department of State. Some of the activities of diplomats and policeman cannot be observed or measured (e.g. sensitive conversations with foreign leaders, and interactions with citizens on the street), and the outcomes are also difficult to judge (e.g. changes in foreign perceptions of US interests, and the level of order on a policeman's beat).

An agency's type substantially impacts its approach to its mission, (i.e. the degree to which its members are devoted to accomplishing the agency's stated mission) and to compliance with the law and existing policy.

Views on the Concept

In a letter of July 1, 1790, the German Baron von Grimm declared: "We are obsessed by the idea of regulation, and our Masters of Requests refuse to understand that there is an infinity of things in a great state with which a government should not concern itself." Jean Claude Marie Vincent de Gournay sometimes used to say, "We have an illness in France which bids fair to play havoc with us; this illness is called *bureaumania*." Sometimes he used to refer to a fourth or fifth form of government under the heading of "bureaucracy".

In another letter of July 15, 1765 Baron Grimm wrote also, "The real spirit of the laws in France is that bureaucracy of which the late Monsieur de Gournay used to complain so greatly; here the offices, clerks, secretaries, inspectors and *intendants* are not appointed to benefit the public interest, indeed the public interest appears to have been established so that offices might exist."

This quote refers to a traditional controversy about bureaucracy, namely the perversion of means and ends so that means become ends in themselves, and the greater good is lost sight of; as a corollary, the substitution of *sectional* interests for the *general* interest. The suggestion here is that, left uncontrolled, the bureaucracy will become increasingly self-serving and corrupt, rather than serving society.

Indeed, the cynical Parkinson's Law suggests that bureaucracies grow independent of their function.

Karl Marx

In Karl Marx's and Friedrich Engels's theory of historical materialism, the historical origin of bureaucracy is to be found in *four* sources: religion, the formation of the state, commerce, and technology.

Thus, the earliest bureaucracies consisted of castes of *religious* clergy, officials and scribes operating various rituals, and armed functionaries specifically delegated to keep order. In the historical transition from primitive egalitarian communities to a civil society divided into social classes and estates, beginning from about 10,000 years ago, authority is increasingly centralized in, and enforced by a state apparatus existing separately from society. This state formulates, imposes and enforces laws, and levies taxes, giving rise to an officialdom enacting these functions. Thus, the state mediates in conflicts among the people and keeps those conflicts within acceptable bounds; it also organizes the defence of territory. Most importantly, the right of ordinary people to carry and use weapons of force becomes increasingly restricted; in civil society, forcing other people to do things becomes increasingly the legal right of the state authorities only.

But the growth of trade and commerce adds a new, distinctive dimension to bureaucracy, insofar as it requires the keeping of accounts and the processing/recording of transactions, as well as the enforcement of legal rules governing trade. If resources are increasingly distributed by prices in markets, this requires extensive and complex systems of record-keeping, management and calculation, conforming to legal standards. Eventually, this means that the total amount of work involved in commercial administration outgrows the total amount of work involved in government administration. In modern capitalist society, private sector bureaucracy is *larger* than government bureaucracy, if measured by the number of administrative workers in the division of labour as a whole. Some corporations nowadays have a turnover larger than the national income of whole countries, with large administrations supervising operations.

A fourth source of bureaucracy Marxists have commented on inheres in the technologies of mass production, which require many standardized routines and procedures to be performed. Even if mechanization replaces people with machinery, people are still necessary to design, control, supervise and operate the machinery. The technologies chosen may not be the ones that are best for everybody, but which create *incomes* for a particular class of people or maintain their power. This type of bureaucracy is nowadays often called a technocracy, which owes its power to control over specialized technical knowledge or control over critical information.

In Marx's theory, bureaucracy rarely creates new wealth by itself, but rather controls, co-ordinates and governs the production, distribution and consumption of wealth. The bureaucracy as a social stratum derives its income from the appropriation of part of the social surplus product of human labour. Wealth is appropriated by the bureaucracy by law through fees, taxes, levies, tributes, licensing etc.

Bureaucracy is therefore always a *cost* to society, but this cost may be accepted insofar as it makes social order possible, and maintains it by enforcing the rule of law. Nevertheless there are constant conflicts about this cost, because it has the big effect on the distribution of incomes; all producers will try to get the maximum return from what they produce, and minimize administrative costs. Typically, in epochs of strong economic growth, bureaucracies proliferate; when economic growth declines, a fight breaks out to cut back bureaucratic costs.

Whether or not a bureaucracy as a social stratum can become a genuine ruling class depends greatly on the prevailing property relations and the mode of production of wealth. In capitalist society, the state typically lacks an independent economic base, finances many activities on credit, and is heavily dependent on levying taxes as a source of income. Therefore, its power is limited by the costs which private owners of the productive assets will tolerate. If, however, the state owns the means of production itself, defended by military power, the state bureaucracy can become much more powerful, and act as a ruling class or power elite. Because in that case, it directly controls the sources of new wealth, and manages or distributes the social product. This is the subject of Marxist theories of bureaucratic collectivism.

Marx himself however never theorized this possibility in detail, and it has been the subject of much controversy among Marxists. The core organizational issue in these disputes concerns the degree to which the *administrative* allocation of resources by government authorities and the *market* allocation of resources can achieve the social goal of creating a more free, just and prosperous society. Which decisions should be made by whom, at what level, so that an optimal allocation of resources results? This is just as much a moral-political issue as an economic issue. Central to the Marxian concept of socialism is the idea of workers' self-management, which assumes the internalization of a morality and self-discipline among people that would make bureaucratic supervision and control redundant, together with a drastic reorganization of the division of labour in society.

Bureaucracies emerge to mediate conflicts of interest on the basis of laws, but if those conflicts of interest disappear (because resources are allocated directly in a fair way), bureaucracies would also be redundant.

Marx's critics are however skeptical of the feasibility of this kind of socialism, given the continuing need for administration and the rule of law, as well as the propensity of people to put their own self-interest before the communal interest. That is, the argument is that self-interest and the communal interest might *never* coincide, or, at any rate, can always diverge significantly.

Max Weber

Max Weber has probably been one of the most influentia users of the word in its social science sense. He is well-knowr for his study of bureaucratization of society; many aspects o modern public administration go back to him; a classic hierarchically organized civil service of the continental type is— if perhaps mistakenly — called *Weberian civil service* several different years between 1818 and 1860, prior to Weber's birth in 1864. Weber described the ideal type bureaucracy in positive terms, considering it to be a more rational and efficient form of organization than the alternatives that preceded it, which he characterized as *charismatic domination* and *traditional domination*. According to his terminology, bureaucracy is part of legal domination. However, he also emphasized that bureaucracy becomes inefficient when a decision must be adopted to an individual case.

According to Weber, the attributes of modern bureaucracy include its impersonality, concentration of the means of administration, a levelling effect on social and economic differences and implementation of a system of authority that is practically indestructible.

Weber's analysis of bureaucracy concerns:

- the historical and administrative reasons for the process of bureaucratization (especially in the Western civilisation)
- the impact of the rule of law upon the functioning of bureaucratic organisations
- the typical personal orientation and occupational position of a bureaucratic officials as a status group
- the most important attributes and consequences of bureaucracy in the modern world.

A bureaucratic organization is governed by the following seven principles:

1. official business is conducted on a continuous basis
2. official business is conducted with strict accordance to the following rules:

- the duty of each official to do certain types of work is delimited in terms of impersonal criteria
- the official is given the authority necessary to carry out his assigned functions
- the means of coercion at his disposal are strictly limited and conditions of their use strictly defined

3. every official's responsibilities and authority are part of a vertical hierarchy of authority, with respective rights of supervision and appeal
4. officials do not own the resources necessary for the performance of their assigned functions but are accountable for their use of these resources
5. official and private business and income are strictly separated
6. offices cannot be appropriated by their incumbents (inherited, sold, etc.)
7. official business is conducted on the basis of written documents.

A bureaucratic official:

- is personally free and appointed to his position on the basis of conduct
- exercises the authority delegated to him in accordance with impersonal rules, and his or her loyalty is enlisted on behalf of the faithful execution of his official duties
- appointment and job placement are dependent upon his or her technical qualifications
- administrative work is a full-time occupation
- work is rewarded by a regular salary and prospects of advancement in a lifetime career.

An official must exercise his or her judgment and his or her skills, but his or her duty is to place these at the service of a higher authority; ultimately he/she is responsible only for the impartial execution of assigned tasks and must sacrifice his or her personal judgment if it runs counter to his or her official duties. Weber's work has been continued by many, like Robert Michels with his Iron Law of Oligarchy.

Criticism

As Max Weber himself noted, real bureaucracy will be less optimal and effective than his ideal type model. Each of Weber's seven principles can degenerate:

- Competences can be unclear and used contrary to the spirit of the law; sometimes a decision itself may be considered more important than its effect;
- Nepotism, corruption, political infighting and other degenerations can counter the rule of impersonality and can create a recruitment and promotion system not based on meritocracy but rather on oligarchy;

Even a non-degenerated bureaucracy can be affected by common problems:

- Overspecialization, making individual officials not aware of larger consequences of their actions
- Rigidity and inertia of procedures, making decision-making slow or even impossible when facing some unusual case, and similarly delaying change, evolution and adaptation of old procedures to new circumstances;
- A phenomenon of *group thinking*-zealotry, loyalty and lack of critical thinking regarding the organisation which is *perfect* and *always correct* by definition, making the organisation unable to change and realise its own mistakes and limitations;
- Disregard for dissenting opinions, even when such views suit the available data better than the opinion of the majority;
- A phenomenon of *Catch-22* (named after a famous book by Joseph Heller)-as bureaucracy creates more and more rules and procedures, their complexity rises and coordination diminishes, facilitating creation of contradictory and recursive rules, as described by the saying "the bureaucracy is expanding to meet the needs of the expanding bureaucracy".
- Not allowing people to use common sense, as everything must be as is written by the law.

In the most common examples bureaucracy can lead to the treatment of individual human beings as impersonal objects. This process has been criticised by many philosophers and writers (Aldous Huxley, George Orwell, Hannah Arendt) and satirized in the comic strip *Dilbert, TV* show *The Office*, Franz Kafka's novels *The Trial* and *The Castle*, Douglas Adams' story *The Hitchhiker's Guide to the Galaxy*, and the films *Brazil* and *Office Space.*

Michel Crozier

Michel Crozier wrote The Bureaucratic Phenomenon (1964) as a re-examination of Weber's (1922) concept of the efficient ideal bureaucracy in the light of the way that bureaucratic organizations had actually developed. Whereas for Weber, bureaucracy was the ultimate expression of a trend toward the efficient, rational organization, Crozier examined bureaucracy as a form of organization that evokes:

> *"... the slowness, the ponderousness, the routine, the complication of procedures and the maladapted responses of the bureaucratic organization to the needs which they should satisfy" (Crozier, 1964, p 3)*

He examined a number of culturally specific examples of bureaucratic organizations in an attempt to understand why bureaucracies so often became dysfunctional.

After reviewing the different ways in which the term is used, Crozier describes the sense in which he uses the term bureaucracy thus:

> *"A bureaucratic organization is an organization that can not correct its behaviour by learning from its errors" (Crozier, 1964)*

Adding: "... not only a system that does not correct its behaviour in view of its errors; it is also too rigid to adjust, without crises, to the transformations that the accelerated evolution of the industrial society makes more and more imperative" (Crozier, 1964)

In essence, Crozier presents an argument against the Tayloristic notion of 'the one best way' to organize an activity and Weber's view of bureaucracy as the ultimate expression rationality and efficiency. He notes that in 1964 'advanced organizations' had already:

> *"... been obliged to discard completely the notion of the one best way [and] are beginning to understand that the illusion of perfect rationality has to long persisted, weakening the possibilities of action by insisting on rigorous logic and immediate coherence" (Crozier, 1964)*

From his analysis of his case studies, he develops a theory of bureaucratic dysfunction based on his observations. Although he later extends his ideas to cover other settings, the two main cases on which he bases his theory are both located in France. "The Clerical Agency" and "The Industrial Monopoly". Crozier chose these examples not only because he was French, but also because he claims that socially and culturally France has developed in such a way that it created organizations that closely resembled the Weberian notion of an ideal bureaucracy.

His theory is based on the observation that in situations where almost every outcome has been decided in advance according to a set of impersonal and predefined rules and regulations, the only way in which people are able to gain some control over their lives is to exploit 'zones of uncertainty' where the outcomes are not already known.

> *"[an] unintended consequence of rationalisation [is] the predictability of ones behaviour is the sure test of ones own inferiority" (Crozier, 1964)*

For Crozier, organizations are not autonomous entities but social constructs that are:

> *"... man made and socially created [and] the indirect result of the power struggles within the organization" (Crozier, 1964)*

Attacking both the rationalists and the human relations school for ignoring the role that such power struggles play in the shaping of an organization he argues that organizational relations are in fact a series of strategic games where the protagonists attempt either to exploit any areas of discretion for their own ends, or to prevent others from gaining an advantage:

> *"Each group fights to preserve and enlarge the area upon which it has some discretion, attempts to limit its dependence upon other groups and accept such dependence only insofar as it is a safeguard... [preferring] retreatisim if there is no other choice but submission" (Crozier, 1964)*

The result of this is that goals are subverted and the organization becomes locked into a series of inward looking power struggles. Thus, paradoxically, the result of attempting to design an efficient organization that runs on rational and impersonal lines is to create a situation where the opposite to is true.

Theory of Bureaucratic Dysfunction

Crozier argues that:

> *"... the bureaucratic system of organization is primarily characterized by the existence of a series of relatively stable vicious circles that stem from centralisation and impersonality" (Crozier, 1964)*

He outlines four such 'vicious circles' that he observed in the organizations he studied.

The development of impersonal rules: In an attempt to be rational and egalitarian, bureaucracies attempt to come up with a set of abstract impersonal rules to cover all possible events. Crozier gives the example of the concours (competitive examinations) which mean that, one the exams are passed, promotion become simply a matter of seniority and avoiding damaging conflicts. The result, he argues, is that hierarchical relationships decline in importance or disappear completely which means that higher level in the bureaucracy have effectively lost the power to govern the lower levels.

The centralization of decisions: If one wishes to maintain the impersonal nature of decision making, it is necessary to ensure that decision are made at a level where those who make them are protected from the influence of those who are affected by them. The effect of this is that problems are resolved by people who have no direct knowledge of the problems they are called upon to solve, and so, priority is given to the resolution of internal political problems instead. In this case, the power to influence events over which one has direct experience is lost and it is passed to some impartial central body.

The isolation of strata and group pressure within strata: The suppression of the possibility of exercising discretion among superiors and the removal of opportunities for bargaining from subordinates results in an organization that consists of a series of isolated strata. The notional equality within the strata becomes the only defence for the individual against demands form other parts of the organization and allows groups some degree of control over their own domain. The result is very strong per group pressure to conform to the norms of the strata regardless of individual beliefs or the wider goals of the organization.

The development of parallel power relationships: It is impossible to account for every eventuality, even by the constant addition of impersonal rules and the progressive centralisation of decision making; consequently, individuals or groups that control the remaining zones of uncertainty, wield a considerable amount of power. This can lead to the creation of parallel power structures that give certain groups or individuals in certain situations, disproportionate power in an otherwise regulated and egalitarian organization. Once again, this can lead to decisions being made based on factors separate from the overall goals of the organization.

American Usage

Administration in the United States must be at all points sensitive to public opinion. A body of thoroughly trained officials serving during good behaviour we must have in any case: that is a plain business necessity. But the apprehension that such a body will be anything un-American clears away the moment it is asked. What is to constitute good behaviour? For that question obviously carries its own answer on its head. Steady, hearty allegiance to the policy of the government they serve will constitute good behaviour. That policy will have no taint of officialism about it. It will not be the creation of permanent officials, but of statesmen whose responsibility to public opinion will be direct and inevitable. Bureaucracy can exist only where the whole service of the state is removed from the common political life of the people, its chiefs as well as its rank and file. Its motives, its objects, its policy, its standards, must be bureaucratic. Popular dictionary definitions reflect a popular dislike for bureaucracy. *The American Heritage Dictionary'*, after two traditional definitions of the word, the third and last definition of bureaucracy reads in part: "numerous offices and adherence to inflexible rules of operation;... any unwieldy administration." According to *Webster's New world Dictionary of the American Language*, one of the definitions reads in part "bureaucracy is governmental officialism or inflexible routine." *Roget's Thesaurus* gives among the synonyms for *bureaucracy*: "officialism", "officiousness", and "red tape".

American science fiction writer Jerry Pournelle has proposed a theory he refers to as "Pournelle's Iron Law of Bureaucracy", which states: "In any bureaucracy, the people devoted to the benefit of the bureaucracy itself always get in control and those dedicated to the goals the bureaucracy is supposed to accomplish have less and less influence, and sometimes are eliminated entirely."

This robust tendency is purported to operate to the effect that: "...in any bureaucratic organization there will be two kinds of people: those who work to further the actual goals of the organization, and those who work for the organization itself. Examples in education would be teachers who work and sacrifice to teach children, vs. union representative who work to protect any teacher including the most incompetent. The Iron Law states that in all cases, the second type of person will always gain control of the organization, and will always write the rules under which the organization functions."

Austrian School Analysis

The analysis of bureaucracy by the Austrian school reflects its characteristic focus on economics, and emphasizes the distinction between bureaucratic management and profit management.

Current Academic Debates

Modern academic research has debated the extent to which elected officials can control their bureaucratic agents. Because bureaucrats have more information than elected officials about what they are doing and what they should be doing, bureaucrats might have the ability to implement policies or regulations that go against the public interest. In the American context, these concerns led to the "Congressional abdication" hypotheses—the claim that Congress had abdicated its authority over public policy to appointed bureaucrats.

Theodore Lowi initiated this debate by concluding in a 1979 book that the U.S. Congress does not exercise effective oversight of bureaucratic agencies. Instead, policies are made by "iron triangles", consisting of interest groups, appointed bureaucrats, and Congressional subcommittees (who, according to Lowi, were likely to have more extreme views than the Congress as a whole).

It is thought that since 1979 interest groups have taken a large role and now do not only effect bureaucracy, but also the money in congress. The idea of "iron triangles" has since evolved to "iron hexagons" and then to a "hollow sphere."

The relationships between the Legislatures, the Interest Groups, Bureaucrats, and the general public all have an effect on each other. Without one of these pieces the entire structure would completely change. This relationship is considered "mu", or such that not one single piece can describe or control the entire process. The public votes in the legislatures and the interest groups provide information, but the legislature and bureaucrats also have an effect on the interest groups and the public. The entire system is codependent on each other.

William Niskanen's earlier (1971) 'budget-maximizing' model complemented Lowi's claims; where Lowi claimed that Congress (and legislatures more generally) failed to exercise oversight, Niskanen argued that rational bureaucrats will always and everywhere seek to increase their budgets, thereby contributing strongly to state growth. Niskanen went on to serve on the U.S. Council of Economic Advisors under President Reagan, and his model provided a strong underpinning for the worldwide move towards cutbacks of public spending and the introduction of privatization in the 1980s and '90s.

Two branches of theorizing have arisen in response to these claims. The first focuses on bureaucratic motivations; Niskanen's universalist approach was critiqued by a range of pluralist authors who argued that officials' motivations are more public interest-orientated than Niskanen allowed. The bureau-shaping model (put forward by Patrick Dunleavy) also argues against Niskanen that rational bureaucrats should only maximize the part of their budget that they spend on their own agency's operations or give to contractors or powerful interest groups (that are able to organize a flowback of benefits to senior officials). For instance, rational officials will get no benefit from paying out larger welfare checks to millions of poor people, since the bureaucrats' own utilities are not improved. Consequently we should expect bureaucracies to significantly maximize budgets in areas like police forces and defence, but not in areas like welfare state spending.

A second branch of responses has focused more on Lowi's claims, asking whether legislatures (and usually the American Congress in particular) can control bureaucrats. This empirical research is motivated by a normative concern: If we wish to believe that we live in a democracy, then it must be true that appointed bureaucrats cannot act contrary to elected officials' interests. (This claim is itself debatable; if we fully trusted elected officials, we would not spend so much time implementing constitutional checks and balances.)

Within this second branch, scholars have published numerous studies debating the circumstances under which elected officials can control bureaucratic outputs. Most of these studies examine the American case, though their findings have been generalized elsewhere as well. These studies argue that legislatures have a variety of oversight means at their disposal, and they use many of them regularly. These oversight mechanisms have been classified into two types: "Police patrols" (actively auditing agencies and looking for misbehaviour) and "fire alarms" (imposing open administrative procedures on bureaucrats to make it easier for adversely affected groups to detect bureaucratic malfeasance and bring it to the legislature's attention).

A third concept of self-interested bureaucracy and its effect on the production of public goods has been forwarded by Faizul Latif Chowdhury. In contrast to Niskanen and Dunleavy, who primarily focused on the self-interested behaviour of only the top-level bureaucrats involved in policy making, Chowdhury in his thesis submitted to the London School of Economics in 1997 drew attention to the impact of the low level civil servants whose rent-seeking behaviour pushes up the cost of production of public goods. Particularly, it was shown with reference to the tax officials how rent-seeking by them causes loss in government revenue. Chowdhury's model of rent-seeking bureaucracy captures the case of administrative corruption whereby public money is directly expropriated by public servants in general.

One of the principal objects of administrative law is to ensure efficient, economical, and just administration. A system of administrative law that impedes or frustrates administration would clearly be bad, and so, too, would be a system that results in injustice to the individual. But to judge whether administrative law helps or hinders effective administration or works in such a way as to deny justice to the individual involves an examination of the ends that public administration is supposed to serve, as well as the means that it employs.

In this connection only the broadest generalities can be attempted. It can be asserted that all states, irrespective of their economic and political system or of their stage of development, are seeking to achieve a high rate of economic growth and a higher average income per person. They are all pursuing the goals of modernization, urbanization, and industrialization. They are all trying to provide the major social services, especially education and public health, at as high a standard as possible. The level of popular expectation is much higher than in former ages. The government is expected not only to maintain order but also to achieve progress. There is a widespread belief that wise and well-directed government action can abolish poverty, prevent severe unemployment, raise the standard of living of the nation, and bring about rapid social development. People in all countries are far more aware than their forefathers were of the impact of government on their daily lives and of its potential for good and evil.

The growth in the functions of the state is to be found in the more-developed and in the less-developed countries; in both old and new states; in democratic, authoritarian, and totalitarian regimes; in the Communist countries of eastern Europe and in the mixed economies of the West. The movement is far from having reached its zenith. With each addition to the functions of the state, additional powers have been acquired by the administrative organs concerned, which may be central ministries, local, provincial, or regional governments, or special agencies created for a particular purpose.

Distinctions between Public Administration and Private Action

Activities such as traffic control, fire-protection services, policing, smoke abatement, the construction or repair of highways, the provision of currency, town and country planning, and the collection of customs and excise duties are usually carried out by governments, whose executive organs are assumed to represent the collective will of the community and to be acting for the common good.

It is for this reason that they are given powers not normally conferred on private persons. They may be authorized to infringe citizens' property rights and restrict their freedom of action in many different ways, ranging from the quarantining of infectious persons to the instituting of criminal proceedings for nonpayment of taxes. To take another example, the postal laws of many countries favour the post office at the expense of the customer in a way unknown where common carriers are concerned. Again, a public authority involved in slum clearance or housing construction tends to be in a much stronger legal position than a private developer.

The result of the distinction between public administration and private action is that administrative law is quite different from private law regulating the actions, interests, and obligations of private persons. Civil servants do not generally serve under a contract of employment but have a special status. Taxes are not debts, nor are they governed by the law relating to the recovery of debts by private persons. In addition, relations between one executive organ and another, and between an executive organ and the public, are usually regulated by compulsory or permissive powers conferred upon the executive organs by the legislature.

The law regulating the internal aspects of administration (*e.g.,* relations between the government and its officials, a local authority and its committees, or a central department and a local authority) differs from that covering external relations (those between the administration and private persons or interests). In practice, internal and external aspects are often linked, and legal provisions of both kinds exist side by side in the same statute. Thus, a law dealing with education may modify the administrative organization of the education service and also regulate the relations between parents and the school authorities.

Another distinction exists between a command addressed by legislation to the citizen, requiring him to act or to refrain from acting in a certain way, and a direction addressed to the administrative authorities. When an administrative act takes the form of an unconditional command addressed to the citizen, a fine or penalty is usually attached for failure to comply. In some countries the enforcement is entrusted to the criminal courts, which can review the administrative act; in others the administrative act itself must be challenged in an administrative court.

The need for Legal Safeguards over Public Administration

Statutory directions addressed to the executive authorities may impose absolute duties, or they may confer discretionary powers authorizing a specified action in certain circumstances.

Such legislation may give general directions for such activities as factory inspection, slum clearance, or town planning. The statute lays down the conditions under which it is lawful for the administration to act and confers on the authorities the appropriate powers, many of which involve a large element of discretion. Here the executive is not confined merely to carrying out the directions of the legislature; often it also shares in the lawmaking process by being empowered to issue regulations or ordinances dealing with matters not regulated by the statute. This may be regarded either as part of the ordinary process by which the legislature delegates its powers or as an inevitable feature of modern government, given that many matters are too technical, detailed, or subject to frequent change to be included in the main body of legislation—legislation being less easy to change than regulations.

Whatever the source of the executive's rule-making power, safeguards against misuse are necessary. For instance, the regulation must not exceed the delegated powers; its provisions must conform with the aims of the parent statute; prior consultation with interests likely to be affected should take place whenever practicable; and the regulations must not contravene relevant constitutional rules and legal standards. In some countries regulations are scrutinized by a type of watchdog known as the council of state before they come into force; in others, by the parliamentary assembly; and in yet others, by the ordinary courts.

In most countries the executive arm of government possesses certain powers not derived from legislation, customary law, or a written constitution. In the United Kingdom there are prerogative powers of the crown, nearly all of which are now exercised by ministers and which concern such matters as making treaties, declaring war and peace, pardoning criminals, issuing passports, and conferring honours. In Italy, France, Belgium, and other continental European countries, certain acts concerning the higher interests of the state are recognized as *actes de gouvernement* and are thereby immune from control by any court or administrative tribunal. In the German Empire (1871–1918) the principle that an administrative act carried its own legal validity was accepted at the end of the 19th century by leading jurists. This led to thc doctrine that administration was only loosely bound to the law. The doctrine was rejected in the Federal Republic of Germany (1949), however, and efforts were made to reduce the area in which the executive was free to act outside administrative law.

Bureaucracy and the role of Administrative Law

An inevitable consequence of the expansion of governmental functions has been the rise of bureaucracy. The number of officials of all kinds has greatly increased, and so too have the material resources allocated to their activities, while their powers have been enlarged in scope and depth. The rise of bureaucracy has occurred in countries ruled by all types of government, including the Communist countries, the dictatorships and Fascist regimes, and the political democracies. It is as conspicuous in the new states of Africa and Asia as among the highly developed countries of western Europe or North America. A large, strong, and well-trained civil service is essential in a modern state, irrespective of the political character of its regime or the nature of its economy.

Fear of the maladies that tend to afflict bureaucracy has produced a considerable volume of protest in some countries; and, even in those where opposition to the government or the party in power is not permitted, criticism and exposure of bureaucratic maladministration are generally encouraged.

Bureaucratic maladies are of different kinds. They include an overdevotion of officials to precedent, remoteness from the rest of the community, inaccessibility, arrogance in dealing with the general public, ineffective organization, waste of labour, procrastination, an excessive sense of self-importance, indifference to the feelings or convenience of citizens, an obsession with the binding authority of departmental decisions, inflexibility, abuse of power, and reluctance to admit error. Many of these defects can be prevented or cured by the application of good management techniques and by the careful training of personnel. A whole range of techniques is available for this purpose, including effective public relations, work-study programs, organization and management, operational research, and social surveys.

Administrative law is valuable in controlling the bureaucracy. Under liberal-democratic systems of government, political and judicial control of administration are regarded as complementary, but distinct. The former is concerned with questions of policy and the responsibility of the executive for administration and expenditure. The latter is concerned with inquiring into particular cases of complaint. Administrative law does not include the control of policy by ministers or the head of state. Under Communist regimes, however, this distinction rarely exists. The control exercised by an elected council or a presidium over a similar body at the next lower level of government is regarded as a form of legal control over administration. Internal methods of control are also regarded as falling within the ambit of administrative law. These include an appeal from the decision of an official within the same organization or an appeal to a higher administrative unit. A distinctive feature of Communist countries is that there is no definition of the powers of governmental organs at different levels. They are all assumed to be unlimited in scope but always subject to an equally unlimited right of intervention and restraint by the corresponding organ at the next higher level of government. This contrasts with the explicit definition of powers at each level of government that is found in the Western-type democracies. The admixture of political and legal control results in administrative law having a loose and imprecise meaning in Communist countries.

Judicial Review of Administration

Judicial review of administration is, in a sense, the heart of administrative law. It is certainly the most appropriate method of inquiring into the legal competence of a public authority. The aspects of an official decision or an administrative act that may be scrutinized by the judicial process are the competence of the public authority, the extent of a public authority's legal powers, the adequacy and fairness of the procedure, the evidence considered in arriving at the administrative decision and the motives underlying it, and the nature and scope of the discretionary power. An administrative act or decision can be invalidated on any of these grounds if the reviewing court or tribunal has a sufficiently wide jurisdiction. There is also the question of responsibility for damage caused by the public authority in the performance of its functions. Judicial review is less effective as a method of inquiring into the wisdom, expediency, or reasonableness of administrative acts, and courts and tribunals are unwilling to substitute their own decisions for that of the responsible authority. Judicial review of administration varies internationally. Sweden and France, for instance, have gone as far as subjecting the exercise of all discretionary powers, other than those relating to foreign affairs and defence, to judicial review and potential limitation. Elsewhere, a preoccupation with procedure results in judicial review deciding only whether the correct procedure was observed rather than examining the substance of the decision.

It is of course impractical to subject every administrative act or decision to investigation, for this would entail unacceptable delay. The complainant must, therefore, always make out a prima facie case that maladministration has occurred.

Judicial review cannot compel the state to act in a particular way because the courts concerned cannot impose sanctions on the government, which itself controls the use of force. Such remedies as an injunction, an order for specific performance, or an order for mandamus will not lie against the central government. These inhibitions, however, are of less practical importance than might be supposed. Nevertheless, nearly all governments (even revolutionary ones) are eager to proclaim the lawfulness of the regime and seldom disregard the decisions of an authorized court or tribunal.

In judicial review of administration at a national level, a country's history, politics, and constitutional theory all play their part. There are, broadly, three major systems: the common-law model; the French, or council of state, model; and the procurator model.

The Common-law System

Origins

The common-law system originated in England in the Middle Ages. In the 17th century relations between the courts and the executive developed into a constitutional struggle between the Stuart kings and the judges over the judges' right to decide questions affecting the royal power and even to pronounce an independent judgment in cases in which the king had an interest. Francis Bacon, in his essay *Of Judicature* (written in 1612), put forth the royalist point of view when he declared that the judges should be "lions, but yet lions under the throne."

"It is a happy thing in a state," he wrote, "when kings and states do often consult with judges; and again, when judges do often consult with the king and state: the one, when there is matter of law intervenient in business of state; the other, when there is some consideration of state intervenient in matter of law." The subordination of the judicature to the royal will was strongly resisted by Chief Justice Sir Edward Coke, Bacon's great rival, who refused to comply with James I's wishes in a number of cases in which the royal prerogative was involved. The King harangued the judges more than once on their duty to respect the royal prerogative and power.

In the constitutional conflict that took place a generation later, the judges and the lawyers made common cause with Parliament against Charles I, and eventually the independence of the judges was established.

Henceforth there was to be one system of law to which all would owe obedience. As a result, the executive possessed no inherent powers other than those subject to the rule of law inasmuch as legislation now had to emanate from the crown in Parliament. In addition, the judges were expected to protect the subject against the executive. A more intangible consequence was the belief that "government" and "law" were often thought to be opposed to one another. The earlier conflict between crown and judges survived to become an antagonism between the legal profession and the executive, particularly the civil service.

These developments established the principle that the executive should never interfere with the judiciary in the exercise of its functions. This was, indeed, almost the only strict application in England of the doctrine of the separation of powers.

On the other hand, it was regarded as right and proper that the judiciary should interfere with the executive whenever a minister or a department was shown to have acted illegally. In this way the concept of the rule of law came gradually to be identified with the idea that the judges, in ordinary legal proceedings in the ordinary courts, could pronounce upon the lawfulness of the activities of the executive. Any attempt to divide the seamless web of the law, any suggestion of a distinction between public and private law, appeared destructive of the law's universality and its power to keep the executive within bounds.

The principle that all public authorities are liable to have the lawfulness of their acts and decisions tested in the ordinary courts was applied everywhere the common law prevailed, including the United States, despite the much stricter interpretation given by the Founding Fathers there to the doctrine of the separation of powers—a doctrine embodied in the federal and state constitutions.

A complete separation of powers was not considered feasible by the framers of the Constitution, and they therefore introduced checks and balances, whereby each of the three branches of government would be prevented from growing too powerful by the countervailing power of the others.

This actually strengthened the power of the courts to review the actions of the executive. Elsewhere in the common-law world, the extended role of the courts in reviewing administration was adopted without any public debate concerning the separation of powers or the need to protect liberty by a system of checks and balances. This absence of an explicitly defined role for courts led, in the early post-World War II years in Britain, to real fears that the courts would be unable or unwilling to question the expanded powers of governmental bodies.

Modification of the Common-law System

The common-law system has been extensively modified in the course of the 20th century. Until recently it did not correspond to the realities of the situation in Britain because, prior to the Crown Proceedings Act, 1947, it was not possible to sue ministers and their departments in tort; government ministers in Britain are considered ministers of the crown, and an ancient legal doctrine holds that "the king can do no wrong." Moreover, the development of state-provided social services has been accompanied by the creation of a large number of administrative tribunals to determine disputes between a government department and a citizen.

The jurisdiction of these tribunals is of a specialized and narrowly circumscribed character and relates to such functions as social insurance and social assistance, the National Health Service, rent control, assessment of property for local taxation, the compulsory acquisition of land by public authorities, and the registration of children's homes. Since 1958 a permanent Council on Tribunals appointed by the lord chancellor has exercised a general supervision over about 40 tribunal systems, but they remain an un-systematic and uncoordinated movement.

However, they provide a method of administrative adjudication far cheaper, more informal, and more rapid than that offered by the courts; the members are persons possessing special knowledge and experience of the subject dealt with; they do not have to follow the strict and complex rules of evidence that prevail in the courts; and it is possible to introduce new social standards and moral considerations to guide their decisions.

These tribunals have won general approval for the quality and impartiality of their work. An appeal on a question of law lies in most instances from the decision of an administrative tribunal to the High Court of Justice. There is still no comprehensive administrative jurisdiction in Britain permitting judicial review over the whole field of executive action and decision.

In Australia a similar movement took place with the growth of a large number of administrative tribunals that regulate many different spheres of public administration, such as industrial conditions; the award of pensions, allowances, and other state grants; town planning; censorship of films; fair rents; the licensing of occupations calling for special skills or public responsibility; trade, transport, and marketing; the assessment of national taxes, local taxes, or duties; the protection of industrial design, patents, and copyrights; and compensation for interference with private-property rights in the public interest.

From 1975 these tribunals were managed by the Administrative Appeals Tribunal.

In the United States the courts review administration much more comprehensively than in Britain. Nevertheless, much adjudication is now performed by public authorities other than the courts of law. The movement toward administrative tribunals began with the Interstate Commerce Act (1887), establishing the Interstate Commerce Commission to regulate railways and other carriers. This law introduced a new type of federal agency, outside the framework of the executive departments and largely independent of the president. Other regulatory commissions followed: the Federal Trade Commission, the Federal Communications Commission, the Securities and Exchange Commission, the National Labour Relations Board, and the Occupational Safety and Health Administration.

These bodies have had administrative, legislative, and judicial functions delegated to them by Congress, and the doctrine of the separation of powers can no longer be successfully invoked to challenge the constitutionality of such legislation. The regulatory commissions are often described by American jurists as administrative tribunals. Thus, in the United States, as in other parts of the Anglo-American common-law world, the concept of the exclusive exercise by the ordinary courts of all judicial powers and of the absence of special administrative tribunals has been substantially modified by these developments.

The Council of State System

The French System

In France the separation of powers was given a place of honour in the Declaration of the Rights of Man and of the Citizen (1789). In the French view, however, if a court were permitted to review an administrative act or decision, it would contravene the separation of powers as much as if the executive could override the decision of a court. Just as an appeal from a court lies to a higher court, the reasoning goes, so an appeal from an administrative authority should lie to a higher administrative authority. Only thus would the true separation of powers be observed.

Herein lies the explanation of administrative law as a system of law separate from the body of law administered in the courts. A law of August 1790 declared that the judiciary was distinct from and would always remain separated from the executive. It forbade judges, on pain of dismissal, to interfere in any way with the work of administrative bodies. In October 1790 a second law stated that under no circumstances should claims to annul acts of administrative bodies fall within the jurisdiction of the courts. Such claims should be brought before the king as head of the general administration.

The Conseil du Roi of the ancien regime, with its functions as legal adviser and administrative court, is generally considered to be the precursor of the Conseil detat. The basic structure of the Conseil detat was laid down by Napoleon, however. Among the functions accorded to it by the constitution of the year VIII (December 1799) was that of adjudicating in conflicts that might arise between the administration and the courts. It was also empowered to adjudicate any matters previously left to the minister's discretion that ought to be the subject of judicial decision.

In 1806 a decree created a Judicial Committee of the Conseil to examine applications and report thereon to the General Assembly of the Conseil. These enactments laid the foundation of an administrative jurisdiction that was not clearly established until May 24, 1872, when a law delegated to the Conseil detat the judicial power to make binding decisions and recognized the Conseil as the court in which claims against the administration should be brought.

The Conseil detat is and always has been part of the administration. It has for long had the task of giving legal advice to the government on bills, regulations, decrees, and administrative questions.

It is this that long led foreign jurists into believing that, when sitting as a court, its decisions would inevitably be biased in favour of the executive. Nothing could be further from the truth, and today the Conseil is universally recognized as an independent court that provides French citizens with exceptionally good protection against maladministration. Suits that are directed against the French administration are heard in the Section du Contentieux, or Judicial Division, the successor of the Judicial Committee after restructuring in 1872.

The Conseil detat is the final authority in administrative disputes. Owing to the immense volume of work falling on it, the former prefectural councils, which served as administrative courts subordinate to the Conseil detat, were transformed in 1953 into administrative tribunals of first instance, and the professional qualifications and career prospects of their members were improved. The great majority of cases go before these tribunals, and the Conseil detat is the court of first and last instance only in those exceedingly rare cases when it is specially designated for that purpose.

If difficulty or doubt arises as to whether a case falls within the administrative jurisdiction or that of the ordinary courts, the question is resolved by the Tribunal des Conflits. This is a court specially established for the purpose, consisting of five judges from the Cour de Cassation (the highest civil court) and five from the Conseil detat. The minister of justice, in his capacity as keeper of the seals (*garde des sceaux*), may sometimes preside and cast a tie-breaking vote.

Several other countries have followed France in establishing councils of state. Among them are Italy, Greece, Belgium, Spain, Turkey, Portugal, and Egypt. It must be stated, however, that in no other country has a council of state acquired such high status, powers, authority, or prestige as in France.

The German System

Germany traditionally has had no council of state, but it does have a fully articulated system of special administrative courts. In the states, or *Länder*, there are lower administrative courts and superior administrative courts, and for the federation there is the Federal Administrative Court, which acts mainly as a court of appeals from the superior administrative courts in the *Länder* and even from the lower administrative courts in certain circumstances.

The Federal Administrative Court serves also as a court of first and last instance in disputes not involving questions of constitutionality between the federation and the *Länder* or between two or more *Länder*; it hears petitions by the federal Cabinet on declarations that an association is prohibited under the Basic Law of the Federal Republic, petitions against the federation in matters concerning the diplomatic or consular service, and cases concerning the business of the Federal Intelligence Service.

A *Land* administrative court possesses jurisdiction concerning the acts of the *Länder* administrative authorities and also complaints against officers of the federal government located in the *Länder*. Some of the highest federal organs are exempt from the *Länder* courts. Few cases go beyond the *Länder* supreme administrative courts.

Recourse to an administrative court is available for public law disputes unless the matter has been assigned to another court by federal legislation. (Public law governs the relationship between the state and executive in the exercise of their governmental authority and the individual—insofar as the relationship is not commercial.) The Administrative Courts Code holds that property claims arising from services for the common good and restitution claims arising from violation of duties under public law shall be heard by the ordinary courts. In other words, the German system is complicated by the rule that only the ordinary civil courts can award damages against an official or the executive arm of government. As a consequence, the distinction between the ordinary courts and the administrative courts depends on the remedy sought and not on the subject matter of the dispute or the nature of the parties. The jurisdiction of the administrative courts in Germany is therefore less comprehensive and clear-cut than in France.

The Procurator System

The third system for ensuring administrative legality, called the Procuracy, was founded in Russia by Peter the Great in 1722, who intended it to be the "eye of the tsar." Catherine II issued a directive in 1764 stating that the procurator general and his staff were to supervise the execution of the laws in the provinces, ensure justice, and prevent abuses. This was designated general supervision. In 1864, however, the Procuracy was relieved of its responsibility for supervising administration, its functions being confined to judicial matters, such as acting as public prosecutor in all criminal cases and conducting them on behalf of the government and the law.

The Procuracy was abolished in November 1917 but revived in 1922. The Soviet constitution charged the procurator general with the general duty of supervising the observance of the law by all ministries and institutions subordinate to them as well as by individual officials and citizens.

The procurator general was appointed by the Supreme Soviet for five years. He appointed subordinate procurators at all administrative levels, from union republic to district and town. The functions actually performed by the procurator underwent many fluctuations and vicissitudes after 1922. The role as a public prosecutor continued, but it was exercised mainly to enforce party policies or programs on recalcitrant citizens rather than to punish public officers or authorities for breaches of the law. Sometimes the task of general supervision was emphasized; at other times it was abandoned in favour of more urgent tasks, as in World War II. Finally, the position of the Procuracy was laid down in a union law of May 24, 1955, and a decree of the Presidium of the Supreme Soviet made on April 7, 1956.

The procurator was not the president of a court or a tribunal but rather a watchdog of legality. His organization comprised a department for general supervision; a bureau of investigation for the supervision of preliminary inquiries in criminal matters; a department for the supervision of investigations carried out by the KGB (Committee for State Security); departments to supervise criminal and civil proceedings in the courts; a department to supervise prisons, compulsory-labour centres, and the like; and departments for statistics, administration, and research.

General supervision was defined by Soviet writers on administrative law as meaning supervision by the procurators over legality in administration. Procurators were expected to see that the laws were strictly observed, to oppose their violation by anyone whatsoever, to protect the citizens, and to ensure that they fulfilled their duties. The law of May 24, 1955, required the Procuracy to ensure that the regulations or decisions issued by ministries, departments, their subordinate establishments and enterprises, and cooperative and other public organizations strictly conformed to the constitution and laws of the Soviet Union and the republics as well as to the decrees of the Council of Ministers of the Soviet Union and the republics. They were also to ensure strict execution of the laws by officials and citizens. The procurator was concerned solely with the legality of administrative action.

After the mid-1960s a change took place in the role of the procurator from the handling of complaints by citizens against government bodies to the handling of "economic" complaints (*e.g.*, violations such as filing fraudulent plan fulfillment records) and the monitoring of economic performance. The decline in the number of individual citizens' grievances handled by the Procuracy, as well as the economic and coercive purposes for which it was used, make direct analogy between the procurator and an ombudsman misleading.

Since the Procuracy was not a court, it could not make a binding decision. This point was emphasized by Article 58 of the 1977 constitution, giving citizens the right to take complaints against administrative actions to the courts. The normal procedure (apart from cases of dereliction involving a criminal prosecution) was for the procurator to protest against any illegality that he detected or that was brought to his notice or to initiate disciplinary action against an erring official. Every citizen had a right to lodge a complaint with the procurator, and denunciation and exposure of bureaucratic abuses were officially encouraged by the Communist Party. The fact that the Procuracy could not make a binding decision did not necessarily prevent it from being an effective organ for securing administration according to law. Neither the French Conseil detat nor the courts in any country can enforce judgments against the central government, but this does not prevent the decisions of the Conseil or declaratory judgments of the courts from being observed almost as a matter of course.

The former Communist regimes of eastern Europe established procuracies based on the Soviet model. In Poland an additional institution to maintain administrative legality was the Supreme Chamber of Control, which was independent of the government and subordinate only to the legislature and the Council of State, a political body quite different from the French model. The functions of the Supreme Chamber of Control involved exercising general supervision over public administration and took into account legality, economy, and opportuneness.

The Ombudsman

The ombudsman is a part of the system of administrative law for scrutinizing the work of the executive. He is the appointee not of the executive but of the legislature. The ombudsman enjoys a large measure of independence and personal responsibility and is primarily a guardian of correct behaviour. His function is to safeguard the interests of citizens by ensuring administration according to law, discovering instances of maladministration, and eliminating defects in administration. Methods of enforcement include bringing pressure to bear on the responsible authority, publicizing a refusal to rectify injustice or a defective administrative practice, bringing the matter to the attention of the legislature, and instigating a criminal prosecution or disciplinary action. When Sweden created the office of ombudsman in the constitution of 1809, the holder of that office was occupied with civil affairs and was appointed by the legislature. He was independent of both executive and judiciary and had full powers to inquire into the details of any administrative or executive act and into certain judicial activities if reported to him by individuals as an abuse of rights.

He had effective authority to prosecute civil servants and other public officials—including, on occasion, ministers themselves. The Swedish ombudsman's responsibility now comprises civil affairs, including the judicature, the police, prisons, and the public administration, both central and local, but excluding ministers and the monarch.

He can act as a public prosecutor (although he does not often do so); as a receiver of complaints from aggrieved citizens; or as an inspector of such institutions as jails, mental hospitals, homes for delinquent children, and retreats for alcoholics to discover if they are being administered in accordance with the law.

The institution of ombudsman was first adopted in other Scandinavian countries and then—especially from the 1960s—in many countries throughout the world, including New Zealand (1962), the United Kingdom (1967), Israel (1971), Portugal (1976), The Netherlands (1981), and Spain (1981). Australia, the United States, and Canada have ombudsmen at the state or provincial level, and in the United States several cities have municipal ombudsmen. In Britain there is an ombudsman to investigate complaints against local government, the National Health Service, and administration in Northern Ireland, in addition to the ombudsman operating at the national level. Some specialized ombudsmen have been appointed in the United States to safeguard the rights of prisoners to medical treatment. In Israel the police have an office of public complaints, and there is a military ombudsman; there is also a state controller, who issues annual reports on executive procedures.

There is no doubt about the value of the ombudsman in the states in which the institution has been established. Part of the ombudsman's usefulness lies in his ability to reassure citizens who believe they have been unjustly treated that careful inquiry into their complaints shows their suspicions to be groundless. In most countries the ombudsman has little positive power other than the right to inspect and to demand the fullest information. He may, however, recommend a particular interpretation of, or a particular modification of, the law. He can also recommend that the government pay compensation to a complainant.

Administrative Procedure

An orderly procedure, besides being efficient, allows responsibility to be fixed on a particular officer or body at each stage of the administrative process. It can safeguard the rights of citizens and protect the executive against the criticism of having acted in an arbitrary manner. It can ensure regularity and consistency in the handling of individual cases. Much depends, however, on the quality and purpose of the procedural requirements. Most countries possess only an uncodified mass of administrative law prescribing procedure. Much of it is to be found in the laws and regulations governing particular functions of government, such as taxation, public health, education, and town planning.

Rules of administrative procedure cover such matters as the setting of administrative machinery in motion; methods for lodging appeals; the rights of interested persons; the time limits that must be observed; the conditions to be satisfied by objectors; and the right of legal representation. The leading treatise on U.S. administrative law devotes many chapters to such procedural topics as rule making, requirement of opportunity to cross-examine and rebut, adjudication procedure, examiners, bias, evidence, official notice, findings, reasons, and opinions.

Some countries have a general code of administrative procedure embodied in legislation. Among them are Austria, Poland, Spain, and the United States.

In common-law systems, the doctrine of natural justice influences administrative procedure in two ways: (1) that a person may not be judge of his own cause, and (2) that a person shall not be dealt with to his material disadvantage, whether of person or property, or removed from or disqualified for office, without being given adequate notice of what is alleged against him and an opportunity to defend himself.

An indirect result of the second principle is the public hearing, widely used by government departments (and in the United States by regulatory commissions) in deciding matters involving individual or corporate rights. In the United Kingdom a public inquiry is now a common means of handling appeals to the Department of the Environment against the decisions of local authorities in such matters as planning applications and compulsory purchase of land.

7

Problems of Government

Every day political issues and activities are discussed and debated. What is not often discussed is the underlying concept of government. We put a lot of faith in our government's ability to solve serious problems and manage society effectively. It is a useful exercise to take a look at the origins of the concept of government and investigate its modern day functions, processes, and efficacy.

The Origin of Government

Looking at the historical reasons why government exists assist in the evaluation of its relevant roles in modern society. Below are key reasons for the emergence of government (circa 3500BC):

1. Agriculture enabled the emergence of stationary civilizations (the attainment of food did not require geographic mobility)
2. Families needed ways to most efficiently organize resources and communicate information (centralized resources, defence against outside attackers, planning, trade routes, etc.), so they assigned leaders and groups to do so
3. Clans/tribes turned into city states, city states turned into larger state societies
4. Rule by consent turned to rule by coercion as leaders gained more power

5. In-depth knowledge of concepts such as business and economic science didn't exist, so the best structure for organizing society came through government
6. Communication abilities such as the internet, telephone, books, etc. didn't exist, so reliance on government was integral for trading and information transfer

Because of these circumstances, government has been a natural fixture in all relatively successful societies in recorded history. Today, few question the requirement of a government system to fulfill certain roles in a successful and orderly society.

What is the Proper Role of Government?

Under the constitution, the U.S. government was intended to have limited involvement in society's functions. Take a look at the assumed roles of government in the U.S. today along with their constitutional validity:

1. Military
2. Civil order
3. Infrastructure – No ownership of transportation (roads, bridges, train lines, etc.), water, energy, etc. included in the constitution
4. Education – No public education system included in the constitution
5. Economy – No Federal Reserve or government market influence included in the constitution
6. Social – No redistribution of wealth (Social Security, unemployment benefits, other welfare) included in the constitution
7. Healthcare – No redistribution of wealth (Medicare, Medicaid) included in the constitution
8. Environment – No mention of government protection of the environment in the constitution

The point is not for society to abandon attention to these categories, but to ask if any or all of their related functions can be fulfilled better without government involvement. Most immediately think these functions cannot be fulfilled without government involvement, but there are historical examples and theory that say that they can.

The Nature of Government

To depict the inherent nature of the government, below is a table comparing the attributes of government and private organizations.

Accountability is Minimal in Government

Although most government members may have best intentions in mind, they are human and can still make mistakes and be bad at their jobs. The lack of accountability inherent in government does not allow for the efficient correction of a given failed initiative. When the following fail (lawful failure), there are rarely, if ever, immediate or direct consequences:

1. Political parties
2. Departments and agencies
3. Officials (President, Administration, Judiciary, Senators, Congressmen, Committees)
4. Employees.

Consequences are often overlooked, ignored, and if ever addressed, it may be years before the failed individual or group is replaced through election. Additionally, election does not guarantee their dismissal.

Government Incentive is Warped

Incentive for a government role or position to be successful is largely based on:

1. Reelection
2. The swapping of favors or special privilege
3. Financial contributions and influence from special interests (businesses seeking special advantage, political and non-political groups with moral positions, lobbyists, etc.)
4. Incentive is not tied to measured results.

Short terms of office incent ıocus toward short-term problems and issues ('hot topics' of the day) while sacrificing focus on long-term problems because they:

1. Provide immediate tangibility and appeal to the population to capture votes for reelection
2. Self-serve the politician for optimal lifestyle during the time they hold the office.

There is no direct mutual incentive or trade of value between those that are to receive service from the government (citizens/taxpayers) and those in the government that are supposed to provide it.

Government Fosters Immorality

The key reasons government fosters corruption and immorality are that it is a system that:

1. Lacks accountability
2. Lacks aligned incentives
3. Exists and operates only through coercion and involuntary, unearned payment (taxes and inflation).

Government Regulation of Industry is Ineffective

There are several reasons the government uses to justify its regulatory intervention in private business:

1. Military – the need for technologies that provide military advantage over other nations
2. Economy – the need to prevent poverty and promote economic well-being
3. Safety – the protection of consumers
4. Social – the redistribution of wealth to those in need (welfare, $ocial Security, Medicare, etc.)
5. Environment – the prevention of pollution and environmental safety hazards.

Again, there is no mention of private business or economic government intervention within the constitution. However, the government assumes these roles preaching the protection of its citizens and then turns around to implement them without the ability to do so efficiently. Government regulation is ineffective for similar reasons that the government itself is ineffective:

1. Regulation is not created efficiently-there is no direct economic incentive or accountability to drive efficiency
2. Regulation is not adjusted efficiently when flaws are found-there is no direct economic incentive or accountability to drive efficiency
3. Fosters regulatory arbitrage – a regulated institution taking advantage of the difference between its economic risk and the regulatory position.
4. Fosters regulatory capture – a government regulatory agency created to act in the public interest instead acts in favour of the commercial or special interests (businesses looking for advantage, environmental groups, etc.) that dominate the industry or sector it is charged with regulating
5. Fosters rent seeking – occurs when an individual, organization, or firm seeks to make money by manipulating the legal environment rather than by trade or production
6. When regulation can be created for irrational or irrelevant reasons, businesses face unneeded risk from potential regulation that can harm their business, which will influence their business decisions (including whether to do business in the given industry at all).
7. Businesses are likely to migrate to less regulated areas of the given industry or economy. The lack of regulation (including the lack of private regulation because of anticipated government regulation) enables more potential for corruption and related catastrophic economic effects.
8. The government has a monopoly on regulation-there are no competing regulatory bodies to weed out poor regulation and allow the best regulation to emerge. For example, if the SEC were a private organization competing against another organization with similar oversight, there would be incentive to do a great job of

regulating. Many of the above government regulation problems would be solved through regulatory competition.

Companies are devoting increasing amounts of money and resources to politics for the purpose of influencing regulation for competitive advantage. Productive areas of the economy are then deprived of these dollars and resources causing productivity and progress to decline.

Recent Regulation Failures

A few examples of regulatory problems directly relevant to today's events are:

1. Loopholes within the SEC made the Madoff scam more likely:
   - o How to stop the next Madoff-Ayn Rand Center (2009)
   - o Close securities law loophole-The Post and Carrier (2008)
   - o Madoff and the Failure of the SEC-The Mises Institute (2008)
2. Since their creation in 1968, Fannie May and Freddie Mac (GSEs) have had exemptions from SEC oversight (including Sarbanes-Oxley), ratio requirements, and state and local taxes, while receiving the privilege of access to a line of credit through the U.S. Treasury. In the meantime, their competitors did not have these exemptions and privileges. This double standard gave the GSEs unfair competitive advantage. Also, they were less likely to get caught for corruption than their private competitors that were required to comply.
3. SEC and monopolistic regulation of credit rating agencies increased the probability of low integrity mortgage-related securities ratings.

Regulation is Needed

This analysis is not meant to conclude that there should be no regulation of industry. The point is to show that government is not the institution to do it. Instead, free market principals enable a system of competitive regulatory institutions that constantly adjust to ever-changing market and consumer demands and only exist and succeed if they do their jobs well.

Democracy is not Necessarily the best System

The U.S. was founded as a constitutional republic (not a democracy), which means that the government was to be limited to powers that preserved and defended the individual rights of its citizens. Citizens were not to be governed by the majority of the population, but by the rule of law. The Founding Fathers knew the many flaws of majority rule and defined the constitution and Bill of Rights to protect the rights of the individual.

The system of government paraded today has moved away from the intentions of the constitution to a majority rules democracy.

What's the Nature of Democracy?

Example: John and Sarah decide they would like to have Bob (who has done nothing to John or Sarah) hit over the head with a hammer. They vote to do so and Bob is subsequently hit over the head. This type of injustice can and does happen on a large scale in a democracy.

What Happens when Citizens Vote?

1. Voter decisions can be manipulated by politicians and propaganda
2. Many vote without full information on the issues
3. Some let emotions and irrationality guide them
4. Many let their moral principles (which differ from many others) guide them
5. In the unlikely case that all voters are fully and accurately informed and attuned to their moral principles, the majority's decision will still harm the minority.
6. Once the vote is passed, what is the likelihood that the promised action will be completed or completed correctly?

In a democratic system, because the majority rules:

1. It doesn't matter if the majority's position is wrong for themselves
2. It doesn't matter if the majority's position is right for themselves, but wrong for the minority.

In a close vote, the majority may not win. The electoral college system can allow the minority to win, so in this case the majority is or feels harmed.

Political Parties are Whimsical Monopolies

The U.S. has 2 major political parties that frequently change positions and principals, even swapping at points in history.

This obfuscation can make it very difficult for the busy citizen to be clear about their political affiliation. Additionally, the current political party system in the U.S. makes the emergence of a third party extremely difficult and unlikely. Party alliances with businesses and special interests create a self-sustaining machine supported by endless reservoirs of money and influential ability.

Busy citizens often do not have time to think through the intricacies of the parties, their solutions, and their ability to implement the solutions.

Even if they see that the differences of current parties do not matter (both choices are poor for the future), they often believe there can be no alternative choice and stick with what they believe to have worked in the past.

Voting for the Person, not the Party

Many claim that the character of the person running, rather than the party, drives their vote choice. This is a noble mindset. However, it defeats the purpose because:

1. The candidate of high character aligned themselves with a party that may not necessarily be in line with the voter's morals and ideals.
2. The candidate surrounds their self with an administration that may not have the same intentions or motivations.

3. Their actions while in office could still have little impact as an opposing party dominating. the Congress can make moot their ambitions.

Democracy Allows the Buildup of Power

Slowly but surely through election term after election term, political election campaigns promise large segments of people certain benefits that those people cannot help but desire. Slowly but surely new laws are passed to implement these benefits. Slowly but surely the government is able to build its reach and power in all areas of society. Additionally, in our country and others that claim to uphold a democracy, democracy seems to inevitably devolve toward socialism. The short article below theorizes on this notion part humorously and part seriously-even going a step beyond to tyranny.

U.S. Checks and Balances do not Check and Balance

The Executive, Legislative, and Judicial branches of the U.S. government are intended to provide checks and balances that will prevent the concentration of power within the government. The inherent problem with this concept is that all 3 branches are within the same institution-the U.S. government. The problems of political party affiliation, personal and political interests, etc. apply to enhance the potential of collusion among individuals between branches. For example, with a Legislative and Executive branch made up of the same political party (and in some cases different political parties), there can be collusion for the approval of a federal judge to influence the makeup of the Supreme Court. Another example is possible collusion between the executive and judicial branches to influence a given ruling. As outlined earlier, there is no true incentive to expose collusion between branches. The 3 branches are policing themselves, and there is no competing group or body intimate enough with their activities to keep them in check.

Index

A

C

□□□